I0642310

Conversations with Stanley Kunitz

Literary Conversations Series
Peggy Whitman Prenshaw
General Editor

Conversations
with Stanley Kunitz

Edited by Kent P. Ljungquist

University Press of Mississippi   Jackson

www.upress.state.ms.us

The University Press of Mississippi is a member of the Association of American University Presses.

First printing 2013

∞

Library of Congress Cataloging-in-Publication Data

Kunitz, Stanley, 1905–2006.
 Conversations with Stanley Kunitz / edited by Kent P. Ljungquist.
    pages cm. — (Literary Conversations Series)
 Includes index.
 ISBN 978-1-61703-870-9 (cloth : alk. paper) — ISBN 978-1-61703-871-6 (ebook) 1. Kunitz, Stanley, 1905–2006—Interviews. 2. Poets, American—20th century—Interviews. 3. Poetry—Authorship. I. Ljungquist, Kent, 1948– II. Title.
 PS3521.U7Z46 2013
 811'.52—dc23
 [B]   2013013053

British Library Cataloging-in-Publication Data available

Books by Stanley Kunitz

Intellectual Things. New York: Doubleday, Doran, 1930.

Passport to the War: A Selection of Poems. New York: Holt, Rinehart, and Winston, 1944.

Selected Poems 1928–1958. Boston: Atlantic-Little Brown, 1958.

The Poems of John Keats, editor. New York: Crowell, 1965.

The Testing-Tree. Poems. Boston: Atlantic-Little Brown, 1971.

Akhmatova, Anna. *Poems of Akhmatova.* Translated, and introduced by Stanley Kunitz and Max Hayward. Boston: Atlantic-Little, Brown, 1973.

Vosnesensky, Andre. *Story under Full Sail.* Co-translator. New York: Doubleday, 1974.

The Terrible Threshold: Selected Poems 1940–1970. London: Secker & Warburg, 1974.

The Coat without a Seam: Sixty Poems 1930–1972. Northampton, MA: Gehenna Press, 1974.

A Kind of Order, A Kind of Folly: Essays and Conversations. Boston: Atlantic-Little, Brown, 1975.

Drach, Ivan. *Orchard Lamps,* editor and co-translator. New York: Sheep Meadow Press, 1978.

The Poems of Stanley Kunitz, 1928–1978. Boston: Atlantic-Little, Brown, 1979.

The Wellfleet Whale and Companion Poems. New York: Sheep Meadow Press, 1983.

Next-to-Last Things: New Poems and Essays. Boston: Atlantic-Little, Brown, 1985.

The Essential Blake, editor. New York: Ecco Press, 1987.

Passing Through: The Later Poems New and Selected. New York: W. W. Norton & Company, 1995.

Shapiro, Karl. *The Wild Card: Selected Poems, Early and Late,* editor with David Ignatow. Champaign: University of Illinois Press, 1998.

The Collected Poems. New York: W. W. Norton & Company, 2000.

The Wild Braid: A Poet Reflects on a Century in the Garden. With Genine Lentine. New York: W. W. Norton & Company, 2005.

Contents

Introduction

Stanley Kunitz, the public voice for poetry, certainly became more widely known to a general audience via a conversation with Bill Moyers, "Dancing at the Edge of the Road," part of a series on the Public Broadcasting System in 1989. The title of Moyers's program was drawn from Kunitz's "An Old Cracked Tune," a poem that had come to occupy a significant place in his readings in the later decades of his career. The figure in the poem is Solomon Levi, a name that was taken from an offensive street song, but Kunitz sees him as an outcast, a marginalized outsider who somehow transcends his status. In short, he is a stand-in figure for the poet. The interview was later republished in two books, one edited by Moyers and the other by Stanley Moss. Kunitz spoke with such authority and penetrating insight in this interview about the powerful role of poetry that some viewers and readers may have assumed that the confidence he exuded derived from an uninterrupted pattern of public recognition and appreciation that extended back to the beginning of his literary career. As this collection of interviews shows, however, the trajectory of Kunitz's poetic career is hardly a smooth pathway at every turn from early experimentation to quick acceptance and recognition.

Although his early volumes *Intellectual Things* (1930) and *Passport to the War* (1944) won positive reviews from critics, his poems, even in the decades after World War II, were seldom anthologized. Kunitz's career is unique for several reasons, not the least of which is its expansive connection to several generations of American poets. He began by contributing to periodicals like the *Dial* and *Poetry* in the 1920s when many of the features of high modernism were coming into vogue. In several interviews, Kunitz points out that this was a period of personal and professional isolation. There were no creative writing programs at the time, no poetry readings, and the lack of a sense of artistic community was a condition he bore stoically. There were no public readings of his own poetry even up to the middle years of his writing career, and a sense of exile or "metaphysical loneliness" was an emotional condition with which he was all too familiar.

That sense of personal isolation stemmed, to be sure, from childhood memories of growing up in his hometown of Worcester, Massachusetts. As he notes in one interview, "Memory is each man's poet in residence," and the "vulnerability of [his] own youth" echoes throughout the body of his poetic work and his related comments on his verse. Very much a poet of root images, he recalls the central event of his family life that would hover like a shadow over his childhood and adolescence and assume a lasting impact: his father's suicide six weeks before he was born. His mother's response was to erase all memories of his father's life and the circumstances of his death, but the emotional struggles Kunitz faced in the aftermath of the suicide led him to transform his father—his name is never mentioned outright in the poems—into a mysterious, even mythical figure. This tortuous path of questioning, discovery, and uncovering of personal and family secrets eventually led him to signature themes in his work: the quest for identity and the search for a paternal figure.

There were stirrings to become a writer, he notes, as early as age thirteen or fourteen, and he even began naïve experimentation with adventure stories. The desire to probe inward was probably accentuated by his hostile reaction to aspects of his native setting. Worcester was a city of immigrants, whose seven hills might, the town officers suggested, recall Rome; in Kunitz's mind, however, each hill constituted a separate enclave inhabited by a discrete ethnic group (Irish, Swedes, Poles, Armenians, Italians, and eastern European and Russian Jews), each of which turned inward toward to its own insular traditions rather than outward to a broader world. Long before Kunitz achieved any degree of national notoriety, one of his earliest interviews was with the local Worcester newspaper—for which he had worked after graduating from college. The interview led to a brief exchange about another writer who chronicled memories of experiences from roughly the same local neighborhood. *The Worcester Account* (1956) by S. N. Behrman was a vivid rendering of the immigrant experience of Eastern European Jews, and Kunitz might have noted common concerns in his own work and Behrman's volume: both writers grew up in the Providence Street area of Worcester, they had a common Jewish heritage, and they noted the animosity and even violence among the ethnic groups in the city. Although Behrman was twelve years older than Kunitz, each had attended Worcester's Classical High School and had participated enthusiastically on the school's debating team. The Behrman and Kunitz families even shared the same family physician—Dr. Jim Nightingale—and the fairly exclusive private school prominent in their neighborhood—Worcester Academy—figured in both *The Worcester Account* and Kunitz's poetry (i.e., the "Academy ballpark" in his poem "The Testing-Tree"). The sectarianism and parochialism of Worcester stirred both writers to seek escape, but unlike Behrman, Kunitz could articulate "no sense of belonging to an immigrant family." Despite his mother's Lithuanian roots, she emerges in his poems as a figure erasing the past, and much of that denial excluded any open or probing discussion of her and her husband's ethnic heritage. Later in his career, when Kunitz edited his mother's narrative of coming to the so-called Golden Land of America, her story stopped abruptly with her arrival in Worcester and the fateful marriage to his father—"events still too painful to recall."[1]

Kunitz does acknowledge the first-class education he received in Worcester's public schools and the encouragement afforded him by several teachers, but he also recalls an Irish teacher who railed against dirty foreigners and dirty Jews. In the face of isolation and a challenging emotional situation at home, he sought refuge and found solace in the woods, the public library, and the local art museum. He edited the school literary magazine, the *Argus*, and as he contemplated his college years, he encountered the quota system that limited the percentage of Jewish students at elite universities. Managing to win a scholarship, he entered Harvard and graduated *summa cum laude*, went on to pursue a master's degree, and seemed ideally suited to advance to further study in preparation for an academic career. He was told, however, that "Our Anglo-Saxon students would resent being taught English literature by a Jew."[2] Understandably embittered, or emotionally "shattered," to use his own word, he expresses no great love for Harvard, and "abandoned all thought of an academic career." He was troubled not only by Harvard's official hostility to minorities but by the institution's general atmosphere of condescension and social stratification. Nevertheless, at Harvard, he received support from visiting professor Robert Gay, enthusiastically attended classes in science offered by Alfred North Whitehead, and read avidly the metaphysical poets John Donne and George Herbert. Although the emerging modern poets were not yet taught at Harvard, he discovered them independently. Widener Library, he acknowledges, was his "singing school."

It would be twenty years before Kunitz would return to work again in an academic setting. In the intervening years he made the most of an editorial position with the H. W. Wilson Company, which allowed him to pursue a flexible schedule, work from his home, and even pursue foreign travel. He edited the *Wilson Library Bulletin*, a periodical that established a standard for professional librarians and book enthusiasts. He developed the idea for a series of reference works—containing profiles of American and world authors—which became standard volumes on public and academic library shelves across the nation. His pride in what might be seen a fairly workman-like editorial role for the H. W. Wilson Company is expressed in several interviews. Even when working for the company, however, a spirit of independence was part of his regimen, and when Kunitz returned to academe, he never assumed a permanent post, preferring to project an independent voice separate from established institutions and distanced from mainstream culture. He eventually accepted teaching appointments at Bennington College, Columbia University, the University of Washington, the New School for Social Research in New York, the State University/Potsdam, Brandeis University, and Princeton University. He enjoyed the stimulation and interaction of working with young people and consistently sustained a sense of anticipation upon entering the classroom, but for Kunitz the vocation of poetry in the U.S. challenged the dominant American myth, the powerful mystique of success and power that pervaded so much of society. Preferring an outsider's subversive posture, he earned his keep as a "peripatetic bard." He served multiple roles as consultant, guest lecturer, writing instructor, and workshop director at a series of institutions.

His attitude perhaps still colored by the Harvard experience, Kunitz is frank and direct about the mixed effects of academic approaches to literary study on the reading and appreciation of poetry. He expresses regret for young poets who have no experience of the world outside academe, and he notes how "breeding a generation of poets who have developed a specialized linguistic skill, but not much else" has failed to advance the cause of poetry. For Kunitz activities not directly relating to drafting poems—his interest in the natural world, his avid pursuit of gardening, his reading in modern developments in the sciences, and working to construct and create objects around the home—have fed his own creative impulses and imagination. He questions the dominance of technique and the conversion of poetry into an academic discipline. "If one thinks of oneself as essentially a professor of English, producing verses on the side, the work is bound to suffer," he acknowledges, and thus he never sought or accepted a position with tenure.

By the 1960s the proliferation of creative writing programs, summer workshops, and conferences afforded younger writers something Kunitz lacked when he set out on a career in poetry: a greater sense of belonging and a shared commitment to the value of the creative imagination. Driven by a search for a sense of community, Kunitz was drawn to Provincetown where he became a founder of the Fine Arts Work Center, a haven for writers and artists. This institution fostered an openness and idealistic mission in stark contrast to the constraints of the academic life he experienced early in his career. One can easily detect the appreciation for Provincetown in his response to a question from the poet Mary Oliver about the appeal of that Cape Cod venue:

> Provincetown has a long tradition in the arts, both visual and literary. One thinks offhand of persons like Eugene O'Neill, or of Hans Hoffman as a painter, and each of them represents an era, the history of our society actually. And the town is steeped not only in the tradition of the famous but in the tradition of those who have quietly and obstinately persevered in the arts, who've not chosen to live in urban centers, who have been by choice citizens of the side channels. And this is one of the qualities of the town. It is one of the least oppressive and institutionalized communities alive. Furthermore, it happens to be extraordinarily beautiful. And one has to know Provincetown in order to be seduced by its ambience.
>
> Matisse, I am told, who visited once said there was no place on earth that had the quality of light that Provincetown has. And I fully agree. Those great open skies and that absolutely pellucid light are something one dreams about and never sees anymore in our smog-ridden metropolises . . . Forty miles or so out into the middle of the Atlantic, and one has a sense of the being really at the tip of a civilization with all that detachment from the center that permits one to be one's own free agent.[3]

Kunitz, Oliver, and Alan Dugan were among the earliest leaders of writing workshops for the center, and the poet Louise Glück was among the early recipients of its fellowships. In the ensuing decade of the 1970s, as editor of the Yale Series of Younger Poets, Kunitz brought recognition via publication to a new generation of poetic voices, and he became a mentor and advisor to a rising group of writers. His founding of Poets House in New York City in 1987 continued his efforts to build institutions that afforded a sense of community to poets and students of poetry. The mission of Poets House is to serve as host to poets and literary events that "stimulate public dialogue on issues of poetry in culture."[4]

The subtitle of Kunitz's volume of prose *A Kind of Order, A Kind of Folly: Essays and Conversations* (1975) attests to the value he attaches to the kind of intellectual and imaginative exchange contained in the interview/dialogue form. He includes in that volume two interviews: one with the Russian poet Andre Vosnesensky and another with Robert Lowell. Even before his efforts on behalf of the Fine Arts Work Center and Poets House, he surveyed "American Poetry's Silver Age," and deployed a college setting for an "improbable dialogue" between two figures, designated as the Poet and the Young Man.[5] He was also the prime mover behind a series of dialogues with contemporary poets, aimed at high school teachers and students, about the challenges, questions, and difficulties of modern poetry. Among his interlocutors in the series, sponsored by the Academy of American Poets, were Lowell, W. H. Auden, Anthony Hecht, Howard Nemerov, W. D. Snodgrass, Allen Tate, and Robert Penn Warren. If Lowell and Theodore Roethke were counted among Kunitz's closest colleagues, Tate's name may seem far removed from this trio of American poets. Kunitz does mention the Fugitive Group in a 1989 interview,[6] and he would have known of the influence that Tate's and John Crowe Ransom's traditionalism and formalism had asserted on Lowell. The unique dialogue with Tate is included in this volume as a sample from the academy series, and the exchange includes Kunitz's suggestive comment: "The poems I love are those that keep their secrets; their motivations and meanings are hidden in the design." The speaker of Kunitz's "The Science of the Night"—the specific subject of another interview here—mentions "mines of secrecy," suggesting that valuable ore can be drawn from probing for that which is concealed or below the surface of things. Kunitz, who acknowledged that "one of my great influences was Plato, and I was very deep in Platonic lore,"[7] in all likelihood, found in the dialogue form a means of probing and uncovering that might serve some ultimate purpose, and in this volume Kunitz can be observed as both interview subject and questioner. [A triangular discussion on the teaching of poetry among Kunitz, Donald Hall, and Marvin Bell is included here.] As Stanley Moss observes, Kunitz "blooms with questions, his own to himself and those of others."[8] Moss implies further that the image of digging, associated with Kunitz's favorite activity of gardening, has more than metaphorical significance for a writer whose process of self-discovery leads him inexorably to offer some disclosure, partial or complete, of what has been long buried but not totally forgotten. His activities as poet, teacher, and workshop leader ultimate point to a purpose of ultimate sharing: "The hard inescapable phenomenon to be faced is that we are living and dying at once. My commitment is to report that dialogue."

Interviewers of Kunitz tend to probe their subject by asking him whether his work falls neatly into accepted poetic categories. His grappling with their questions and rejection of certain labels point to a more nuanced understanding of what kind of poet he aspired to be. In an early interview[9]

Kunitz acknowledges how he willed himself to become a hermetic poet. At this point in his career, he seemed to see poetry as a noble, occult calling that incorporated secret knowledge, magic, and mystery. The intensely autobiographical roots of Kunitz's poetry and his childhood and adolescent conflicts and emotional traumas led interviewers to ask whether he was a confessional poet like Lowell or Sylvia Plath. He erupted with passion in rejecting that label. Calling much "confessional poetry raw and embarrassing—bad art,"[10] he replied with particular force to the notion that his friend Roethke might be linked with the confessional school. When asked by Gary Pacernick if he considered himself a Jewish poet, he notes, "the noun 'poet' does not require a qualifying adjective, either 'Jewish,' 'American,' or 'modern.'" Poetry becomes both a means and an end in finding one's personal center, and one point of entry for understanding his or any poet's work is the cluster of key images at the heart of a body of work. Perhaps with the "feast of losses" of his poem "The Layers" in mind, he points out that his poetic perspective does not signify a lament for any specific loss or circumstance; he nevertheless accepts the notion that he becomes more an "elegiac poet" late life, what he characterizes as his natural tone. Reflecting his preference for natural over urban settings and his fascination with the creature world, he describes varied forms of life, specifically animals (both great and small) that appear in his poems (e.g., whales, raccoons, snakes, crickets, dragonflies, hookworms). If like many poets he once again rejects convenient labels, he nevertheless acknowledges that he is a poet of the natural world, if not explicitly a nature poet.

If Kunitz tends to challenge or reject the fixed categories of so-called poetic schools, there is nevertheless considerable inspiration to be found in some of his more affirming comments on the poet's vocation. The poet, he notes, pursues a quest to discover the secret self, the hidden self, the voice behind the mask. With a self-defined posture of being an outsider, a subversive voice distanced from mainstream culture, it is the writer's role to suffer and to bear witness to suffering and dispossession. Poems can be "vessels of compassionate imagination," a defense against forces of dehumanization, a contribution to human wholeness. Whatever bitterness colored his early life, it can be clearly seen from these comments that Kunitz never abandons the higher vocation of the poet, aligning himself with a visionary tradition he identified with William Blake.

Kunitz took great pains with his interviews, often insisting on several stages of revisions. For the interview with Gary Pacernick on his Jewish background, for example, he met with the interviewer in 1995, wrote down answers to Pacernick's questions in advance of their face-to-face exchange, and referred to the texts of his prepared answers during their discussion. In 1997 there was a follow-up discussion and subsequent additions and revisions.

Interview responses also served as source material for subsequent writing projects for Kunitz. In his foreword to *A Kind of Order, A Kind of Folly*, the author points out that a volume of reflective prose bears some of the features of a random miscellany. In that vein, "Recapitulations" in that volume is a series of apparently disconnected ruminations, reflections, observations, and aphorisms on a variety of subjects—aesthetic motifs, the roots of his poetry, his friendships in the sister arts of painting and sculpture, his comments on a host of poets. Entitled "Seedcorn and Windfall," many of these statements take an aphoristic turn, and when asked about his own aphoristic style, Kunitz notes, "Blake is a great model for anyone who wants to write aphoristically, and he has no rival in that sphere." "Seedcorn and Windfall" includes the following statement: "One of the prevailing illusions is that youth itself is a kind of genius . . . instead of a biological condition."[11] The casual reader would not know that this aphorism came from a more substantial commentary on a fast-paced, youth-oriented culture of obsolescence, part of an interview in the alumni magazine of Bennington College. The following statement, a more complex example than the brief entry just cited, appears to be a discrete comment on guilt and sin:

> When I speak of "the guilty man," I don't mean someone who has sinned more than others. I mean the person who, simply by virtue of being mortal, is in a way condemned; he's mortal and he's fallible, and his life is inevitably a series of errors and consequences. Since he cannot really see the true path—it is not given him to see it, except in the moments of revelation—he is denied the rapture of innocence.[12]

This passage, taken from a volume of prose published in 1975, derives from an interview that appeared in *Contemporary Literature* in 1974. Serving as a self-contained statement, it can also provide a gloss on Kunitz's "The Guilty Man," a poem that appeared in his volume *Passport to the War* and much revised for republication in subsequent volumes. Moreover, that poem first appeared in *Poetry* magazine in 1934, one in a trio of poems called "Nameless Men." In "The Single Conscience," an essay published in *Poetry* in 1938, Kunitz refers to the artist-poet as "the true, recurrent undying wanderer, the eternally guilty, invincibly friendly man."[13] From this one example in

"Seedcorn and Windfall," one can see how from a singular interview excerpt one can connect various strands of association, meaning, and implication—guilt, conscience, names, and namelessness—that reverberate among Kunitz's works in several genres and forms. The value Kunitz attaches to these observations, derived from interviews and notebook entries over many decades, is underscored by Kunitz's resurrection of "Seedcorn and Windfall" for a second installment in *Next-to-Last Things*. Once again, many of the observations derive from interviews conducted over the decades. Kunitz, moreover, developed a tentative plan, never fulfilled, to publish *A Poet's Miscellany*, a fuller and more complete assembly of his aphorisms and journal notes sometime in the late 1990s. The poet Susan Mitchell, noting that a concise journal entry precedes Kunitz's "The Wellfleet Whale," has written perceptively on how an interplay of suggestion and meaning among various genres—poem, essay, journal entry, aphorism—illuminate the fuller body of Kunitz's work.[14]

The circumstances that led to Kunitz's interviews are varied. Because of his friendships with painters like Philip Guston, Mark Rothko, Franz Kline, and Robert Motherwell, he was asked to contribute to symposia on art and sculpture.[15] Having contributed his series "Words for the Unknown Makers" to complement a Whitney Museum exhibition on American folk art, he was asked to respond to questions on the crafts tradition, an interest in folklore that went back as far as his days as a reporter for the *Worcester Telegram*. In that interview for *Craft International* magazine, he told the story of his encounter with the Old Darned Man, a Connecticut folklore figure, and this description later appeared as a prose poem in the *American Poetry* Review and *Next-to-Last* Things.[16] As a teacher at various colleges and universities, he was interviewed by students for literary magazines and alumni publications. After his visit to Russia in 1967, he was asked to comment on that experience by Sherwood Harris, deputy editor of *Ameryka*, the Polish language version of a magazine published by the United States Information Agency. He was interviewed by the poet and critic Richard Kostelanetz. By the 1980s, his growing reputation and his work as a translator led to measure of international recognition, and he was interviewed by the distinguished Indian author Ayappa Paniker. By that time each year seemed to bring a new prize, honor, and recognition, and he was sought out by the editors of distinguished journals in literature and the arts and figures in the electronic media.

The Moyers interview mentioned at the outset of this introduction appeared in *Interviews and Encounters with Stanley Kunitz*, edited by Moss.

Moss's volume includes many significant and illuminating interviews, including Kunitz's exchange with Christopher Busa on the art of poetry (*Paris Review* 1982), which was republished with revisions in *Next-to-Last Things*. I am grateful to Chris Busa for calling to my attention to (and for his willingness to reprint here) a later interview with Kunitz that appeared in *Provincetown Arts*. The current volume includes interviews from the various phases of Kunitz's career, including the two decades since Moss's volume appeared. Many of the items reprinted here have not been listed in previous bibliographies, and their inclusion is based on research into the Stanley Kunitz Papers, 1919–2003. For guidance to specific items in the Kunitz Papers, I gratefully acknowledge the cooperation and assistance of the staff of the Manuscripts Division, Department of Rare Books and Special Collections, Princeton University Library.

KPL

Notes

1. Kunitz, *Next-to-Last Things: New Poems and Essays* (Boston: Atlantic Monthly P, 1985), 175.

2. "Kunitz, Stanley (Jasspon)," *World Authors 1950–1970*, ed. John Wakeman (New York: H. W. Wilson Company, 1975), 822–26. Since Kunitz wrote the biographical entry for this volume, it has served as a standard source for information about his career.

3. Kunitz, Interview with Mary Oliver, circa 1970, Stanley Kunitz Papers, Department of Rare Books and Special Collections, Princeton University Library, Box 19, Folder 1.

4. www.poetshouse.org/about/mission.

5. Kunitz, "American Poetry's Silver Age," *Writing in America*, eds. John Fischer and Robert B. Silvers (New Brunswick, NJ: Rutgers UP, 1960), 27–45.

6. Fran Quinn and Jonathan Blunk, "Interview with Stanley Kunitz," *Worcester Review* 13 (1992), 63–64. The conversation with Tate appeared as "Communication and Communion: A Dialogue," *Southern Review* 21 (April 1985), 404–14.

7. Cynthia Davis, "Myths and Monsters," *Interviews and Encounters with Stanley Kunitz*, ed. Stanley Moss (Riverdale-on-Hudson, NY: The Sheep Meadow P, 1992), 33–34.

8. Moss, *Interviews and Encounters*, ix.

9. Robert Boyers, "Imagine Wrestling with an Angel: An Interview with Stanley

Kunitz," *Salamagundi* 22–23 (1973), 71–83. When this interview appeared in *Interviews and Encounters*, Kunitz excised the hermetic reference.

10. Davis, "Myths and Monsters," *Interviews and Encounters*, 41.

11. Kunitz, "Seedcorn and Windfall," *A Kind of Order, A Kind of Folly* (Boston: Atlantic Monthly P, 1975), 304.

12. "Seedcorn and Windfall," *A Kind of Order, A Kind of Folly*, 310.

13. First appearing in *Poetry*, "The Single Conscience" was reprinted in *A Kind of Order, A Kind of Folly*, 187–93.

14. Mitchell, "A Visit to the Poet's Studio," *Interviews and Encounters*, 149–51.

15. "A Symposium on Pop Art," *Arts Magazine* April 1963, 41–44; Oral History Interview with Stanley Kunitz on Mark Rothko, Archives of American Art, Smithsonian Institution, conducted by Avis Berman, 8 December 1983.

16. "The Tumbling of Worms," *American Poetry Review* 14 (September–October 1985), 24, resurfaced in *Next-to-Last Things*, 9–10. For background on "the legendary figure, known throughout the country as the Old Darned Man," see *A Treasury of New England Folklore*, ed. B. A. Botkin (New York: American Legacy P, 1989), 287–91.

Chronology

1905 Kunitz is born on July 29, in Worcester, Massachusetts. He is the son of Yetta Helen and Solomon Z. Kunitz, European immigrants. His father commits suicide before his son's birth.

1918 Kunitz's mother remarries, a man named Mark Dine; stepfather dies only a year later.

1920 Moves out of house and finds a room at YMCA; works various jobs.

1922 After graduating from Classical High School, enters Harvard to pursue a degree in English; minors in philosophy.

1925 Submits writing samples to Roland Andrews, editor of the *Worcester Telegram-Gazette* in hopes of a position as a newspaper reporter. Works cooperatively with staff members Francis P. Murphy and William H. Guilfoyle.

1926 B.A., Harvard University, *summa cum laude*; receives Garrison Medal for Poetry from the university; interviews rocket pioneer Robert Goddard for *Telegram*.

1927 M.A., Harvard University; denied access to further graduate study after being told, "Our Anglo-Saxon students would resent being taught English literature by a Jew." Covers Sacco-Vanzetti trial for Worcester paper; travels to New York in attempt to find publisher for Vanzetti's letters and to seek new prospects. Begins an association with H. W. Wilson Company, which included editorship of *Wilson Library Bulletin*, the leading periodical in the library field.

1929–1930 Allowed great freedom by H. W. Wilson Company, Kunitz lives abroad in France and Italy.

1930 *Intellectual Things*, first book of poems published. Marries Helen Pearce, and moves to a farm in Mansfield Center, Connecticut.

1931 Under the pseudonym "Dilly Tante," a name he used in columns for the *Bulletin*, he edits *Living Authors: A Book of Biographies*,

	the first of seven reference works he published with the H. W. Wilson Company.
1933	Coedits with Howard Haycraft and Wilbur C. Hadden *Authors Yesterday and Today*.
1934	Edits with Howard Haycraft *The Junior Book of Authors*.
1935	Moves to New Hope, Pennsylvania. Meeting with poet Theodore Roethke begins long-term correspondence and friendship.
1936	Edits with Howard Haycraft *British Authors of the Nineteenth Century*.
1937	Divorced from Helen Pearce.
1938	Edits with Howard Haycraft *American Authors 1600–1900*.
1939	Marries Eleanor Evans.
1941	Receives the Oscar Blumenthal prize from *Poetry* magazine.
1942	Edits with Howard Haycraft *Twentieth-Century Authors*.
1943–1945	Serves in the U.S. Army in charge of information and education for the Air Transport Command, Gravely Point, Washington.
1944	*Passport to the War*, second book of poems inspired by wartime experience, published.
1946	Recipient of fellowship in creative writing from Guggenheim Foundation. Spends time writing a novel in house on large estate of naturalist Ernest Thompson Seton in Santa Fe, New Mexico.
1946–1949	Teaches at Bennington College, replacing Theodore Roethke.
1949–1953	Teaches at Potsdam State Teachers College (now State University of New York, Potsdam). Advises English Department on curriculum and teaches summer seminars.
1950–1958	Taught at New School for Social Research, New York City.
1950	Birth of daughter Gretchen.
1950–1957	Directs poetry workshops, New School for Social Research, New York City.
1952	Edits with Howard Haycraft *British Authors Before 1800*.
1953	Wins Amy Lowell Traveling Scholarship.
1954	Travels in Europe.
1955	Edits with Vineta Colby *Twentieth-Century Authors: First Supplement*.
1955–1957	Poet-in-residence, University of Washington.
1956	Receives Levinson Prize, *Poetry* magazine.
1956–1957	Poet-in-residence, Queen's College, New York City.
1957	Spends a summer in Provincetown, Massachusetts. Receives *Saturday Review* award.

1958   *Selected Poems* published. Marries Elise Asher, a painter. Receives a fellowship award from the Academy of American Poets. Receives Harriet Monroe Award, University of Chicago.

1958–1959 Poet-in-residence, Brandeis University. Receives Ford Foundation grant.

1958–1962 Poetry workshop, Young Men's Hebrew Poetry Center, New York City.

1959   *Selected Poems* wins Pulitzer Prize.

1961   Receives honorary doctor of letters degree, Clark University, Worcester, Massachusetts.

1961–1963 Danforth lecturer at U.S. colleges and universities.

1962   His appreciation for Cape Cod having been whetted five years earlier, he takes a property in the west end of Provincetown. He would then divide time between Provincetown and his apartment in New York's Greenwich Village for the rest of his life.

1963   Begins long association with Columbia University, first as lecturer in School of General Studies; then as teacher of creative writing in School of the Arts. Selected to the National Institute of Arts and Letters.

1964   Editor of *Poems of John Keats*.

1965   Receives Brandeis University Medal of Achievement.

1966   Leads a series of dialogues with twelve poets, sponsored by the Academy of American Poets, on teaching poetry in American high schools.

1966   Contributes as translator to *Anti-Worlds and the Fifth Ace*, by Andrei Voznesensky; edits with Vineta Colby *European Authors, 1000–1900*.

1967   Visits Russia as part of a cultural exchange program. Reads his poetry and lectures on poetry.

1968   Fellowship Award, Academy of American Poets. One of the figures who organize Fine Arts Work Center in Provincetown, Massachusetts; Founding chairman of the FAWC Writing Program; this association would extend to the end of his career.

1969–1977 Editor, Yale Series of Younger Poets (Yale University Press).

1970   Elected chancellor of the Academy of American Poets. Visiting lecturer, Yale University.

1971   *The Testing-Tree and Other Poems* published. Contributes as translator to *Stolen Apples* by Yevgeny Yevtushenko.

1973   Collaborative translation (with Max Hayward) of *The Poems of Anna Akhmatova*.

1974–1976   Poetry Consultant, Library of Congress.

1974   Publishes *The Terrible Threshold* in Great Britain. Collaborative translation of *Story under Full Sail* by Andre Voznesensky. *Robert Lowell: Poet of Terribilita* published as a limited edition pamphlet by J. Pierpont Morgan Library. Illustrated edition of *The Coat without a Seam* published.

1975   *A Kind of Order, A Kind of Folly* (essays) published. Elected to the American Academy of Arts and Letters. Editorial consultant, *World Authors, 1950–1970*, edited by John Wakeman.

1976   Collaborative translation of *Orchard Lamps* by Ukranian Poet Ivan Drach; lectures on reading tours in Africa.

1978   Kunitz's poem "The Lincoln Relics" published as chapbook by the Graywolf Press; Senior Fellow in the Humanities, Princeton University.

1979   *The Poems of Stanley Kunitz 1928–1978* published. Wins the Lenore Marshall Prize.

1980   Receives Lenore Marshall Prize from the Poetry Society of America. Guest of honor, *The Poet in Society*, University of Virginia. Edits *Selections: University and College Poetry Prizes 1973–1978* for Academy of American Poets.

1981   Reads Phi Beta Kappa poem at Harvard University.

1983   *The Wellfleet Whale and Companion Poems* published as chapbook by Sheep Meadow Press.

1985   Honored in week-long series of readings, lectures, musical programs in Worcester, Massachusetts. Reads poetry in Worcester's Mechanics Hall, where he debated as a high school student.

1986   *A Celebration for Stanley Kunitz on His Eightieth Birthday* published by Sheep Meadow Press, a collection of poems and tributes from other authors.

1986–1988   Chosen first State Poet of New York, Walt Whitman Citation of Merit.

1987   Author of introduction, *The Essential Blake*. Wins Bollingen Prize conferred by Yale University Library. With Elizabeth Kray, founds Poets House in New York City. Publishes "The Quest for the Father" in the *New York Review of Books*.

1992   Centennial Medal, Harvard University.

1993   Receives the National Medal of the Arts from President Clinton.

1995   *Passing Through* published. *Passing Through* awarded National Book Award. Receives Shelley Memorial Award from Poetry Society of America.

1998   Receives the Frost Medal from the Poetry Society of America.

2003   In the spring experiences a health crisis from which he emerges "transformed," a favorite Kunitz term.

2005   Publishes *The Wild Braid*, which includes conversations, reflections, and related poems that deal with his passion for gardening. "Stanley's Century," a feature section edited by Cleopatra Mathis and Parker Towle, appears in the *Worcester Review*.

2006   Dies of pneumonia at age one hundred at New York City home.

Conversations with Stanley Kunitz

Pulitzer Prize Poet Stanley Kunitz Started Career in Worcester

Margaret Parsons / 1960

Stanley Kunitz, a native of Worcester, was mentioned as the most underrated poet of today in a special supplement of the London *Times* on "The American Imagination," published November 8, 1959, this in spite of the fact that he had just won the Pulitzer Prize for his *Selected Poems*, as the best book of poetry published in 1958. He was described as "the poet's poet" in an article on "A Vocal Group, the Jewish Part of American Letters."

Last year he won the Ford grant as one of the ten American writers whom the Ford Foundation is subsidizing for two years, that they may devote their time and energy to writing.

He returned to his New York home from Boston, where the previous college year he had been on the faculty of Brandeis University.

Among his many awards is the Amy Lowell Traveling Scholarship, which he received in 1953. He was enabled thereby to spend the next year in Europe.

Kunitz was born in Worcester and lived on Providence Street until he graduated from Harvard, summa cum laude in 1926 and he has taken a master's degree, also from Harvard, in 1927.

His early education was in the Worcester public schools and he was valedictorian in his class at Classical High School, from which he graduated in 1922. While there he edited the school magazine, played on the tennis team, and won several debating prizes. He won a scholarship from Harvard, was named to Phi Beta Kappa, the honor society for scholastic achievement.

While he was at college, he had been working during the summer vacations as reporter on the *Worcester Telegram*. After receiving his master's degree in 1927, he was a staff writer for the *Telegram* until early 1928, when he went to New York. He wanted to be a writer and decided to try to get into the publishing world.

Not even when he was teaching at nearby Brandeis did he come back, though, as he was driving about the countryside, the signposts beckoned him to Worcester.

We have been following his career with interest for the thirty-one years we have been editing the *Sunday Telegram* Book Page, carrying reviews of all his books and noting his rising success and recognition in the *Evening Gazette* Book Chat. We had corresponded but had never met. So we called him last spring at Brandeis, but just missed him. Barely had the students registered last fall when we were on his trail again, only to learn that he was still in New York, by virtue of the Ford grant.

So we wrote to New York and made plans to see him there during National Book Awards, on which he was a judge. He is one of the distinguished Worcester authors—along with S. N. Behrman, Esther Forbes, and the late Bob Benchley—and we want to introduce him to Worcester people, many of whom know him only by his poetry.

We found him at his home on West Twelfth Street, near Seventh Avenue in what is loosely termed Greenwich Village. It is one of a block of brick houses built in the 1880s, with large rooms and high ceilings, which give a pleasant air of spaciousness, after one has been visiting the more compact modern New York apartments.

Our eye was attracted at once by the many paintings of such variety as to suggest different artists. So we were not surprised, on meeting his wife, to learn that she is an artist and poet, Elise Asher. Some of the paintings are by her and some by friends with whom she has swapped. They have been married three years. She has a daughter by a previous marriage, and so has the poet, whose daughter is now in California.

The house is large enough to provide a studio for her, a study for him. From the back windows in his study on the second floor we see the outline of his garden, in which he takes particular delight. From the window we noticed the entrance with a bas-relief sculptured head on the wall and the shape of the oblong garden beyond, spacious for the heart of New York. Making things grow and playing tennis are two things Kunitz likes best to do.

Conversation naturally started with Worcester. We had to tell Kunitz about the wholesale destruction of Providence Hill, where his old home was, and we broke the big news that it looks like we were really going to have a new public library. Of his fellow workers on the *Telegram*, there aren't many left now.

He spoke of his interest in Sam Behrman's book, *The Worcester Account*, and said life on Providence Hill described by Behrman was entirely different from what he knew a half a generation later. The picturesqueness and the foreign flavor of the transported people keeping their old language and their old customs had yielded to the Americanization process of ironing out the differences between the old settlers and new neighbors.

When Kunitz left for New York and its publishing world, he had behind him the practical experience of his newspaper work here and training in writing under "Copey" (Charles Townsend Copeland) and other Harvard professors.

We came across a story told by Kunitz in *Copey at Harvard*, a new book by J. Donald Adams. Kunitz recalls the time when he was taking Copey's advanced course, English 12: "I was much involved in the world of private fantasy and my stories were written in a high-flown style with which Copey could have little sympathy. As I look back now, I see how patient he was with me when I resisted his efforts to pull me down to earth.

"My pride was hurt by his criticism; but just then when I was prepared to yield to utter dejection, he would permit himself to cluck approvingly at the appropriate places in my manuscript. 'Write out of what you know,' is the admonition that sticks in my mind.

"We were not easy with each other in these intimate conferences—some of my classmates were much closer to him—but in the end he gave me an 'A' with his blessing and with a gift to boot, *The Art of Thought* by Graham Wallas. The volume, in which he inscribed an unexpected compliment, is still in my possession.

"Perhaps I owe a great debt to a less famous teacher Robert Gay of Simmons College, who (if memory serves me right) substituted for Copey the following year, with the title of visiting professor. It was he who returned a manuscript of mine with the comment 'You are a poet—why don't you write poems?' I did thereafter."

But one doesn't make a living writing poems, as Kunitz explained to me, years after the incident above took place. At fifty cents a line, which he says is a good rate for poetry, the poet who sold a thousand lines a year would make five hundred dollars.

His apprenticeship in the publishing world was on the staff of the H. W.

Wilson Co. of New York, where he began to write sketches for the excellent series of biographical dictionaries of modern literature, which have been coming out ever since *Living Authors*, the first, edited by "Dilly Tante." (Kunitz wished in those early days to make his name known by more original work.) Perhaps their enthusiastic reception induced him to use his own name on the many succeeding volumes.

We are glad that the increasing time he gives to poetry has not entirely diverted him from these indispensable books of reference (in the eyes of a book reviewer). He is now at work on one of even larger scope, treating the lives and works of many different authors of many different lands and going back to past literary history.

By the way when he first went to New York seeking a start to his literary career, he carried with him the makings of a manuscript which he thought would be eagerly received by the publishers. He had covered phases of the Sacco-Vanzetti case for the *Telegram* and had been given Vanzetti's letters to his mother to edit or dispose of. But not a publisher was to be found who would touch them. (Like many, he felt the defendants had not had a fair trial. Furthermore, he believed them innocent—a subject on which there is still a division of opinion.)

It was then that he sought and secured a job with Wilson and was the founder of the *Wilson Library Bulletin*, which is still going and is considered the most successful library bulletin in the world. He was then living in Mansfield, Connecticut. His first volume of poetry, *Intellectual Things*, was published in 1930 and got a very nice reception.

Came the second World War, and he entered the army as a private, became staff sergeant and was in the information and education division in Washington. He edited a weekly magazine, *Ten-Minute Break*. On leaving the army in 1945, he was given a Guggenheim Fellowship and went to New Mexico, where he lived in an abandoned Pullman car on the Santa Fe ranch of the Ernest Thompson Seton.

Suddenly out of nowhere came an invitation to become a teacher at Bennington College where he had once given a poetry reading. Feeling that he had learned what he needed of the publishing business, he accepted, although the pay was much less. He has never regretted the change. After being at Bennington for three years, he taught at the University of Washington.

Mainly he taught poetry and conducted poetry workshops, so that today he finds a substantial percentage of young poets are his former students. In nearly every magazine using poetry or in collections of the work of young poets, he finds names of his former students cropping up.

He is also active in conducting poetry readings at the YMHA and other New York centers. A brochure on the Kunitz poetry has recently appeared in the Yale Series of Recorded Poets, edited by Louis Martz, chairman of the Yale English Department where Kunitz has recorded his own works.

We were interested in hearing his opinion of the state of poetry today.

"The best modern poetry is complex," he explained, "because it is dealing with the manifold tissues of experience. This problem of the obscurity of modern poetry is not the responsibility of the poet, but of the reader. It is an encouraging symptom that more interest is shown in poetry than ever before, partly because of the readings in poetry centers throughout the country, partly because of recorded poems. The vogue of reading started with Thomas at the YMHA in nonsectarian meetings, freely and generously devoted to the arts themselves without any kind of dogma."

We were interested to hear his high opinion of the poetry readings of the YMHA, because we attended the first reading by Dylan Thomas when, as Kunitz says, "Dylan Thomas taught the audience that you didn't have to understand all the poems said, for the music of language is an intrinsic point."

Kunitz gave a very hopeful picture for poetry in a recent article in *Harper's*: "This happens not to be a time a great innovation in poetic technique; it is rather a period in which the technical gains of past decades, particularly the 1920s, are being tested and consolidated."

"Despite all the lamentations about the state of poetry in America today, the general level of quality, I dare say, is higher than it has ever been in our literary history. It isn't a Golden Age for several obvious reasons, including the absence of one or two monumental geniuses in their prime to concentrate the poetic energies of the age; but it may well be a Silver Age . . . My guess is—my wild guess, if you will—that only the Elizabethans will make a better showing."

He is referring here especially to the Elizabethan lyrics. He is himself engaged this year in writing a long narrative poem.

When we saw Kunitz in New York, he was just back from Washington, where he had given a poetry reading under the Gertrude Clarke Whittall Fund, which takes us back to Worcester. Mrs. Whittall, formerly of Worcester, was present and took great pleasure in hearing the young poet (as she called him in a whisper to her companion overheard by Kunitz). We wonder if she realized that he came from the city where for so many years she had made her home.

Communication and Communion: A Dialogue between Stanley Kunitz and Allen Tate

Allen Tate / 1966

In the spring of 1966, because poets were persistently complaining that poetry was badly taught, the Academy of American Poets and Stanley Kunitz organized, in conjunction with the New York City Board of Education, a series of weekly dialogues between Mr. Kunitz and twelve American poets as an accredited course for high school teachers. This course was preparatory to the inception of the now nationally renowned "Poetry-in-the-Schools" program, which began the following year in New York City under the direction of Elizabeth Kray, who was then executive director of the academy. Among those who participated in this series of dialogues were: W. H. Auden, Anthony Hecht, Denise Levertov, Robert Lowell, William Meredith, Howard Nemerov, Henry Rago, Louis Simpson, W. D. Snodgrass, Allen Tate, and Robert Penn Warren. The tapes of this entire series, which have only recently been transcribed, are now housed at the Poetry Room of Harvard University along with the academy's complete archive of recorded poets. This conversation with Allen Tate took place on March 30, 1966.

Kunitz: I can think of no better way of introducing Mr. Allen Tate than by reading a paragraph from an essay of his entitled "The Man of Letters in the Modern World":

> A man of letters has, then, in our time a small but critical service to render to man: a service that will be in the future more effective than it is now, when the cult of the literary man shall have ceased to be an idolatry. Men of letters

and their followers, like the parvenu gods and their votaries of decaying Rome, compete in the dissemination of distraction and novelty. But the true province of a man of letters is nothing less (as it is nothing more) than culture itself. The state is the mere operation of society, but culture is the way society lives, the material medium through which men receive the one lost truth of what Jacques Maritain calls the "supra-temporal destiny" of man. It is the duty of the man of letters to supervise the culture of language, to which the rest of culture is subordinate, and to warn us when our language is ceasing to forward the ends proper to man. The end of social man is communion in time through love, which is beyond time. [Tate, Allen, *The Forlorn Demon: Didactic and Critical Essays*, Chicago: Regnery, 1953, 9.]

Tate: I don't know what I'm supposed to say now. I wrote those words a long time ago, and I am rather astounded at the rhetoric of the passage. It seems a little high-flown, but I think I still believe what I said insofar as I understand it. I have a clearer recollection of another passage which discussed the difference between communication and communion. Now when you turn on the radio or the TV and you hear some commentator discussing Vietnam, he's engaging in communication, isn't he? He may not quite know what he's communicating, but that's his purpose, If you're reading a poem, you are not receiving a communication, you're participating in a discovery, and as a reader you participate in that discovery as a collaborator. We *use* communication; we *participate* in communion. Any work of art, any genuine work of art, poem, picture, or sculpture, is a discovery of a kind of knowledge about the human condition that we didn't have before. On the contrary, the mass-medium commentator is trying to move us toward some course of action, which may be deplorable or of uncertain consequences. We had better beware of these people who communicate. I think it's best to go off and sit by ourselves alone and read Shakespeare.

Kunitz: Communicators have an ulterior purpose in mind: they want to persuade you to believe something, do something, or maybe, under optimum conditions, buy something. The information that poetry conveys is incidental to its design as an instrument of aesthetic pleasure.

Tate: I think I. A. Richards made a good point about that many years ago. He said that a poem obviously contains ideas about human conduct, but a genuine work of art, a genuine poem, puts us in a state which he described as a readiness to act—but we don't act. I remember that Wystan Auden wrote years ago that "poetry makes nothing happen." Outside us, that is—something does happen inside us.

Kunitz: Before we came here, Mr. Tate and I were discussing a way of beginning our talk, and I suggested it might be seasonal and proper to open with a reading of a poem that is a celebration of the spring, at least in one of its aspects: A. E. Housman's "Loveliest of Trees":

[Kunitz reads three stanzas from A. E. Housman's "Loveliest of Trees."]

Kunitz: What made me think of the poem is that I've just learned it's the subject of a quiz, prepared by Science Research Associates, that is being given to college students. This is to determine who should and who should not be sent to Vietnam. One of the justifications for deferment would be the ability to reply to the questions about this poem, or poems like this, in the way that Science Research Associates expects you to reply. The first of the true and false questions reads:

> How old was the poet when he wrote this poem? Here are the options:
> A) Twenty
> B) Forty
> C) Fifty
> D) Seventy
> E) One cannot tell

Now the right answer, according to Science Research Associates, is what you might guess. Twenty, of course, because,

> Now, of my threescore years and ten,
> Twenty will not come again,
> And take from seventy springs a score,
> It only leaves me fifty more.

Fifty from seventy leaves twenty. Simple! But what has this to do with the age of the poet? The calculations concern the speaker of the poem, who is a dramatized creation, a persona. This confusion of the poet with the speaker of the poem is, I think, an elementary misconception.

Tate: That's very true. Some years ago I was out in Salt Lake City, reading some poems of my own. A pretty young lady in the back row held up her hand rather timidly and said, "Mr. Tate, you seem so cheerful. Why are your poems so gloomy?" She was assuming that I wrote the poem, you see. I wrote the poem. Somebody else wrote the poem with my hand.

Kunitz: We both agreed before we came into the hall here that Housman's poem is one we found great pleasure in, and yet it is not the kind of poem either of us can write or that anyone we know can write in our time.

Tate: Perhaps the reason is simply the whole sense of the human condition has changed since the end of the nineteenth century when this poem was written, and there's been a revolution in poetry. The simple romantic lyric seems almost impossible to write today because there's always—on at least the periphery of one's mind—immense complexities of experience, tied to the circumstances of modern life, that seem to inhibit the lyrical impulse. The revolution initiated by Pound and Eliot around the time of the First World War, shortly before that, made it possible for poets to put into poetry a much more inclusive experience than even the great Victorians had been able to accomplish. I don't mean to say that the modern poets have written longer poems and that they're more comprehensive in that respect. Modern poets don't write long poems. There are few distinguished long poems in our time. But line by line in the whole texture of the language there's a much more inclusive sense of the ambiguities of the human situation, and that accounts for what is sometimes referred to as the obscurity and difficulty of modern poetry. It's actually in the long run not more difficult than poetry of certain periods in the past, but it is at any rate quite different. I think of many different lyrical passages in the *Cantos* of Ezra Pound. But they are all somehow qualified by an undercutting of irony. He takes it back, he doesn't quite, he can't quite sustain it. I think the *Cantos* is a series of beautiful fragments—some parts of it not so beautiful, just dead, flat prose, which seems to be a kind of commentary on the lyrical impulse, as if to say, I don't believe in it. Or if I do believe in it, I can't sustain it. Something in our world will not allow me to sustain it.

Kunitz: The nineteenth-century household poet tended to use materials in his verse that were rather obviously poetic and which evoked conditioned responses, whereas the poet in our time would rather build his universe of language out of materials that do not present themselves as being on the surface poetic. In that light I sometimes feel that poetry is the enemy of the poem.

Tate: I think that is very true. We know that early in T. S. Eliot's career, one of his purposes was to build up a language which would permit him to put into his poetry, to convert into poetry, the discordant and even the sordid aspects of urban life, which was probably a lesson he learned from Baudelaire, from *Les Fleurs du Mal*. But his purpose was definitely to have a non-poetical language, and yet make it poetry, If we read one of his early poems like "Prufrock," we'll see that he has done that. There are some conventional properties of poetry, but he presents them ironically. That is to say, you can no longer believe in these things. That is true of Pound also, and Hart Crane, and most of the poets we are interested in our time.

Kunitz: The opening lines of "Prufrock," with the image of the evening "spread out against the sky/ Like a patient etherised upon a table," struck some members of this audience last week as atrocious. They seemed to regard it as a violation of the poetic contract.

Tate: Their assumption was that the properties of the poem must be intrinsically poetic. But it's up to the poet to make them poetic. Eliot begins his poem, "Let us go then, you and I/ When the evening is spread out against the sky/Like a patient etherised upon a table." It becomes poetic as the context of the poem develops because of what Prufrock is saying. He's not actually describing the sunset or the twilight, he's saying something about himself, that he is passive and scarcely conscious.

Kunitz: In a state of anesthesia.

Tate: It's almost anesthesia. And that prepares the way for the brilliant conclusion of the poem when Prufrock comes back to reality and drowns in reality. He's lived on illusion and fantasy, you see.

Kunitz: In making your distinction between communication and communion, I gather that by the word communion you imply the sharing of a felt experience.

Tate: Yes.

Kunitz: You have taken over into the medium of poetry some of the language of religion.

Tate: Yes, I think I have. It's analogous to the idea of communion, religious communion, and I think it is somewhat related to it. That is to say in a religious service of any kind, nothing is communicated. People gather together and share through certain symbols a common experience or a renewal of a common experience. I think that is what happens between the poet and his reader. There's something shared, a discovery or something that is not quite of the naturalistic order of experience, something a little beyond that, something arrested in time. It's outside the relation between cause and effect in which most of our ordinary experience takes place.

Kunitz: It is abundantly clear that one of the profound differences between poetry in our own time and the poetry of other times is that we are no longer living in an age of faith. When a community has a common faith, a common set of beliefs, poetry has a natural advantage in that it can spring from the assumption of common responses to given situations or symbols. In a fragmented society we can no longer act on that assumption.

Tate: I'm not averse to what you say. I think that the discussion of this point in our time frequently has brought us back to Dante and *The Divine Comedy*. Many years ago, I. A. Richards and T. S. Eliot had an amiable controversy on this subject, and I can't think that people have added very much to it since then—the relation of poetry and belief.

Mr. Eliot's conclusion was—I think he won the argument—well, Mr. Richards said that one reason why he liked "The Waste Land" was that it was a poetry without any beliefs whatever. Here was a poetry for modern man; you see, it was not embarrassed by beliefs which he couldn't share. Well, I think that's wrong. "The Waste Land" is full of implicit beliefs of all kinds—partly Christian, partly from the *Upanishads*—but Eliot's point was that in reading *The Divine Comedy* it was not necessary to be a believing Catholic. What was necessary was to *understand* the philosophical and theological background of the poem because the poem doesn't consist of those beliefs. The acts of the poem refer to them, and the conduct of the characters whether in Hell or Purgatory or Paradise has been motivated, or at least made rational, through these beliefs. The poem itself concerns the characters whom Dante presents in each Canto as the poem progresses toward the end. And there's no doubt that Dante had a very great advantage.

At the same time, while there was a shared community of beliefs, it's been proved that Dante was not merely a servile follower of Thomas Aquinas.

Etienne Gilson has shown that Dante was a philosopher on his own account and constructed his own philosophy, which suited his needs as a poet. So this relationship between the poet and belief is always a very shifting one and difficult to reduce to a formula.

Kunitz: Once you take faith out of the society, the arts become the vessels of those displaced mystical yearnings. And the problem of the poem is how to become transcendent at the same time that it takes its matter from the things of the world around us, the phenomenal experience.

Tate: That's very true because there's so much modern poetry that can't assume a body of belief, and the poetry itself is a kind of dialectic between doubt and faith. The conflict gets into the poetry. It's not settled before the poetry is written. Now we know that the great Victorians had this conflict, but their poetry was still more traditional. That is, it tells them the two voices, Tennyson's *In Memoriam* was dealing with this whole thing. But it is not so much an interior experience for him. It was something he was merely aware of without being deeply affected by it; whereas a poet like T. S. Eliot has been profoundly affected by it. Gerard Manley Hopkins was, and he was the only English poet of that time whose religious experience got into the poetry.

Kunitz: Blake, in a way, is the grandfather of the modern poet when he says, "I must create a system myself or be enslaved by another man's."

Tate: And Yeats continued that by constructing a system of his own, partly suggested by Blake.

Kunitz: Perhaps it would be interesting, in juxtaposition to the Housman poem, to read a lyric that comes out of the same tradition but that satisfies us less. What of Wordsworth's "I Wandered Lonely as a Cloud"?

Tate: I'll take a perverse delight in reading it because I think it so bad.

> I wandered lonely as a cloud
> That floats on high o'er vales and hills,
> When all at once I saw a crowd,
> A host, of golden daffodils;
> Beside the lake, beneath the trees,
> Fluttering and dancing in the breeze.

Continuous as the stars that shine
And twinkle on the milky way,
They stretched in never-ending line
Along the margin of a bay:
Ten thousand saw I at a glance,
Tossing their heads in sprightly dance.

The waves beside them danced; but they
Out-did the sparkling waves in glee:
A poet could not but be gay,
In such a jocund company:
I gazed—and gazed—but little thought
What wealth the show to me had brought:

For oft, when on my couch I lie
In vacant or in pensive mood,
They flash upon that inward eye
Which is the bliss of solitude;
And then my heart with pleasure fills,
And dances with the daffodils.

How shabby the whole thing is! That a great poet could write that is an appalling thing.

Kunitz: Why do you call it shabby?

Tate: Well, because it's made up of clichés, and the versification is bad, and it's padded out: "a crowd,/ A host, of golden daffodils." He should have chosen one word, a great difference between "a crowd" and "a host." Which are we to choose? The poem isn't written, he's left it up to us.

Kunitz: It's true that the poem has a number of double epithets like "stars that shine/ And twinkle."

Tate: I suppose he thinks we'll see them shining and twinkling at the same moment.

Kunitz: What about that passage, "The waves beside them danced; but they/ Out-did the sparkling waves in glee"? Who can believe in those glee-ful daffodils? "A poet could not but be gay,/ In such a jocund company."

Tate: "Jocund" is one of those dead eighteenth-century words.

Kunitz: Notice that the rhythm never changes. The poem maintains its tidy metrical beat, in disregard of the grain of the feeling. Now it's true that this is a poem that appears in all the traditional anthologies, is taught in all the schools, and remains to this day a sentimental favorite. Some poems, it should be said, make people feel comfortable simply because they are familiar. There's a certain passive gratification in not having to cope with the unexpected, in not having to struggle toward understanding.

Tate: A Wordsworth scholar would say this poem illustrates certain Wordsworthian ideas. They read all poetry, these scholars, to illustrate something else. That's one reason why this is in the Wordsworth canon. It's so easy. Characteristic, romantic ideas are expressed, squeezed out.

Kunitz: This makes me think of a passage in one of your essays entitled "Understanding Modern Poetry." The passage reads:

> The weakness of the Romantic sensibility is that it gave us a poetry of "po-etical" (or poetized) objects, predigested perceptions; and in case there should be any misunderstanding about the poetical nature of these objects, we also got "truths" attached to them—truths that in modern jargon are instructions to the reader to "respond" in a certain way to the poetical object, which is the "stimulus." And in the great body of nineteenth-century lyrical poetry—whose worst ancestor was verse like Shelley's "I arise from dreams of thee"—the poet's personal emotions became the "poetic stimulus." The poem as a formal object to be looked at, to be studied, to be construed (in more than the grammatical sense, but first of all in that sense), dissolved into biography and history, so that in the long run poetry was only a misunderstood pretext for the "study" of the sexual life of the poet, of the history of his age, of anything else that the scholar wished to "study"; and he usually wished to study anything but poetry. [Tate, *On the Limits of Poetry* (New York: The Swallow Press and William Morrow, 1948), 121.]

Tate: I think I have a little anecdote that I could add to that. Many years ago I made some rather rash remarks about Shelley's "Ode to the West Wind," as animadversion against it. "I fall upon the thorns of life! I bleed!" Well, a Shelley scholar. (Isn't it a curious thing among the scholars—there's the Shelley man, the Keats man, the Pope man, the Dryden man. Isn't there something suspect about a man who studies one poet only all his life?)—Yes, anyhow, this Shelley scholar had an introduction to selections from Shelley. He said, "Mr. Tate, when he wrote this paragraph about 'I fall upon the thorns of life! I bleed!' evidently wasn't aware that Shelley's little boy was ill, and Shelley was rather depressed."

Kunitz: In your essay you go on to say,

> So it is not "modern" poetry which is difficult; it is rather a certain kind of poetry as old, in English, as the sixteenth century, and, in Italian, much older than that. It is the kind of poetry that requires of the reader the fullest cooperation of all his intellectual resources, all his knowledge of the world, and all the persistence and alertness that he now thinks only of giving to scientific studies. [Ibid., 123]

And the last few sentences of the essay are central to what we have been discussing.

> I would say then, in conclusion, that modern poetry is difficult because we have lost the art of reading any poetry that will not read itself to us; that thus our trouble is a fundamental problem of education, which may be more fundamental than education. We may be approaching the time when we shall no longer be able to read anything and shall be subject to passive conditioning. Until this shall happen, however, we might possibly begin to look on language as a field of study, not as an impressionistic debauch. If we wish to understand anything, there is only the hard way; if we wish to understand Donne and Eliot, perhaps we had better begin, young, to read the classical languages, and a little later the philosophers. There is probably no other way. [Ibid., 128]

Tate: Consummate perfection, isn't it? I wish I could live up to it.

Kunitz: If we didn't have a dream of perfection, how would we perceive all the things that are wrong with us? Poets are the most dissatisfied people I know. That's what makes them responsible human beings, despite the myth to the contrary.

Tate: I think the poet is responsible first to himself and now to what other people think he ought to be responsible for. He's not responsible for politics, and I think it is a great mistake for poets to become politicians. My friend Shelley, you know, was a wonderful example of that. As soon as he was sent down from Oxford for atheism, in London he made little toy boats and floated them on the pond in Hyde Park. They had tracts on these boats, and they would just sail across. People would read the tracts, and the whole world would be reformed. That's the way poets deal in politics. And I think also of a passage in a poem by the late Phelps Putnam, a very fine poet who's been forgotten. His work hasn't been in print for years, but he has a poem about a group of young men, and they have been at a party. One young man is going home just as the sun is rising. He's not in very good shape, and he looks up and sees the sun rising in the wrong direction. He says "You always knew a time would come when he/ Would grow damned tired of rising in the east," . . . "And I cried 'Pour la Reine' and drew my sword./ But, Christ, I had no sword." That's the poet: as politician, he has no sword.

Kunitz: Imagination is a sword, but of course it's usually stuck in the poet's own heart—at best not too conspicuously. The poems I love most are those that keep their secrets: their motivations and meanings are hidden in the design. There was that French mathematician, you will recall, who, after seeing one of the great plays of Racine, threw up his hands and said, "What does it prove?"

Tate: Well, it doesn't *prove* anything. It just makes it possible for us to participate in a human situation, which is rendered far more comprehensible to us by being given shape and form, interior form. It doesn't prove anything.

Kunitz: The other day I was reading about a certain tribe in New Guinea who have no technology except for the stone axe and the bamboo dagger—no clothes, no pots or pans or dishes, and a language so rudimentary that the word for "joy" is also the word for every other emotion. Now that seems to me a kind of revelation. Suppose that the only word we had to describe the entire spectrum of our feelings was "joy." What a confusion, what a frustration it would be!

Tate: Perhaps if we had only that one word for emotion, we would feel nothing but joy, because words have a magical power.

Kunitz: I'm skeptical about that.

Tate: I am, too.

Kunitz: Part of the whole quest of the poet is to create a language which is so subtle, so fine, that it can project every nuance of feeling, even for feelings for which we have no words. The feelings are diffused through the whole system of the poem.

Tate: And particularly through the interrelation of the words. In the context of the poem, through the harmony of its parts, common words surpass themselves, take on new meanings.

The Poet in the Classroom

Robert Russell / 1967

College English 28 (May 1967), 580–86. Originally published by the National Council of Teachers of English.

Recently while on a lecture tour of some eastern colleges, Stanley Kunitz, Pulitzer Prize–winning poet, stopped at Franklin and Marshall College in Lancaster, Pennsylvania. As an instructor in the English Department, I naturally looked forward to his visit. Since I was then teaching a course in the analysis of poems, I mimeographed Mr. Kunitz's "Green Ways" and passed it out to the class before his visit, saying that, if we were lucky, Mr. Kunitz might attend our meeting.

All good poetry is difficult to read and understand, but not all difficult poetry is good. A large part of the students felt that all "modern poetry" was merely difficult. Still, spurred by the prospect of meeting the poet himself, they outdid themselves in struggling with the lines. Mr. Kunitz agreed to join us for that hour, and the students were eager, loaded with questions.

I introduced the poet. "Mr. Kunitz," asked one of the students, "what did you mean when you said, 'The trellis of the crystal/ In the rose-green moon'?"

"Excuse me," he replied politely, "but I didn't come to explain the poem. I came to listen and perhaps to join in *your* discussion."

They lapsed into silent disappointment. Sensing this, he went on, "You see, it isn't *my* poem now. It's published. It belongs as much to you as to me."

Encouraged, the students began offering their interpretations of the lines. When we were talking freely, Mr. Kunitz interrupted. "Maybe it would help," he said, "if you thought of 'crystal' as being a kind of building block in the mineral universe. 'Trellis' is an accurate image of the architecture of a crystal."

This was the key, and as we talked the shape and power of the poem gradually revealed themselves. It is a cry of pain and exaltation—pain at being trapped in the great cycle of life and death, and exaltation in the joyful knowledge that, even in his own disintegration, the poet gives birth through love to new life and art.

> Let me proclaim it—human be my lot!—
> How from my pit of green horse-bones
> I turn in a wilderness of sweat,
> To the moon-breasted sibylline,
> And lift this garland, Danger, from her throat
> To blaze it in the foundries of the night.

When the hour had raced by, even the most conservative felt that there was at least one great modern poem, and that was "Green Ways" by Stanley Kunitz. Although the poet himself had helped us, he had done so not as the omniscient author, but as an acutely sensitive reader. This hour had been so stimulating that I later thought that I ought to offer a seminar in the poetry of Stanley Kunitz with visits from the poet himself. It was only three hours by train from his New York home to Lancaster, so it might be arranged.

It was, in fact, arranged. The money was put up by the Shell Assists Program, I was shaken free from some of my regular teaching, and the seminar was scheduled. Eight students signed up—an ideal number.

We met in a quiet, book-lined room furnished with a long table, ten chairs, ash trays, a hot plate, a jar of instant coffee, and a stack of cups. We gathered around the table with our copies of Kunitz's *Selected Poems*, published by Little, Brown and Company, the volume which won the Pulitzer Prize for poetry in 1959. This was our reading for the semester—116 pages. We would read and reread every poem, every line of every poem, and every word of every line until we understood.

The collection opens with "The Science of the Night," forty-six lines dramatizing a lover's agony when he realizes that, even in the act of love, he cannot really possess his mistress. Even in his rhythmic ecstasy, no man can bridge the gulf which eternally isolates his identity from hers.

> And even should I track you to your birth
> Through all the cities of your mortal trial,
> As in my jealous thought I try to do,
> You would escape me—from the brink of earth
> Take off to where the lawless auroras run,
> You with your wild and metaphysic heart.

My touch is on you, who are light-years gone.
We are not souls but systems, and we move
In clouds of our unknowing like great nebulae.
Our very motives swirl and have their start
With father lion and with mother crab.

This longing for "my own lost rib"—this is the knowledge or "science" of the "night," which is also his dark ignorance of his beloved. The intensity of the longing and the certainty of failure sent the class reeling from the room leaving half empty coffee cups beside the ash trays. In "Hermetic Poem" Mr. Kunitz writes, "Who enters by my door/ Is drowned, burned, stung, and starred." They had begun to enter.

I had scheduled the poet's first visit for the beginning of our second month. He arrived on a chilly Sunday evening early in March. Nervous about the morrow, he asked what the students were like as people, how they had been responding, and which poems they were likely to want to talk about.

It is hard enough for a man to put on paper the secret struggles of his heart and mind, but, once done, he can turn with relief to the privacy of his study. Mr. Kunitz, however, was being asked to face not a few casual readers, but a group which had done its utmost to pry into every heartbeat of every line. It was as if a mature and passionate lover were asked to meet a group of youngsters who had been studying his letters to his mistress.

I knew that they had understood, but did not know how they would act in the presence of the poet. After all, they knew me quite well, and I had not the poet's stake in the poems. I tried to quiet his concern and hoped for the best.

The next morning Mr. Kunitz huddled tensely in my usual chair at the head of the table, and the students filed in. They were dressed in white shirts, ties, and jackets—a bad sign. They didn't expect to relax either. I did my best to capture the warmth, ease, and good-humored seriousness of our regular meetings, but it was no good. They were too embarrassed. Mr. Kunitz was nervous. I was disappointed in my own inability to bring them together.

"Well," he said after the class, "that ordeal's over."

"It will be better next time," I hoped.

His next visit was as fruitful as the first had been all but fruitless. Everyone was more relaxed. "Mr. Kunitz, we had quite an argument about 'Prophecy on Lethe' on page 61," I began. "There were two camps. If I can summarize their positions, maybe you would talk a little about the poem." I explained the arguments with help from the others and then gave Mr. Kunitz the floor.

"I must confess," he responded, "that I find those interpretations interesting, particularly since I had never thought of them before. That poem is a long way from me now. I'm glad I don't remember what I had in mind."

"Why are you glad, sir?"

"Because I want you to keep on asking questions, which are so much more important than any answers I might give you."

"But don't you have the right answers?"

"There aren't any. My intentions, even if I could remember them, are irrelevant; and my afterthoughts are not necessarily to be trusted. What matters—I say this hopefully—is the poem itself, in the give-and-take of each new encounter, as it struggles to come alive in your consciousness. The mistake is in supposing that the poem began as an idea, which was then transposed into verse. If that were true, we might as well publish the original idea and dispense with the poem that paraphrases it. Usually the poet doesn't really have what could be defined as an explicit intention. The poem demands to be written and gives no peace until it's done. Our subliminal drives are more likely to provide the motives for an action than any rationalization we can offer. Writing a poem is a very complex action, and I don't think I understand my subconscious any better than you do yours."

"Then you can't help us with this particular poem?"

"Not much . . . except to say that I suppose it's some kind of revelation, or epiphany, that I had at the time: an unusually deep awareness, sudden and fleeting, not a chronic condition. There are poems that don't seem to want to come up to the surface where they can be talked about."

"Actually," confessed one of the students, "I was really horrified by the last line, 'Your jelly-mouth and, crushed, your polyp eyes.' I think that's revolting!"

"I think it's beautiful," Mr. Kunitz laughed.

The time sped by. The class officially broke up at noon, but adjourned to a small dining room where the college had provided lunch for us, and our talk ran on for two hours.

When the last student had left to catch his next class, Mr. Kunitz said, "It went much better, don't you think?"

"Much better," I said. "They're more relaxed; but they're still too embarrassed to let you see how your poems have gripped them. But anyway, they'd have to be poets themselves to express that."

His last visit was scheduled for the meeting after we were supposed to have finished his book. He was to come on a Monday, but by Friday we still had four poems to go. I suggested that they simply work through those over the weekend by themselves.

"We need another class," they insisted.

I invited them to come to my house on Sunday evening.

Mr. Kunitz arrived on Sunday afternoon. I explained our plans for the evening. Other members of the English Department had offered hospitality so that he needn't sit through an extra session.

"I'd like to stay, if you don't mind, but I won't say anything. I just want to listen."

At 7:30 the students arrived, exchanged friendly greetings with Mr. Kunitz, and settled down on the living room floor with their books. They were sufficiently at ease in his presence now. Their voices soon rose in anger and excitement, turning the living room into the arena of our classroom. As usual, I was moderator, steersman, and, when our ship threatened to founder on a hopeless controversy, I interrupted, stated both sides, gave my opinion, and tried to move the group on. Sometimes this worked, but sometimes it didn't, for any or all of them were as ready to argue with me as with one another. Tempers flared, sometimes shedding light and sometimes only heat.

We were soon locked in a struggle over the identity of the "him" in the first stanza of "The Way Down."

> Time swings her burning hands
> I saw him going down
> Into those mythic lands
> Bearing his selfhood's gold,
> A last heroic speck
> Of matter in his mind
> That ecstasy could not crack
> Nor metaphysics grind.
> I saw him going down
> Veridical with bane
> Where pastes of phosphor shine
> To a cabin underground
> Where his hermit father lives
> Escaping pound by pound
> From his breast-buckled gyves;
> In his hermit father's coat,
> The coat without a seam,
> That the race, in its usury, bought
> For the agonist to redeem,

By dying in it, one
Degree a day till the whole
Circle's run.

"I think the 'him' is Apollo," said one. "The burning hands are the hands of the sun by which we measure time, and Apollo is the god of the sun."

"It couldn't be Apollo. It must be Christ; the 'agonist' is certainly Christ, and he 'redeems.' Apollo doesn't redeem anything."

"But how do you know that the agonist and the 'him' are the same?" asked another.

Then one of them turned to the poet." We're making an awful mess of your poem. Won't you help us out?"

"I shouldn't call it a mess," he replied. "All your speculations are sensitive, which leads me to think they must be at least partly true. I can't expect you to know that I began to write the poem after making the steep descent down to the Grotto of Neptune in Tivoli, not far from Rome. The actual physical setting is of no consequence, for 'the way down' of the poem is into a mythic underground, older than self or history. Down there the protagonist confronts the mystery of his roots, endures his fate, and is restored to life."

"It's surprising that a modern poet should be so involved with the past. Shouldn't he cut himself off from the past so that he can be truly modern?"

"You might as well expect a tree to blossom and bear fruit after it has been hacked off at the base. Of course a poet has to be of his time—timely—before he can hope to achieve timelessness; but language itself continually reminds him that there can be no actual separation between past and present. Every word he conjures up comes dragging the chains of its history behind it."

After a pause, he continued, "Fertile ground is a place of many deaths. The past dies into poetry. In the end it is all imagination. Any tailor can stitch a coat; the miracle is to sew it without a seam."

We stopped at 11:00 and I turned to Kunitz. "I hope this wasn't an ordeal too."

"It was just as fascinating as it was difficult," he confessed. "The joke is on the poet who fancies he has written a poem. He finds instead that it is as many poems as it has readers."

Toward the close of our class the following morning, one of the students said, "Mr. Kunitz, may I ask you a personal question?" Everyone laughed.

"Shoot!"

"If you had your life to live over, would you live it differently? We can guess that things haven't always been easy for you. Would you change anything?"

"I guess I was stuck with myself," he said, "and did what I could with it. I made plenty of mistakes, but at least they were my own. I don't have much hope of changing the world, but I can try to change myself. I am changed by the poems I write. And I want to keep on living my life—and changing it."

"Would you say that your life has been happy?"

He hesitated. "I've had my joys. But that's a different story. Swift said that happiness is the art of being well deceived. Only the young care about it passionately, perhaps because they are so miserable most of the time. Despite the philosophers, I should say that happiness is an overvalued condition."

Standing by the waiting train in the full sweetness of a hot May afternoon, we shook hands.

"This has been an experience that none of us will forget," I said lamely.

"It's I who must thank all of you," he replied.

He was gone, and I returned to what seemed an empty college. It was over. But not really. The essays that soon appeared on my desk proved that it was only beginning. All bore postscripts saying, in one way or another, that this seminar had changed their lives. One of the students, certain that he could not have said all that he meant in his paper, paid me a visit that no teacher would ever forget.

"I feel," he said, "as though I have been walking through the world in a stupor for twenty-one years. I'm just beginning to wake up to what I am—to what a man is, and to what his world is. I know I can't understand or predict all the consequences, but I do know that this has been one of the major experiences of my life."

The primary reason for our success was a simple one—the careful study of great art produces great impact, and our work had convinced us that Mr. Kunitz is a great poet. His poems are intensely personal, unflinchingly honest. He exemplifies the doctrine that only the most profoundly private experience is worth the artist's struggle to express. This alone is universal. While having this strong appeal, his poems also convey a sense of the vastness of the stage on which the individual has his instant of drama and the hugeness of the cycle of birth and death in which he is caught.

> . . . What the deep heart means,
> Its message of the big, round, childish hand,
> Its wonder, its simple lonely cry,

The bloodied envelope addressed to you,
Is history, that wide and mortal pang.

The question presents itself—can an individual have any value in such cosmic expanses? The answer is yes—by living, by grasping both poles of the paradox, the ultimate value of the individual and, at the same time, his incredible insignificance, and letting the charge burn. And if, while burning, one can leave a clear and structured record of that experience for others to read, so much the better.

It wasn't only the "content" of the poems that was responsible for their impact. It was the content in motion, the movement preserved in static structure, for Mr. Kunitz is a consummate craftsman. As we worked together, the students came to realize this. They continually had that great, slow pleasure that comes from discovering a poem which at first seemed utterly confusing. After long serious work, the thoughts, the shape of the thoughts and the electricity that played back and forth among them, gradually became clear till at the end they had the sense of possessing the poem or of being possessed by it.

All this is only to say that we succeeded because Mr. Kunitz is a great poet and that we worked hard on his poems. There was another reason— a nonliterary one, but nevertheless important. It was that Mr. Kunitz was more to the students than a signature. He was actually a person, and he proved it by coming down the hall, walking into our classroom, and sitting down. Above all, he proved it by listening to what we had to say, by being surprised, pleased, uncertain, and by laughing. All this said to them in language that could not be misunderstood, "I am he."

The poems stepped from the page into the eyes, the voice, and the substance of a man. The tumult and beauty over which we had struggled had become flesh. What other proof of truth remained to be given? And so the students walked from the seminar still shaking from the impact of the realization that literature was life and that they were actors in the same drama.

This is not to say that literature can be taught to students by parading great living writers through our colleges and universities. The physical presence does almost nothing to educate people who are unfamiliar with the man's work. Such occasions may be valuable from the point of view of public relations, but they are practically useless as far as education goes. This is no reason to put an end to the evenings when visiting poets come to give readings. They serve the very worthy purpose of lining the poet's pocket with a little much needed gold. How much more sensible, though, for an audience to be properly prepared by serious study for the coming of a Russell Vliet or a James Wright. It would even be worth it if the students and faculty had to put down their copies of Milton and Keats to study the work of the next visitor before he arrived.

Our colleges and universities have traditionally been defenders of the truths of the past. They sit in the present facing backward with broad-bottomed ease, and they say to the young, "Let us teach you about the mighty dead." And the young listen, if at all, with only one ear, for they are alive here and now. It might be well if some of our institutions recognized that not all the mighty are always among the dead—not all the giants have been slain. When a college invites a poet for any length of time, it asks that he disguise himself as a lecturer on his famous predecessors. Surely we can find some rooms in our halls of learning that are high enough for the artist to enter on the strength of his own stature and to stand up in—as himself.

Presenting the Poet: Stanley Kunitz

Richard Kostelanetz / 1969

Ameryka 121 (July 1969): 33–36. Reprinted with permission of Richard Kostelanetz.

A poet who stands as "an anomalous figure" in American literature, Stanley Kunitz, born in 1905 in the industrial city of Worcester, Massachusetts, belongs to the fertile generation that lies between the old masters—Eliot, Frost, Stevens, and Pound—and today's poets, such as Lowell and Berryman. He attended public schools in Worcester, and then graduated from Harvard University, *summa cum laude* (1926). He stayed at Harvard for a master's degree and pursued his interest in poetry.

Like his late friend Theodore Roethke, Kunitz sometimes wrote in conventional and traditional forms, but many of his works exploit materials from the human unconscious. Roethke and Robert Lowell had their poetry evaluated and critiqued by Kunitz.

On returning from a visit to Eastern Europe, Kunitz talked about the trip, his own work, and projects he is just beginning.

We talked over a couple of afternoons in his book-filled office in Greenwich Village.

He occasionally jumped up to talk to his wife Elise Asher (poet and painter). He recently traveled in the Soviet Union as part of a cultural exchange, and our conversation often touched on that experience.

Q: Could you summarize your impressions of Russian poetry?
A: I was surprised that Russian poetry is not what Americans expected. Americans know only two Russian poets: Yevtushenko and Voznesensky, both of whom are platform poets, rhetorical poets in the Mayakovsky tradition. I tried to reach the young poets—and they indicated that were losing interest in this rhetorical style. (Voznesensky is still very popular.) In seeking models for their own work, they are going back to the rejected lyric poets of an earlier generation like Osip Mandelstam, Boris Pasternak, Anna

Akhmatova, Marina Tsvetaeva. When I listened to the private readings of the young poets, I enjoyed their musical character. It was lyrical, about love, often about disappointment in love, poems about longing, about nature, about the ugliness of cities, subjects and experiences that appeal to any American.

Q: What is your process of writing a poem?
A: The problem is that I have to submerge under the surface of conscious-ness—surely that is why I start so slowly.

Q: Can you will yourself into that state?
A: No. During the night I try to confront exhaustion and go deeply to the source of creativity. It starts with images, phrases. Sometimes I find something in my notebooks that strikes a chord and resonates. I will start saying these words, trying to link them with other words, other phrases. At a certain point I put them down, usually in handwriting, in a notebook. After a few lines have accumulated, sometimes, nine or ten lines, I usually go to the typewriter and I see how they look on the page—very important moment.

Q: This usually happens in the middle of the night.
A: Yes, I retype, examine the manuscript. Then I add other verse by typing them directly—I work until I notice that what I have written may not be good. Then I rip up the draft and start from scratch. Sometimes it takes fifty or sixty sheets—the room gets buried in paper.

Q: By copying a poem so many times you strain it through your fingers.
A: Exactly. The sense of touch is very important to me. I think that tactility is the keenest of my senses.

Q: In what way is tactility reflected in your poetry?
A: I sense that certain lines are rough, others sharp, others shiny or silky. A poem joins several textures. Sometimes a poem is an intersection of several layers and that variety gives changeable impressions.

Q: Does a clearly defined impression derive from that tactile sense in your poetry?
A: For me those tactile impressions or sensations are inseparable from my poems, some less, some more. Look at the beginning of "Invocation" (long "o" sounds and labial consonances); there is no hard sound that would give

an impression of contact, until you get to the third line. The opening is: "Soul of my soul in the ancestral wood/ Where all the trees were loosened of the leaves/ I strayed, discovering my winter form." I hear in these lines the movement of water and the touch of my fingers in water. But in the next stanza, everything changes: "Webbed in a dream, stagnating like a worm,/ Offensive to myself, to the grey bird-drifts/ Melting from the boughs, with rhyming calls,/ Ancient and hoarse, beslimed, glued to a rock/ Five hundred years, fainting, struggling with mist/ Self-woven, issue of death, ghost of my name." This is composed almost solely from tactile sensations inseparable from sound. In the very next line—"Heard then the pods clack hollow blistered skins"—each word is so separate and noisy.

Q: But which sense is more real to you, sight or hearing?
A: I believe it is the ear, but the ear needs the support of the eye. I wished people listened to my poems read with a supporting text—then both senses contribute to a combined experience.

Q: Now it's been a decade since your *Selected* Poems?
A: In the last decade I tried to develop a personal style. I am no longer writing in the style that dominates the *Selected Poems*. It took me five years to break away from it—I felt a need to free myself of the rhetoric.

Q: What were your motives for this change? Personal, intellectual, or a wish not to repeat your earlier style?
A: I think I was done with the old style, exhausted its possibilities and did not want to focus on construction.

Q: Was the change simply a matter of maturity?
A: Possibly. If you want to discuss it in personal terms: in the beginning I was terribly shy and ingrown. I was groping. Nobody knew me; I did not know other writers. My only friend was Theodore Roethke. This friendship was very significant. He was the only other poet that I felt close to. We exchanged manuscripts over many years.

Q. Were you a recognized poet, a reasonably well-known poet at the time?
A. I always had a reputation among poets, but not by the general public. I was not included in any anthology, except the one I worked on in the 1930s with Harriet Monroe. Only recently they started including me in anthologies. In between I was not widely read because I wrote in a style quite different from Eliot or Auden—very influential poets of the 1940s.

Q: But by the 1950s your standing markedly improved?

A: The move to the city was a major event which changed me a lot. Before marrying Elise I was a country man. As you know during the crisis I was a farmer. I had one helper. I was growing medicinal herbs and other plants—I sold them in Hartford, Connecticut. From 1958 onward I changed—as if I grew and straightened out.

Q: So around 1958 two events influenced you: the move to the city and the second marriage.

A: Also one's age. A person feels at home in his body and does not want to jump out, as during one's youth.

Q: That same year you published *Selected Poems*.

A: It was not my first book. What was important is that I got some recognition; yet I don't think this was the main reason for my change. I think that there is continuity even though I am writing differently. I am not even certain that others believe I write differently.

In some new poems one can recognize my old voice. However, from a technical point of view I tried to modify my latest poems in *Selected Poems*. For example, "Revolving Meditation" was meaningful since I discovered that I could develop a work not constrained by prosodic considerations or verse forms. I did not worry about rhyme or meter. This approach opened new possibilities. It opened a pathway for experimentation.

Q: So what are the qualities in the new poems?

A: Sincerity replaced rigidity. Also, an art for a less specialized audience rather than an esoteric art.

Q: Have you suggested that you were stimulated by an initial interest in music?

A: Yes, that's right. That was certainly where I got a sense of both sound and form. But when I became enchanted with poetry, I suppose I felt that music would no longer interest me as a performer because I would rather write my own songs, and I hadn't really studied music to the point where I could compose. And, then, language itself, as I look back, has always been my primary concern from the very beginning, even in grade school. I was the one who was always involved in writing. I have manuscripts of poems and stories I was writing when I was ten.

Q: Were you encouraged?

A: Oh, yes, by my teachers in grade school and in high school. I edited, in fact, and founded the high school literary magazine, called *The Argus*.

Q: Tell me about your parents.

A: My mother was an unusual woman—she ran the family thanks to the energy she established in her dressmaking workshop. And, of course, my father killed himself before I was born. Six weeks before I was born. So that I had no real father at all. That's why the father theme is so strong in my book. I did have a step-father for a short while—between the ages of nine and fourteen—a beautiful man, very generous, a scholarly sort of person, who was dominated completely by my mother who ran this dress factory and who designed her own clothes and eventually built up a business, an elaborate one, something like two hundred machines.

Q: Did she own or manage it?

A: She owned it; she was extraordinarily competent. First of all, Mother had an education, but she was not a very good business woman. And she was always expanding. She never fired anybody. And during the bad years, she always kept her staff completely under her. The result was that anytime there was an economic decline, my mother went bankrupt.

Q: This happened more than once.

A: Oh yes.

Q: Were there other relatives?

A: I had two sisters, older sisters, of course. I was, naturally, the last. My mother was forty-four when I was born. My sisters were considerably older. Both of them died young, in their twenties. My mother apparently had had six children. And I was the only one that survived.

Q: You survived her.

A: I survived her; she lived to the age of eighty-six.

Q: Where was your mother from?

A: Mother was from Lithuania, actually. Her name was Jasspon.

Q: Jasspon?

A: Based on family legend, my mother claimed that we were Sephardic Jews from Spain, who were spread throughout Europe. I guess that there is some truth in the story.

Q: How were you influenced by Harvard?
A: I first came under the spell of Blake's poetry, then of the English metaphysicals—John Donne, George Herbert, and Henry Vaughan. Of course, I was reading all new writings of the era. I decided not to imitate Eliot's style. He interested me, but I preferred William Butler Yeats. Both were great poets, yet I resisted Eliot. I was attracted to an existentialist art—on that basis I developed my future work—the struggle between living and dying. I also go back to the metaphysicals and to Hopkins, who was the other major influence on me. And I was also very much interested in philosophy. In the beginning, I suppose, Plato was my philosopher, and then I became interested in Kant, Schopenhauer, and then Peirce among the moderns. I never cared for Dewey. And then in a later period I was fascinated by Ludwig Wittgenstein's writings and linguistic theories.

Q: What role does this knowledge play in your poetry?
A: I think nothing. When you write poems you must not rely too strictly on everything you learned intellectually. However, the knowledge becomes part of the material of the poem. Creation comes from intuition, not conscious ideas. One's knowledge gives the material grit, friction.

Q: What poems of the past are most important to you?
A: William Blake. I write quite differently, but we are joined by the visionary function of poetry.

Q: Does any contemporary poet have a similar approach?
A: Only Roethke.

Q: Could there be others trying to translate the subconscious into conscious thought?
A: I know of no American poets nor any Russian poets—except for someone like Pasternak, who did actually have some of that quality but not in the visionary sense that goes back to Blake. I think you will find it in Rene Char and Henri Michaux among the postsurrealists. Even though they differ stylistically, they, like other poets, are interested in the continuation of a postsurrealistic French tradition.

Q: In the United States most well-known poets are college teachers. You have been teaching twenty years. In your opinion, is an academic environment helpful to the poet or vice versa?

A: First, let me tell you that I was not always teaching. A poet can become sterile if one relies on the academy unless one is disorganized and needs the discipline. I started teaching in 1946 after the army. Roethke suggested I take over his lectures at Bennington. I quit after three years—after a quarrel with the new president. I was then the dean of the Department of Literature, so I was disappointed and resolved never to become so deeply engaged in academic life, to always preserve my independence. I believe that pedagogical work is useful for a poet on a part-time basis—lectures or week-long engagements. I did not take engagements for more than one year, part-time (like now at Columbia or at the New School). Now at Columbia I teach one term a year in the graduate school, one class a week.

Q: What can be taught about poetry?

A: Two things. First, some lessons in craft, which is part of the activity and principles of workshops—important in poetry even though the task is not solving problems. Then a mastery of words, control over expressions, a certain control over the medium of language is teachable through discipline.

Q: Do you teach by suggesting how to do something, or how not to do things?

A: Actually I use the materials that are supplied by the students. General opinion of given texts is not enough—it has to be submitted for detailed analyses. I'm likely to say this line doesn't sound right to my ear, or that I see errors. I ask why the author left a hole in the middle of this poem. I indicate that a phrase is a cliché; this image is dead, or not deep enough.

Q: Do you feel at all obliged to inculcate a certain style, a possible technique similar to your own?

A: No, I must say that this is one of the cardinal principles of my teaching style. My students don't write like me; nor do I try to have them write like me, God forbid; nor do they write like anybody else. I just help them to discover who they are and what they want to achieve as poets. What they can do best? Which use of language is natural to them? It is vital to me that each student creates in his personal way.

Q: Do you tell them about the poet's role in the contemporary world?

A: I believe that this can be done only by example. For instance, I am very much involved in the political scene. I always have been—and I am just as likely to talk about Vietnam in a class as I am about Housman, Creeley, or any other poet. Often I insert scientific information about discoveries, the creation of cells, new experiments in nuclear physics . . .

Q: How do you know about these topics?
A: From reading. I read voluminously in scientific literature. Perhaps I read as much science as I do poetry. Unfortunately there is not enough time, so I try to sleep less. You really can't be a good poet if you have no knowledge of contemporary painting, sculpture, dance, and film. These are parts of civilization.

Q: Do you write much criticism?
A: From time to time I feel a need to organize my thinking, and this forces me to clarify reflections about the arts or the world around me. For several years I have been working on an extensive essay, maybe forty typewritten pages, about aspects of order and disorder in the arts, all the modern arts, relating to scientific discoveries and the natural sciences. I see a close connection between what is happening in art and in the highest levels of scientific research.

Q: Where do you see similarities?
A: This is very difficult to explain in a few sentences. First of all is the problem of the dematerialization of the universe. The breakdown of solid forms in an atomic universe, governed by laws of quantum mechanics. I do not try to relate physical theories with tendencies in contemporary art, but I do suggest that we are entering a period in which we need to accept a new concept of order. I am trying to say here is that what's happening in the arts today is based on new forms containing more and more disorder.

Q: Is it unnecessarily hard to be a poet in America?
A: It was always hard to go against the prevailing current in America, and the artist must struggle for a bit of recognition, particularly in poetry. Also, anybody born like me at the beginning of the century found himself in the shadow of a great dynasty of elders who had achieved the new poetry after World War I and the twenties, and these poets survived as indestructible for thirty or forty years.

Q: Was this the generation born around 1885? T. S. Eliot, Robert Frost, Ezra Pound, Wallace Stevens, and others.

A: Of course, since they dominated for years, it was harder for younger poets to be noticed. Roethke and I were saying that we will not be noticed until Frost, Pound, and Stevens pass on—we really thought that. Now that all except Pound are gone, the kingdom of poetry is a little less cluttered.

Q: It's rather well known that several major poets now in their early fifties have experienced acute mental distress. What accounts for this phenomenon?

A: First of all, I think, in terms of their struggle, that generation was particularly vulnerable because they had a much harder time than the poet of today has, partly for the reason I've just given. There were giants who dominated the scene. A second reason was the Puritan ethic that dominated the whole country, so many people felt the problem of censorship and other restraints. Also they didn't have the outlets into the academy, all the opportunities for lectures that are open to the poet today. To all these causes the poet was particularly vulnerable.

Furthermore, madness became a kind of refuge. The ordeal of one's life could become so difficult that really it was easier to say I'm mad so don't blame me for my sins. I do think there was for some a kind of entrance into madness as a hope rather than as a despair because this seemed better than the alternative which was to know that you lived in a society that despised you.

Q: How would you describe the life of the young poet in America today?

A: All modern societies, in a sense, are more open because there is a crumbling of the establishments of the state throughout the world. The arts have a lot do with it, as they nibble at the edges of the state; for the artist above all has to be the conscience of the tribe. I think unless the artist serves that function he is really abdicating his role. To be that conscience means always to speak the truth that is in you and not to fear the consequences, to oppose even the greatest power around you, which is the state, and to build a life on a principle of dissent rather than compliance.

In America one cannot always be recognized, but one is surrounded by a circle of friends who understand his work. Some work may appear in a friendly periodical. Sometimes it is just mimeographed, but since it is circulated and becomes available, it can win an audience. And there always is hope that some work will be picked up by one of the more widely circulated magazines or one of the trade publishing houses. The path is not easy, but then I don't see any reason why it should be. Most of the work at the beginning isn't good enough, and the pains of apprenticeship are valuable to the artist. If the artist doesn't know something about suffering, I don't think he's going to be much good in the long run.

Finally I wish to add: the world of art is a continuous seamless web woven from subtle fibers—because life on our planet is also a continuous web—starting with the lowest creatures, even lower—at the level of viruses, and evolving into more complex forms. In this continuum of life I see no chasms or interruptions—it also applies to political institutions, independent of geography or race. All life forms on our planet react similarly to hardships, so art should be above nationality. It may be influenced by the immediate scene, but art becomes truly great when it speaks for all mankind, as Tolstoy and Shakespeare still speak to us today. And speaking of the continuous web of the arts, it is also true that any injury done to the arts or to an artist, anywhere in the world, triggers a shudder and makes the whole web tremble.

An Interview with Stanley Kunitz

Candace DeVries Olesen / 1972

Quadrille (Bennington College Alumni Magazine) 6 (1972), 7–11. Reprinted by courtesy of Bennington College.

The following interview with Stanley Kunitz was held on a sunny November afternoon in his delightful brownstone in New York City's Greenwich Village. There is, as readers of Mr. Kunitz's poetry might expect, a veritable forest of greenery within and without his attractive living room. The walls are covered with paintings, including those of his wife Elise Asher (a painter of considerable sensitivity, who combines her oils with calligraphy), and the shelves are crowded with books. Climbing the long, red-carpeted stairs to the softly lit book-lined studio where the interview was given, one could not help but feel that the wall adjacent to the staircase, alive with innumerable photographs of family and friends, was like a fascinating novel, to be fallen into and "read" for days. It should be added that besides owning a home that seems to reflect his poetry perfectly, Stanley Kunitz is also the owner of cat called Celia, who must be the fattest cat in the world!

QUADRILLE: Last March your picture appeared on the front page of the *New York Times Book Review*, illustrating Robert Lowell's review of your newest volume of poetry, *The Testing-Tree*. According to Mr. Lowell, "Stanley Kunitz is now writing in a language that cats and dogs can understand." Do you agree?

KUNITZ: My cat Celia understands every word of mine, but I won't try to speak for the dogs. It's true that I've been working now for several years, since my *Selected Poems* toward a more open style . . . a style based on familiar speech rhythms, as uncluttered and lucid as I can make it. The difference between *The Testing-Tree* and my earlier work is not so much in the substance as in the tone, the pitch of the voice. My model is the conversation between friends.

QUADRILLE: According to the painter Edward Hopper, "In every artist's development a germ of the later work is always found in the earlier . . . what he was once, he always is with slight modifications." I noticed, comparing *Selected Poems* with *The Testing-Tree* that a constant "concern" (if you will) is dealt with much more directly in the new poems.

KUNITZ: Maybe time itself compels a man to confront the great simplicities. At a certain stage in his maturity he frees himself from the knots and complications, the ambiguities, of his youth. So that it is easier then for him to say what he has to say without fussing too much about it.

QUADRILLE: But you say it still with a deep commitment to craft.

KUNITZ: The object is to learn the controls of language, so that you don't have to tell lies. Like any skill, if you master it early enough, it will eventually become second nature—which doesn't guarantee that you will have anything left to say. Incidentally, I don't enjoy being praised for craftsmanship. An old poet ought never to be caught with his technique showing.

QUADRILLE: Stanley Moss, in a review of your new poems, comments that much of the literature of our time is drawn to suicide or the fires of hell. You, on the contrary, "dance for the joy of surviving." How do you respond to the poetry being written today, particularly by young writers?

KUNITZ: There's so much wrong with the world that anyone can find plenty of reasons to despair. But I'm not really tempted to play the role of Jeremiah. Much of my time is spent with the young, and I consider myself a partner in their disaffections and their hopes. This generation has extraordinary gifts, including beauty. It isn't about to give up. I admire many young writers, among them several who survived my classes. My inclination is to feel reasonably sanguine about the course of modern literature.

Not that I close my eyes to the amount of showmanship, self-indulgence, and sloppy craftsmanship that gets into print. The vainest ambition is to want an art separated from its heritage, as though the tradition were a cistern full of toads instead of a life-giving fountain. A poet without a sense of history is a deprived child. Of course, given the polluted planet that the young have inherited, I can't very well blame them for believing that their elders were horribly nasty or stupid caretakers of a civilization. The arts, in fact, have been saying precisely that since the dawn of the Industrial Revolution.

QUADRILLE: Do you think that younger teachers can be reproached for failing to give adequate instruction in the craft and history of poetry?

KUNITZ: The truth is that even if one wants to teach a sense of craft, the typical young writer today won't buy it. He sees art as a kind of spontaneous combustion. The study of prosody, for example, strikes him as a waste of time, a stereotype imposed on him from above . . . the dead hand of convention. There are exceptions, to be sure, and they stand out in the crowd.

QUADRILLE: This might apply to painting, too. Some young people say, "But I just want to express myself," when they haven't yet learned to see— which takes a long time and is a discipline.

KUNITZ: One of the prevailing illusions is that youth itself is of kind of genius . . . instead of a biological condition. We live in an accelerated age, with astonishingly fast rates of obsolescence. Anyone involved with creative young people soon realizes how accurately they reflect a culture, in their impatience with slow development or ripening, in their rush to become superstars overnight. They have been led to believe that all they have to do is concoct a novelty . . . a new sensation . . . or make a big enough noise . . . and tomorrow they will be rich and idolized. In this respect the visual and performing arts are worse than literature. But everywhere the young, and then the ones who are no longer quite so young but who like to think of themselves as belonging to a fashionable avant garde, are preoccupied with "making it"—a vile sort of enterprise. It's so much a part of the contemporary scene. The arts tend to become a commodity like any other manufactured thing.

QUADRILLE: You once wrote in an essay: "The hard, inescapable phenomenon to be faced is that we are living and dying at once . . . my commitment is to report that dialogue."

KUNITZ: I guess that pretty much tells the story of what I'm up to in the course of a lifetime . . . or should I say death time?

QUADRILLE: In your poetry you move from the comical-ridiculous to the tragic in the space of two lines: "That coat hanger neatly whisked your coat right off your back. Soon it will want your skin," And again, in "The Bottom of the Glass"—a sort of tragic-comic title in itself, I think—you say: "Life aims at the tragic:/ what makes it ridiculous?/ In age as in youth/ The joke is preposterous." Do you think that because we are born to die that life is a joke? Or, sadly, a dirty joke?

KUNITZ: To say that one is aware of the comedy of life is not to deprive it of its dignity. The comic vision requires a certain distancing from the object. It enables us not to fall into the grotesquerie of self-pity or to become sentimental about our losses. The fatal temptation for any poet is to become grandiose, to write only in inflated emotional states. Holderlin said that the way to achieve nobility in art is through the commonplace. Not to over-reach, not to strain for high-flown epithets or resolutions, but simply to be as true as we can to the grain of the life.

QUADRILLE: I noticed, thinking about *The Testing-Tree* in terms of auto-biography, that you manage to suggest the first-person even when the "I" isn't there.

KUNITZ: But "I" is always is there. It's a spiritual pressure . . . where the language bends to the force of the life within.

QUADRILLE: At this point I would have to agree with Stanley Moss in his *Nation* article when he suggests you deal with two selves . . . the "I" who definitely planted the trees or song to a daughter, and the figurative "I"—the salmon who swims upriver.

KUNITZ: There is an aspect of one's Becoming that has nothing to do with personal identity, but that falls away from self, blends into the natural uni-verse. To be human is not to be apart from or superior to the whole mar-velous show of creation, which includes the salmon and the robin and the green ways of plants.

QUADRILLE: In some of your poems—I'm thinking particularly of "After the Last Dynasty"—are you at all influenced by Chinese or other poetry of the East? There is a delicacy, simplicity, economy of words that reminds me of their art.

KUNITZ: I've read a good deal of the poetry of the Orient and even in-quired into its techniques, but I suppose I'm too much of a Western man to regard it as a major influence. Certainly I admire the sparseness . . . the power of understatement . . . the tendency to let the natural image and its juxtapositions speak for themselves rather than to force the issue. "Never try to explain," I advise in one of my poems, and that's a good lesson—if I may say so—for any poet.

QUADRILLE: In Stevie Smith's obituary in the *New York Times* a year ago, she was quoted as saying that "pain is the origin of poems, because no one writes or wishes to who is one with their desire." Is that consistent with your understanding of the poetic process?

KUNITZ: What I chiefly understand is that I have to fight for my poems. I begin with the supposition that memory is each man's poet-in-residence. It's curious how certain images out of the life—not necessarily the most spectacular—keep flashing signals from the depths, as if to say, "Come down to me . . . and be reborn." The words that reveal they've made that descent, when the mind is shaken, come up wet and shimmering and alive. They've been down in that well, where they've made the child you were. And there's another aspect to note. The writing of a poem is an attempt to transcend the day itself, its bombardment of impressions and distractions and annoyances, the telephone, the negotiations, the frivolities. Not that this material is alien to poetry—all of it may become embodied in the work—but that it must attach itself to your secret life.

QUADRILLE: In your note to the title poem "The Testing-Tree" you report that a friend of yours told you that what you had recorded there was recognizable as an ancient ritual, and that your patriarchal scarred oak was transparently a manifestation of the King of the Wood. Then there's your "King of the River," which has been described as your major poem concerning aging and dying. What lies behind your choice of a title for your latest book?
KUNITZ: I like the sound and the sense of "The Testing-Tree." It has intimate ramifications, a private context, apart from the mythic. Keats, you will recall, thought of the poet's life as allegorical.

QUADRILLE: You thought of this new collection as a sort of test of yourself?
KUNITZ: Every poem is. I had gone back to Worcester, my native city, and looked for the old house and those Indian woods. It was a most depressing adventure. The place had turned into a technological nightmare . . . an express highway running through my childhood. On the site of my nettled field stood a housing development, ugly enough for tears. That's one reason why I had to write "The Testing-Tree."

QUADRILLE: You seem to be confirming Stevie Smith's assertion that "pain is the origin of poems."
KUNITZ: How can one separate awareness from suffering? To be aware of mortality itself, the running down of the universe, the horrors of poverty, the abomination of bigotry, the monstrousness of war . . . that alone is suffering enough to last a thousand lifetimes. People don't have to be taught to suffer—they have to be taught how to live. Then they can begin to discover what joy is.

QUADRILLE: One final question. This particular issue of *Quadrille* is based on "Continuing Education." You have already hinted at some of the disciplines and insights that are demanded of those who would pursue a career in the arts. Do you have any further advice?

KUNITZ: One thing I have learned is that talent is about the cheapest thing we have. There is so much of it around. It's a blessing to be born gifted. But it won't be enough if you lack the character to endure. You'll need all the courage and faith and patience you can muster. And you'd better be lucky, too!

Stanley Kunitz on
"The Science of the Night"

Adele Slaughter / 1974

From *Calvert*, Maryland Media (Spring 1975), 6–9.

Stanley Kunitz, Pulitzer Prize–winning poet who is this year's Poetry Consultant at the Library of Congress, gave a reading of his poems on the "Writers Here & Now" series on November 19, 1974. After the reading, Adele Slaughter conducted the following interview with Mr. Kunitz.

AS: Mr. Kunitz, when you wrote "The Science of the Night," how many drafts did you write? Can you remember?
SK: Oh, that poem went on for a long time, through dozens and dozens of drafts. Maybe I could start by talking about how I usually work on a poem. I remember very well working on "The Science of the Night." I usually start in my notebook, writing with a pen and more or less registering the first impulse that comes to me, a phrase or line. I started with that first phrase— "I touch you in the night"—the germ of the poem. But I didn't know where the poem was going. A poem won't go anywhere until it takes on a life of its own. At that point I turn to the typewriter and start pecking away until I hit a block; then I rip out the first sheet and start all over again. Meanwhile, I'm building up these rhythms; I'm saying them aloud at the same time, a sort of incantation, I'm trying to get enough momentum to jump over the next hurdle. At the end of a poem of this length, I may have a hundred sheets of paper on the floor . . .

AS: You mean, working yourself up to it?
SK: I always have to start at the beginning because I need that whole increment of rhythm and imagery in order to work up enough speed. Otherwise,

I'd never clear the hurdle. That's pretty much the way this poem was written. Actually, I have exhibited some of the sheets of the poem . . .

AS: You have?

SK: At the New York Public Library. They once did an exhibition of that kind, as if to prove that inspiration is such hard work. When I look at a manuscript of mine, I wonder how anyone could possibly decode it.

AS: The line in that poem that seems the turning point to me is "Caught in the calcium snows of sleep." I was wondering if you had anything to say about that.

SK: What I remember is that when I wrote that line I felt pretty good about it. Actually, like so much of the poem, it comes out of information I had read somewhere, in a paper on insomnia, that during deep sleep there is a precipitation of calcium in the brain. It's one of the little bits of knowledge that we store, and suddenly—it seemed just the right place!

AS: This poem is full of bits of knowledge. There's the shifting of the spectrum. "As through a glass that magnifies my loss/ I see the lines of your spectrum shifting red."

SK: Oh, the red shift, yes. We need to learn as much as we possibly can about the world around us. Poetry is not only acts of perception, but also bits of information, concrete instances, embedded in the whole imagery. Any kind of information can be valuable to a poet. Poetry that is all mood or all feeling, empty of any kind of knowing, is much too vaporous and dissipates its energy. But the red shift: I don't know how many readers understand what is going on there or would even be able to tell me what the red shift is. Can you?

AS: Rod Jellema told me what it was . . . going so fast that the spectrum shifts?

SK: That's right. (*laughter*) In a reading of the light from distant galaxies the shift of the spectrum to the longer waves—toward red indicates that the celestial object is moving away from us. It is adduced as evidence that we live in an expanding universe, an infinitely expanding universe—which is a frightening thought. I'm pretty sure that this is the first poem to make use of the red shift, but that alone wouldn't make it any better. No nugget of information in a poem is worth anything unless it's incorporated into a structure of feeling and imagination.

AS: I was wondering about that line, "from hooded powers and abstract flight" . . .

SK: A tough question. Sometimes one goes back to a poem and asks, "What exactly did I have in mind?" Not everything is subject to clinical analysis. There are parts of a poem that are mysterious even to the writer. The *image* is clear to me, the hooded powers speak to me of daemonic adversaries, those secret enemies of the life that rebel against the person and attack his selfhood. I see them as Klan figures, agents of the destructive will; *Abstract flight* is another kind of image. Of course, it's tied in with the red shift: it's the movement away from the gravitational center of love. *Flight* is obviously associated with the idea of the expanding universe, and the worst kind of flight would be a coldly abstract one: into the reaches of the mind, the mind turning away from all feeling and becoming cold and abstract like the skies themselves. It's a kind of death of the heart that I'm talking about here, I would suppose. But I wouldn't bet my life on it . . . (*laughter*)

AS: Well, I think the best thing about the poem is the way it maintains different levels—like "Bring me the mornings of the milky way/down to my threshold in your drowsy eyes" . . . You create two levels in the use of the milky way—both the stars and the milkman coming.

SK: Once the astrophysical imagery gets into the poem—you see it gets in very early—the first image has the night in it . . .

AS: Yes, and then that next image—"star-bemused" . . .

SK: I think that "star-bemused" is the phrase that led on to everything else. You have to trust your own imagination. You mustn't sit on it and say, "Well, I don't want to write *that* kind of poem." If the poem decides to go that way, you have to ride along with it. You give it all the rein it wants until it's just about ready to run wild. From that point on you keep hauling it in and letting it go out again. A bad poet pulls back when he should be letting go, and vice-versa.

AS: Would you explain the tone you have adopted in your poetry and how has it transformed?

SK: The tone of voice I now seek in my poems approximates the tone of an intimate conversation between friends, a voice that doesn't strain too hard for nobility or resonance, but that makes a music out of its purity of diction and modulations of breath and pitch. The rhythms of my earlier poems were more self-evident, I suppose. Most people, unfortunately, haven't the slightest idea how to read a poem that doesn't go thumpety-thump. More ought to be done in the schools with reading poems aloud in order to capture their rhythms. The trouble is that teachers are among the worst offenders on this score. The young need to be given the opportunity, before their imaginations are crushed and their ears tuned out, to hear the poets themselves—in the flesh, or in recordings. I would much rather hear a poet read his own poetry, no matter how faulty, no matter how poor a performer he is, than to hear Richard Burton do it for him. I learn from a poet's reading about the sound in his head and the pulse of his feelings.

AS: I read "The Science of the Night" many times; it had many more dimensions when I heard you read it. The poem became so much more personal.
SK: Poetry in its origins is a highly personal medium. That's why it has a capacity to enter the secret life of others.

AS: This poem seems highly metaphysical. I was wondering whether you had been influenced by John Donne.
SK: Most of my early poems were influenced by the metaphysical poets, Donne in particular, Herbert; also Vaughan. Those three. Then, later I was under the spell of Gerard Manley Hopkins, who never ceases to astonish me. From your poetic ancestors you learn to test your possibilities. One of the most important of the apprentice disciplines is in studying how the action of a poem develops. The imagination operates in bursts—it is an explosion—a sudden cluster of words. But how to achieve momentum? How to produce the sense of a continuing process? Each poet has a different syntax of the imagination, not necessarily one that he understands himself, or should even try to understand. It is best left to others to probe the ways things happen, the links between the clusters, the nature of the propelling energy. Once you have done that, you've really penetrated into the arcanum of a poet. It doesn't happen too often.

AS: But it's different for every poet?
SK: Inevitably.

AS: Some of the things you mentioned about momentum sound very familiar to me, which makes me feel good.
SK: Yeats is the poet who gave me the word "momentum." Each of us has his own way of working up steam. I know some poets for whom poems flow daily like water, but then they usually resemble water, not wine. My Russian

friend Andrei Voznesensky—who doesn't belong in this category—writes all his poems in his head, walking around. Then he comes home and puts them down and that's the end. He never touches them after that. Wallace Stevens used to compose his poems in his head on his way to the insurance office; he would walk to the office every morning in Hartford and improvise lines en route. On his arrival at the office he would dictate them to his secretary—that's how some of the best poems in the language got to be written—incredible! There are some poets who consider it heresy to touch a typewriter. But I love the feeling a typewriter gives me, because I can see my lines on the page in clean typography. My handwritten manuscript is such a mess! That wonderful look of a poem after you've finally licked it into shape and transposed it onto the typewritten page! It's a joyful experience, a beautiful moment. That's what one fights for all the way through the morass.

AS: I guess that's why most people write—to see that.

SK: But meanwhile you've been swamped by all that crud on the page, and you've doubted you would ever escape into the clearing.

AS: Do you think your poems are totally finished before you get to the typewriter?

SK: By no means. A poem never forgives you for giving up too soon.

Interview with Stanley Kunitz

Cleopatra Mathis, Anne Cherner, and Elmaz Abinader / 1977

Columbia Journal 1 (1977), 1–7. Reprinted with the permission of Cleopatra Mathis, Anne Whitehouse, and Elmaz Abinader.

Columbia: We're interested in your thoughts about young poets today. You seem so involved in what young poets are doing.

Kunitz: Why not? I feel more compatible with them than with the generation I was born into. The imagination lives by its changes and is always looking for a home. Perhaps the writers I feel closest to are those who remind me of the vulnerability of my own youth. I like to think of Yeats, with his characteristic mix of poignancy and arrogance, saying towards the end of his life that when he was young his Muse was old: but now that he was old, his Muse was young. That's a paradox worth testing, if you have the right collection of genes.

Columbia: How do you feel the women's movement is affecting the poetry establishment today?

Kunitz: The only social dynamite we have. The civil rights movement and the antiwar movement are still with us, but they're no longer explosive forces as they were in the sixties when they instigated a semi-insurrection on the part of a whole generation against the old guard.

Columbia: What else is happening now?

Kunitz: After Vietnam and Watergate it's a rather ambiguous period, one of disenchantment and cynicism, distrust of the elders, distrust of the social order, but no flag to wave, and very little idealism.

Columbia: Is this a general condition or specific to poetry?

Kunitz: There's always a connection between history and the arts. Except for the women, the poetry of protest and rebellion seems to have exhausted its vitality.

Columbia: Do you think that the best poetry now is being written by young women?

Kunitz: It's foolhardy to generalize, but I don't suppose it's a coincidence that my first five Yale Series choices were men and my last three have been women. Furthermore, in these past few years most of the top contenders have been women. The explanation seems to me simple enough. Women are writing their emancipation proclamation. They don't have to look for a theme— they've found it inside their skins.

Columbia: Do you think this infusion of energy into women's poetry is going to be permanent?

Kunitz: No revolution keeps its militancy and euphoria forever, but I don't doubt that from now on women are going to play a much more central role in all the arts.

Columbia: Should literary magazines have a quota for women and blacks, as demanded in the recent manifesto to the *American Poetry Review*?

Kunitz: That concept of proportional representation seems to me an aesthetic nightmare. Literature has to defend its values even from the best of causes, and certainly from the statisticians. I've always feared the tyranny of the righteous.

Columbia: Was Louise Bogan a victim of the male establishment in poetry, or were there other reasons she did not get the recognition she deserved?

Kunitz: She herself—especially in her later years—felt neglected and thought that being a woman had much to do with it. The evidence is confusing. Other women poets of her generation were extravagantly praised— Edna St. Vincent Millay, for example. But Millay was easier to accept, for she played a bohemian part that was attractive sexually. Elinor Wylie, now all but forgotten, also had a great reputation, coinciding, with her role as an ornament of society. Maybe it's time for reappraisal. As for Bogan, though she never became a popular poet, she was always respected by her peers. The trouble may have been that she was too fine.

Columbia: Fine in what way?

Kunitz: In her sensibility, her mind, her control. If her art had been coarser, she would have had more readers. And that would be true whether she was male or female.

Columbia: Does the future of poetry lie with the small presses?
Kunitz: Probably so. The major publishers are tripping over themselves in their haste to abandon poetry. The old private firms, with their individual taste and literary aura, have practically vanished from the scene. They've been swallowed up by vast conglomerates, interested only in profits and geared exclusively for the mass market. The consolation is that when all, or nearly all, poetry is relegated to the small presses, poets can be freed from the delusion that they are producing articles of commerce. That may be good for their souls.

Columbia: Isn't it true that small press poetry is usually read by poets?
Kunitz: The same has been said about poetry published by the big houses. Actually, a few of the small presses are showing the way by reaching a new market for poetry. With the infusion of federal money, through the National Endowment for the Arts, they are gradually improving their system of distribution. The irony of this growing dependence on subsidy is that poetry is essentially a subversive activity and must remain so. We need to guard against its becoming a polite art, or a hopelessly eccentric one.

Columbia: Do you think the loosening of form in twentieth-century poetry has had anything to do with making poetry more accessible to a wider audience?
Kunitz: I'm not so sure of that. The flight from meter and rhyme has made poetry easier to write but harder to remember. If poetry is more accessible, it must be because it has become a more conversable medium, less lofty and grandiloquent. Intimacy is our touchstone. We feel more compatible with sand than with marble.

Columbia: How does this relate to the conduct of your workshops?
Kunitz: In a classroom I follow Goethe's dictum that "art exists in limits," but with this qualification: that the limits are a changing phenomenon. My premise is that we are liberated into poetry, not imprisoned by it. The young need to be instructed about limits, but prodded to keep testing them. I stress that the imagination itself is infinite and inexhaustible and that its supreme faculty, realized in the forms of art, is to achieve transcendence.

Columbia: Do you feel that we are moving into a new concept of form?

Kunitz: The "new" concept is more than 150 years old. Coleridge led the way, in one of his lectures on Shakespeare, when he drew a careful distinction between mechanic form, which is arbitrary and imposed, and organic form, which he defined as innate, inseparable from the properties of the material, shaping itself from within. As our society becomes more and more mechanized and computerized, the modern arts insist more and more on vaunting their organic nature. To be an artist is to defend the life principle against dehumanization, against becoming a statistic. It is to be free and whole, the freedom being inseparable from the wholeness.

Columbia: Free and whole, how?

Kunitz: Free to assert one's conscience; free to be ruthless with oneself and compassionate with others; free to change. A whole person is one who pivots on the center of his being, who dares to be human.

Columbia: Almost all young poets today are connected in some way to university programs, particularly workshops. Do you think this is beneficial?

Kunitz: Sometimes, when I'm in a bad mood, I feel we've reached the saturation point with poets and that it's time to apply some sort of Malthusian doctrine to eliminate the excess. I don't suppose that any civilization before us has ever cultivated so bountiful a crop—we must have at least ten thousand persons living in America today who think of themselves and describe themselves as poets. About 1,500 of them are listed in the official catalog of Poets & Writers, Inc. It has to be remembered that any earlier generation that delivered as many as five or ten poets to posterity is celebrated as a great one. One has to conclude that we're in the midst of a cultural revolution, the literary consequence of the democratic process. We may be entering into a new quantitative era of the creative arts. As for schools of writing, they are an inevitable part of the process. No one can deny their potentiality for abuses, their tendency to confuse self-indulgence with imagination, to encourage nonexistent talents, to put the stamp of academic approval on a machine-made product. If I thought I were involved in any such enterprise, I'd give up teaching tomorrow. Obviously, I am convinced that, through my years of trial and error, I have acquired a few grains of knowledge about "my craft or sullen art" that I can share with others. Does that sound arrogant? In my seventies now I still haven't forgotten the lonely apprenticeship of my youth. I want my students to enjoy with me the sense of belonging to a noble and visionary company. What are the disciplines for? A language separated from human awareness and aspiration leaves me cold.

Columbia: What's your appraisal of the quality of poets produced by the various writing programs?
Kunitz: As I've indicated, their level of accomplishment is high.

Columbia: You mean technically proficient, not good?
Kunitz: You're putting words into my mouth, but I won't argue with you. There's less of the idiosyncratic power that comes from working alone.

Columbia: You say, in *A Kind of Order, A Kind of Folly*, that though you teach order to your students, you realize that only "the troubled spirits" in your classes have a chance of becoming poets. Why?
Kunitz: Order is teachable, and there's no denying that reasonably good poems, the kind that editors prefer to publish, can be built on reasonable foundations. But I was referring to the rare and true genius who immerses himself in "the destructive element"—Conrad's phrase—and brings us news of his wilderness. I like to quote Paul Tillich's precept, that "the self-affirmation of a being is stronger the more non-being it can take into itself."

Columbia: You've spoken of the poet's "finding his center." Can you explain what you mean by that?
Kunitz: I'll try. You have at the center of your being a conglomeration of feelings, emotions, memories, traumas that are uniquely yours, that nobody else on earth can duplicate. They are the clue to your identity. If you don't track them down, lay claim to them, bring them out into the light, they'll eventually possess you, they'll fester, or erupt into compulsive behavior. The farther you stray from your center, the more you will be lost. That's one of the teachings of Lao-tzu. When you're there, at the existential core, you'll know it. Hopkins said in one of his letters that he could taste himself, and the taste was more distinctive than the taste of ale or alum, or the smell of walnut leaf or camphor. You can tell the poets who are working at their center by the distinctiveness of their voice, their constellation of key images, their instantly recognizable beat.

Columbia: What of your own education as a poet?
Kunitz: At Harvard there were no courses in modern poetry and no elders to turn to for criticism or advice. In the curriculum, English poetry stopped

at Rudyard Kipling and American poetry at Amy Lowell. The Widener Library was my singing school. At no time was it conceivable to me to show my poems to masters like Frost or Robinson or Stevens or Eliot—they were out of reach and had no contact with the young. During that period and long after I was graduated, poetry readings just didn't happen. In fact, until my middle years I was never once asked to read my poems in public. Ted Roethke, my first literary friend, and I used to get together in the country and read to each other. I remember his saying, "Someday the bastards will be sorry they didn't ask us." Perhaps I should explain that after college and a short period of newspaper and editorial work, I fled from the cities and lived in isolation as a countryman, free-lancing and learning about plants and animals and drafty old farmhouses. Twenty years passed—along with World War II—before I was invited, by an odd set of circumstances, to teach my first class. That was at Bennington. When I look back on it, I wonder how I survived or why I didn't come to a silent and morose end. My joy in the natural world had a lot to do with saving me. And now, in retrospect, I'm grateful that I was thrown back upon myself and forced to shape a life, out of small resources, but on my own terms. I'm always sorry for young poets who go through college and then through a graduate writing program and then back to the university as teacher, without any experience outside the academic order. How much they've missed! They'll die of hothouse anemia. I want to tell them: "Do something else, develop any other skill, turn to any other special branch of knowledge. Learn how to use your hands. Try wood-working, bird-watching, gardening, sailing, weaving, pottery, archeology, oceanography, spelunking, animal husbandry—take your pick. Whatever activity you engage in, as trade or hobby or field study, will tone up your body and clear your head. At the very least it will help you with your metaphors!

Columbia: Have you ever felt yourself "blocked" as a writer?
Kunitz: Indeed I have. All of us reach a dead end at times. First you think you've exhausted your material, written yourself out. Then you begin to wonder about your style. Perhaps it's too restrictive, perhaps it prevents you from coping with a broad enough range of experience, so that a good portion of yourself, your variety of interests and feelings, is excluded from your writing. It may be time for you to risk a change of style, to crack it open and make it new again. Even more drastically, you may have to question the kind of life you lead. We are always so busy, so preoccupied. The writers of another age had fewer distractions and were, as a rule, more productive. How

many poems have been lost to the telephone! It's difficult to be with yourself, to be lonely enough. The world of Becoming threatens to annihilate the world of Being. And yet the solution isn't to reject the turmoil of modern life. We need to be in it and out of it, the same secret of alternation that the great mystics discovered, shuttling between the Many and the One.

Columbia: You've been teaching for a long time. Do you still enjoy it?

Kunitz: After thirty years I still walk into a classroom with a buoyant sense of anticipation and excitement. I know some poets who tell me they are intimidated by a workshop, with its cast of sensitive psyches, its tensions, its interplay of pent-up feelings—rivalries, fears, desires, aggressions, etc. They see it as a threat to their own psyche. To me it's a place of drama and possibility. I suppose the moral is that you need to care, and you need to feel fairly sure of yourself, but not too sure. Of course, you give a lot, but you take something too, from all that youth and energy and hope. Maybe it helps keep you vulnerable and alive.

Columbia: You seem to be functioning on a spiritual level, something that goes beyond form and order. In the workshop, when you read a poem, one you're particularly close to, it's almost as though you were being seduced by it. There's a tone . . .

Kunitz: Well, there's something about the music of a poem I love.

Poetry in the Classroom:
A Symposium with Marvin Bell,
Donald Hall, and Stanley Kunitz

Alan Loxterman / 1977

American Poetry Review 6 (January–February 1977), 9–13. Reprinted with permission.

The following is a transcript of the soundtrack from a videotape recording made during a symposium held in the Robins Center, University of Richmond, in Virginia. This symposium, entitled "The Continuing Revolution in American Poetry," was only one of the events during the Tucker-Boatwright Literary Festival, a series of poetry readings and classes given during the week of January 19 to January 23, 1976, by Arthur Vogelsang, Maura Stanton, Thomas Lux, Jane Shore, and the participants in the symposium: Stanley Kunitz, Marvin Bell, and Donald Hall. The Festival was organized by Maura Stanton and Alan Loxterman, an English professor at the University of Richmond, who was also moderator of the symposium.

LOXTERMAN: I would like to begin by asking you what poetry is.

BELL: Poetry is anything these gentlemen say it is. You could say poetry is what looks like poetry except for poetry that isn't in lines and that's poetry too. Obviously there are a great many definitions, depending on what your interests are, and you probably have more than I can think of, so . . .

KUNITZ: I think that is an impossible question. Poetry is whatever poets write when they say they're writing poetry.

LOXTERMAN: All right, some background then. Is American poetry today revolutionary after the fashion of T. S. Eliot and Ezra Pound (or put in your own names, if you will) at the beginning of the century? In other words, I'd like you each to define, in historical terms, to what extent American poetry has been revolutionary (if you think it has), in terms of certain significant figures, schools, and esthetic theories—whatever seems important to each of you.

HALL: To me the great revolutionary of American poetry is neither Eliot nor Pound, but Walt Whitman. That revolution is still in process, I hope. We enter it and leave it and come back to it again. Eliot and Pound seem to me not so revolutionary. Perhaps I quarrel with the question: I don't like political and military metaphors in the arts, not just on political grounds—I think they are misapplied very often. It's not exactly revolution. It's discovery, it's originality, it's exploration, creative tentative exploration, into new territory—which is, I think spiritual and inward. It's revolutionary because it overthrows current modes, then the revolution becomes a current mode and gets overthrown again. Eliot was certainly revolutionary to Harriet Monroe and the readers of *Poetry* in Chicago, the readers of the *Atlantic Monthly* in 1912. But he was, after all, picking up from French poetry. He was not being vastly original in terms of international poetry, but in terms of American poetry he was. I think it's essential for the modern artist to keep moving, to keep changing, for the arts to keep moving and changing. I don't know why that should be so. Probably it's linked to societal change, the rapidity of industrial and political change. If you look at the *arts* internationally (not just poetry) for the last hundred years, you see that the greater the artist the more he tends rapidly to change at his most creative periods. I use the word "change" instead of "revolution." In that way I think the best of poetry now in America is continually changing, continually revolutionary. I think I am sanguine about the immediate future of American poetry. It will continue to change, continue to explore, continue to discover.

BELL: Everything that Donald Hall has said makes sense to me. There's a question in my mind too about whether there was as much of a poetic revolution going on as we think. It seems to me that history is really the history of the times and of a few singular figures, and that the influence of any poet who has a great influence while he or she is alive is really an influence on second-rate poets. That's where the influence shows up, it seems to me, and that may not matter. But I tried to think of ways in which significant changes seem to be going on that are common in some way to the first-rate poems of many first-rate poets, and which are different in some way from the interests that Eliot and Pound and other people had. It's true that Eliot and Pound had more influence, certainly on criticism and perhaps even on the writing of poetry, at one time, than Whitman ever had while he was writing—perhaps much to our detriment. Nonetheless I tried to make some little distinctions, and I thought I came up with five, three of which go together. What Pound contributed most, I think, is that he liked to invent schools, so one day he invented a school called Vorticism. Vorticism, translated into crude terms, means that you can leave the transitions out. That kind of jump-cut, what they call in the film industry a jump-cut, that kind of film cut is so easy for us to apprehend now that we take it for granted; we stop questioning whether or not there is any other way, in fact. I think that was a great interest of that time. Now I think something very unusual is happening in the work of a great many contemporary poets and, without saying too much about it now, I think that there are a number of poets who are finding a way of trying to do everything at once. Many kinds of things are going on at once in the poem, as distinct from an emphasis on how to get from one place to another without having to show you all the stages. Eliot—and, if you like to, think of Joyce and some other people—thought of art as an escape from personality. Joyce is always quoted in terms of his remark about the artist paring his nails somewhere behind a work of art, and so forth. Well. Obviously that has changed. Not merely with the publication of books like Robert Lowell's *Life Studies* and the books of W. D. Snodgrass and Anne Sexton and others, but in the whole tone of contemporary poetry, which is much more personal and doesn't think of art as an escape from personality at all. I would like to go further and make a distinction between personality and character, but I won't do it for now. The third thing that goes with those two, somehow I thought, is that the emphasis that Eliot and Pound and the rest of their generation put on poetry was very much an emphasis on the excellent finished product. A stay against confusion, if you like. A perfect jewel, an anthology piece. I think there's an emphasis now on the process and I'm not trying to be judgmental here, whatsoever. I'm not taking sides. But I think there's an emphasis now on process that shows up in certain ways—in the way the poetry is written. Not for everyone, but for many. I think there's a continuing movement that existed then, and has simply picked up speed (logarithmic speed, if you will) to welcome what was formally thought unpoetic or even antipoetic into poetry. A great many people have done it in a great many ways. And finally, I think there's a movement that would never *call* itself a movement in existence now, by which poetry is being redefined in terms of prose. And in fact a great deal of poetry is prose now. But that's enough of that.

KUNITZ: Well, I too want to repudiate the word "revolutionary" because I don't think it is applicable to the condition of poetry. Poetry, of course, is forever changing. All the arts are forever changing. It doesn't mean they're getting any better, but they're changing. And if they stopped changing they'd go dead. I think this is in the nature of the thing we're talking about. Yes, I suppose inevitably, if you think of American poetry as a cultural phenomenon, modern American poetry must be traced back to Whitman as the big paternal figure, the one who had the cosmic vision. Every great culture requires an epic poet. At least it yearns for one; and if it didn't have one back in the shadows, in the dawn of history, it is forced to create one. We had to create Whitman or inspire him to create himself in order that democracy might have its sustaining myth, its poetry that belongs specifically to us as a people. Therefore he really stands at the very gates of our literature. But you cannot stop at any moment and say this is where modern poetry begins. If you look at the broad canvas you see that Whitman is certainly there, but Hopkins is also there, and Baudelaire and Rimbaud are there. The search for the fathers keeps going on; you are always finding new ones, and every new assemblage of them somehow modifies the tone of what is being written in one's own time. And the ancestors of poetry aren't limited merely to poets. Darwin and Marx and Freud are certainly among the fathers of the modern mind, and the modern mind is what shapes our poetry. And Einstein, too, you'd have to add to that trio—there's a quartet, really. The other arts work in the same way. You have to think of Cezanne and Picasso and Matisse and others as being generators of the special vision that makes for the modern arts, and all the arts move in a phalanx; they're not separate activities, and that is why one has to perceive that they are related to the whole movement of a civilization, they do not happen in isolation. Each age generates its own voice and you'd better care about it because it's the only voice you're going to get. And therefore those who say, "Well, I liked it better when they were writing in a different fashion, back in those good old Victorian days, or when they were painting those nice realistic pictures," are really yearning for something that is unattainable. Each generation has to find its own soul and its own conscience. Well, that's enough . . .

HALL: Can I do a little arguing? I want to argue with Marvin a bit. A symposium without argument is hapless. I used to argue for the discontinuity of, say, Eliot and Pound with modernism and present-poetry, and now I find more and more continuity. Is the poetry of process a new thing? I'm not so sure. When we hear poets talking about their poetry we hear Robert Duncan telling us he will not revise—Allen Ginsberg too, and many other people—that the dictates of the spontaneous mind at the moment are not to be violated. And I don't believe it; I never believe anything a poet ever tells me about how he writes his poems. I'm *interested* in what he tells me, because it often gives me a clue as to how he *wants* his poems to be taken, but I will immediately look for the opposite: if a poet tells me, "I write always late at night, drinking gin," I believe that he writes early in the morning, drinking coffee. And that it's important to him, and allows him to write, to lie about it.

About poetry of process: I'm interested in what I can see in the texts, and it seems to me that Romantic poetry to modern which is a continuation of it—is continually a poetry of process: the form of the Wordsworthian ode (the "Immortality Ode") or the form of the "Lapis Lazuli" is an imitation of process. This memory occurs to me and then reminds me of something else, and then I think of this event. "A funny thing happened on the way to the tower!" This form is the imitation of spontaneity and spontaneous process, and it seems to me continuous with Ted Berrigan, believe it or not. And the *Cantos* (not, say, the Pound of *The Return*, which is certainly a jewel, or much earlier Pound) is in its form an imitation of discursive conversation. I'm not talking about the actual process of writing. I find the process of composition irrelevant, partly because I really don't know anything about it and I never will; certainly I won't know it if the poet tells me about it.

Also, I want to say that *The Waste Land* is an extremely personal poem, almost a confessional poem. Eliot was telling us that art is an escape from personality; and when he told us, the lie allowed him to write the most personal poem ever written.

KUNITZ: What about (to corroborate what you're saying), what about Coleridge's odes, for example, the "Dejection Ode," or Wordsworth's "Prelude"? Certainly these are discursive poems, and poems of process representing the way the mind moves, so that I don't think that process is a modern invention. But the *consciousness* of process is a modern concept. Therefore, the very thought of process activates and, in a way, changes the quality, to a degree. It's like becoming self-conscious about one's own ego; the moment you do that, you're no longer writing in a state of innocence.

HALL: But haven't we had two hundred years of that consciousness?

KUNITZ: Sure, but it has been accentuated. It has become self-knowledge, even guilty knowledge. Freud saw to that.

BELL: I think that it is a question of emphasis, and the poems that have been named are a few good examples of thousands, of course, that do exhibit the process by which the poet observed and thought and wrote, even as the poet and the poems themselves go forward. I have no quarrel with that. I think there is a greater self-consciousness, to use Mr. Kunitz's term, about the process, which in turn allows the poet, if he or she wishes to, to speak about the process itself, even as it goes on, so that the speaking of the process becomes the process, and so forth and so forth—I mean, we're making false distinctions, thanks to language here. But I think I'll have to name someone whose work will probably be unfamiliar to many of you; nonetheless, I don't think the poetry of John Ashbery could well have existed before that kind of self-consciousness, though he shows in any case the strong influence of Stevens—one of the two or three poets writing in America who I think show a very strong influence of Stevens. (Despite our homage to him, I think that few really show a severe influence.) Ashbery does, but in addition he is a poet of great self-consciousness who is also very often a difficult poet because he is articulating subtle distinctions, almost at the moment they come on him it would seem. Now obviously, artifice is part of it and some of that's an illusion. I think a very different poet, a poet who seems to be a folksy poet and a poet of the common term and the common idea, but who really is something else, does the same thing, and that's William Stafford. I think Stafford is a poet, a very cagey poet who—well, there's a great deal that has to do with the way thoughts come into being, which has been articulated, brought to the surface, and welcomed into the poem. Sometimes to the detriment of the whole poem, seen as a final product. Sometimes not. By Stafford, by Ashbery, and by a great many other people—including, I think, in individual poems, the people who sit before you now. I guess that I don't think, after all, that it's only a matter of emphasis, though I don't find myself in disagreement with anything that Donald Hall said.

KUNITZ: There's a famous passage in Valery writing about poetry when he talks about a man looking in a mirror and seeing himself look in a mirror. Well, that's an image, I think, of a good deal of modern art; when you see that in the paintings of De Kooning, when you don't know whether it's the inside of the room or the landscape that is really being abstracted in the painting. The inside and the outside are interchangeable.

LOXTERMAN: So, then, none of you would recognize a particularly aggressive experimental tone to poetry in the twentieth century which might even distinguish it, say, from nineteenth-century poetry, entitling us to call it revolutionary in that sense? Why not?

KUNITZ: Except in terms of the growing self-consciousness about change, about self-knowledge, and about the avant-garde. I think there is a cult of novelty and a cult of the avant-garde, and that does change the picture considerably. And that may be the most important modification that we have seen; whereas other generations really venerated the tradition and the poet who was writing in the tradition, the modern tendency is always to find something new and to praise whatever is new, regardless of whether it's better or not. But the fact that it's new is itself an affirmation of its interest and excitement. So that the avant-garde who used to be the outsiders looking in are now the insiders looking out.

HALL: Novelty is an institution.

KUNITZ: It's become an establishment.

HALL: That doesn't mean novelty is all bad; it's simply an observation, it's true.

KUNITZ: There's a question from the audience.

AUDIENCE: Isn't what you are describing in the twentieth century somewhat the same as the decadent and the esthetes in the 1890s? It's really different, but those people all distinguished themselves as being antibourgeois.

HALL: I think we write better poetry. There's one other answer to that, which is that the nineteenth-century esthetes were actually a minority; they did not dominate the scene of art. They were regarded as being disreputable in their own Victorian frame, which conforms to the definition of an avant-garde; it's not true of poets now, because our society is not Victorian.

LOXTERMAN: All right, now what part would you say that readers and publishers play in this element of experimentation? And I suppose we could include criticism here, too, particularly in the twentieth century. Do they encourage or discourage aggressive experimentation? And you can separate the readers from the publishers, if you wish.

HALL: Every magazine editor is looking for something new to make his name. You distinguish yourself, as a publisher or editor, by recognizing novelty—since novelty is an institution. Or "originality" or "revolutionary work." Now that sounds cynical, but in fact novelty or originality can be good work or it can be bad. Most people most of the time, including editors and publishers, don't have any taste and they print a lot of bad stuff. Almost always, I think, they print it because they *think* it's really good. They look for what they consider the new thing, the wave of the future. This helps original-appearing work to be published. Not necessarily truly original, but original-*appearing* work; it does operate against, say, someone like William Stafford whose work, while it has great elements of originality, doesn't *look* original. Stafford was something like forty-three or forty-four before his first book was published by a commercial publisher. Because the institution of novelty wouldn't accept it.

KUNITZ: I don't feel there are any objective criteria that can be dissected and framed and that are of any use to any poet. Any poet that I know distrusts criticism, the whole act of criticism. I don't know of any poets who have really been helped by criticism, I mean from professional critics—particularly academic critics. The only words about one's poems that really matter are the words from other poets. I truly feel that that's the only kind of reaction to your poems that can be helpful to you. Then, there is the reaction from a group of persons in a room when you're reading your poems. If you sense that response, that is an act of criticism in itself. And it's the most human of all the critical acts. But all the efforts to create schools of poetry, to pass arbitrary judgments about the one kind of poetry that is better than other kinds, or to rate poets on a descending scale according to how they fulfill these *a priori* criteria: I think all that is an affliction rather than any kind of blessing.

HALL: It's an industry.

KUNITZ: Indeed. Consider the industry of Harold Bloom and company. All that fantastic scholarship seems designed to glorify the act of criticism beyond that of creation and to redefine the tradition as a sacred kingdom to which only a favored handful of poets are seen as qualified for admission.

BELL: That's true. I agree with both statements. I would add only this. It is true that there are a great many magazines now which publish poetry, and so forth, and that editors are on the lookout for good poetry and idiosyncratic poetry too, perhaps. Yet I think it would take someone of enormous character to become as expansive and as humane and accomplished, all at once, as Williams or Whitman. For the very reason that one is rewarded for juvenilia now, we all are. It's a cultural thing I'm talking about now. I think there is a certain level of accomplishment that, while very important to oneself, produces self-imitation through the rest of one's life if one doesn't have the character to withstand that temptation. And it is true that Stevens didn't publish *Harmonium* until, I think, he was forty-four. Frost was forty before he published in this country, and Williams really didn't write most of his great poems until he was in his fifties—even the *Selected Poems* is not where most of the great stuff is. It comes out to that, and Stafford was at least in his forties; I think he was closing in on fifty. And there are good reasons for that, as you all know. Someone once asked the great Japanese potter Hamada how long it takes to make a pot and he said, "A hundred years."

HALL: That's great. You know, you said it takes character. I think it takes criticism too. It takes hard-nosed friends to keep it going, too. Otherwise, you will be rewarded for your bad poems. After you've published a few books you can publish anything you want. And if you have the brains you then realize that you can't put any trust in editors any more. When you're young you think, "If I publish a poem that means it's good, right?" Then you see the magazine that printed your poem and you see it's got lots of crap in it and you realize that, no, that didn't mean it was good because if he liked those people then maybe I'm as bad as they are. You have to give up on that.

I have profited enormously by criticism, from the criticism of my friends, most of them poets. Not all of them. Some of my friends who are teachers have helped me with my poems. I haven't learned much from criticism in print—very little from book reviews. When I finish a poem or get it almost finished, I seize upon everybody, take advantage of everybody that I can, to read that poem, and to be hard on me. Some of my friends, out of their own fear of criticism, probably, just say, "Oh, wonderful! Wonderful!" I don't show them anymore; they're not any use to me. To keep on going, you've got to seek out criticism, you've got to seek out toughness—criticism and toughness that try to find the criteria within the poem itself. It can sound weak-minded to say the criteria don't come from the outside but from the poem itself, but that's what happens. You read a poem, say well and thoroughly, not just with your brain, not with your critical brain; you read it with your whole body and your whole experience, trying to find assent or dissent with it. When you feel that assent, which is inspiriting and discovering, the poem adds up to you and fills you up, and you read it again: it fills you up more and more. After that, after you've had that experience, you may not even know what the poem is about. You could not *talk* about it. Then if you want to learn from it, you go back to it and pick the poem apart for its criteria, for its particular embodiments of excellence. And you may, as a poet and as a person, learn from the act of criticism, or reading, for your own person.

AUDIENCE: A professor at the University of Richmond was quoted as saying that the only interesting form of language now would be in graffiti and advertising.

KUNITZ: The only form is advertising?

HALL: Graffiti and advertising.

BELL: It's the same thing, isn't it? Well, I suppose if your test is whether you sell anything then advertising is obviously a superior language. But I don't think that the poet is selling anything; and in fact if he is, even if it's a "pure" message, I think something goes wrong with the poem.

LOXTERMAN: Is it even the interesting language which sells in advertising?

KUNITZ: It is a calculation about an induced response. I don't agree with Auden's pronouncement, in his lines on Yeats, that poetry makes nothing happen. But of course he was right in opposing poetry to oratory or advertising. He was defending the language of poetry as an intrinsic reality, which doesn't use itself up by being translated into action. A poem's energy doesn't leak out, it renews itself at every reading. Form is what holds that energy in and prevents it from leaking. When you confront a true work of art, you are not moved to do *anything* except give yourself to that work. To respond to it in the most human way you possibly can. With all your resources, all your inner resources.

LOXTERMAN: You are speaking now of the reader and the poem?

KUNITZ: Yes.

HALL: I disagree with the man who said that very much. Graffiti are often lovely, witty, funny. I like jokes, I like fun. I like poems even better. Perhaps some poems are just jokes and fun, for that matter. That's ok, but it's not the only interesting use of language. I think there is excellent, oh, even great, poetry being written. Obviously I disagree that graffiti are better! And advertising is, oh goodness, it's sometimes interesting to figure out what they're doing and how they're doing it and admire their venal cleverness. But that it be interesting language or good language—no I don't think so, any more than it is good language to be a successful lying politician. Sometimes it's *interesting* at the same time as it's appalling. But it's not *good*.

AUDIENCE: I've never met anyone who never wrote a poem. In fact most people have a whole sheaf of them. And yet the audience for poetry is tiny. Why?

KUNITZ: That's easy to answer. The child in them wrote those poems. But our educational system is designed to kill the imagination. After a few years of indoctrination, children begin to feel guilty about their fantasies. These are equivalent to lies, the sign of a mind that isn't coping with reality—reality, which consists of information, facts, statistics. What we see gradually is the dying out of the child. And a dying out of the imagination at the same time. The poets, the artists in general, are the tough ones, the stubborn ones, who resist having their imaginations stomped on, and who manage somehow to keep their childhood alive in them. But they are relatively only a handful. The same is true of readers. As a percentage of the population I doubt that our audience for poetry is greater than what it was when we were a frontier society. In proportion to our numbers, and in proportion to our educational opportunities, that audience is shamefully low. It's a commentary on what has gone wrong with the so-called American dream.

BELL: I'll go even further. In describing the circulation of poetry, I think the sales of individual books don't accurately reflect the readership. Unlike newspapers, which are read by more than the person who buys each one, most poetry books are bought but not read. Most poetry books are sold to undergraduate students, I think, and they're used for a course and then abandoned. I don't think one has many readers; and I'm not quite bemoaning it personally, but I do think it's true. On the other hand, there are some benefits to proceeding in an art form that is a gratuitous activity. There are some real benefits to it. So it's true—

KUNITZ: There are contradictions, though. Look, here in this hall are persons who really care about poetry, or else they wouldn't be here, I suppose. On any campus you go to, there they are. But they don't buy books of poetry.

HALL: They don't buy books. But all of us now who publish books of poems keep reading our poems, performing our poems to thousands of people every year. That simply was not true twenty years ago. It's more true now than it was *ten* years ago. The audience is larger, the audience is increasing. I'm quibbling: it's small, yes, but it's vastly greater than it used to be in America. It's vastly greater, it's greater not by 10 percent or 20 percent, but by a factor of ten times, twelve times.

KUNITZ: I'm not so sure.

HALL: The number of books sold is considerably more than it was. A book of poetry published in the forties was published in an edition of five hundred or so, wasn't it?

KUNITZ: My first book of poems was an edition of six hundred.

HALL: Six hundred. O.K. The edition now is very likely to be—it depends on whether it's paper or hard-three thousand soft, three thousand hard. That's a factor of ten: six thousand copies to six hundred. I just proved my point, didn't I? Wonderful mathematics. But the audience is greater still, the *real* audience, not the metaphorical audience: the hearers, the listeners. My goodness, back when I was in college, there were very few poetry readings. Mr. Frost made his living reading his poems; Mr. Sandburg made a part of his living reading his poems. Very few other people, the poets of that time—the people who published, like the people who publish now—were reading once or twice a year, for the most part, and for very little: small audiences and little money. Now the poetry reading is almost an institution, surely. It's *common.* Most colleges have to have a poetry reading now and then during the year. So the whole publication—the making public—of poetry has greatly increased. I don't say that therefore we have arrived at Utopia. The audience *is* small but it has grown, and we ought not to forget that.

KUNITZ: Don, I think one fact that modifies the picture is that there is no doubt a growing awareness among the young, a growing awareness of poetry and a growing response to it. But our population as a whole is dominantly older than it used to be so that when you measure the *whole* population you see this island of youth that is responsive to poetry; but, in terms of the general population, it is not sweeping the country, let me assure you.

HALL: I didn't mean to say that.

AUDIENCE: Is one of the primary interests in poetry today stretching the kinds of meaning that language can carry?

(*Pause.*)

HALL: I don't know if I can understand the question. Silence bothers me so I have to talk. Each separate attempt to write a poem involves new associations, new linkages, juxtapositions of words, an expansion of the possibility of a particular word. But I don't understand the concept (perhaps it *would* be correct if I understood it) of a particular endeavor in contemporary poetry that could be called expansion of the meaning of language. I could quibble and argue that there is a contraction also, an attempt to fix, to use words exactly. Not to fix the meaning of words but to use words exactly and with respect for the wholeness of the word, its physical presence in your mouth, in your ear, as well as the history and the family connections of the word. That "contradiction" might be, in terms of the relation of literature to the spoken language or to the ordinary written language, a kind of meaning of "expansion."
Somebody else talk, please.

BELL: Well, poets often find it difficult to use those terms in which you ask the question, so it is hard to answer. Any one of us who writes poetry is always trying to satisfy one's own demands, you know: psychological, linguistic, and emotional. And that includes probably what you might think of as stretching language or compressing more meaning into a shorter space or something. You might think of it that way, but we, I think, tend to talk in different ways when we're talking about writing.

KUNITZ: I once wrote a sentence that I'm trying to recall now and that will have to serve as my answer to your question. "The language of poetry is language surprised in the act of changing into meaning." That goes back to the concept of process that we were talking about earlier. So you're not dealing with fixities of meaning; you're dealing with language which is saturated with your own self and your own being, and in that sense certainly you are charging it with your own energy; and, perhaps, in your phrase, "stretching" it. But if you *consciously* set about stretching language in writing a poem, I think you'd better give up writing poetry.

AUDIENCE: Is the small audience for poetry caused by the fact that poets are consciously (or unconsciously) writing for a small audience so that we feel the need for a single figure, a popular figure like Robert Frost or Rod McKuen, to focus others' attention upon poetry?

HALL: I'm tempted to try to say that I like . . . I'm not conscious of writing for a small audience. But perhaps I *am*, and that's all right. I'm writing to try to attain an ideal of excellence. That doesn't mean I achieve it, of course. But I'm trying to write a good poem, perhaps even a great poem. And whatever that involves I'm willing to undertake. That endeavor may well involve excluding lots of people; and I take that chance gladly. I will not, I would not, I don't want to try to write the poem that will appeal to the masses as a kind of calculated thing. Poetry is my master, I hope. Not the people. And I defend that.

Marvin said earlier that there are advantages to writing for a minority, and there are, if you don't . . . when some novelists—fiction is pretty much a minority art, too, but let me state this anyway—when some novelists sit down to write, they know that this might be worth seven million dollars or only two hundred thousand dollars. When we go to our desk to write our poems, we are not troubled by such thoughts. We are not troubled by them; those butterflies do not wheel around our heads. We are freer, therefore, and that's a lovely thing.

Now, Stanley talked earlier about educational systems, the American educational system. I want to suggest that what we're dealing with is something of which the educational system . . . is only a symptom. I think it's evolutionary. I think that what poetry is up to is hard to take for the majority of people; that the greatest poetry is too hard to take for the majority of the people; that poetry is a sort of advance guard of evolutionary change. I'll try to make this brief. Poetry is not a regression to a childlike or a primitive state. It is not. Babies do not write great poems, and neither did Australopithecus write great poems, as far as we know—I think we can say with certainty he didn't. There is in the human mind the baby, always. All of us retain the baby in the human mind, and baby-like kinds of thinking which are valuable and useful kinds of thinking: primary process, etc. There comes a time at the—about the fourth or fifth grade—when we must put away childish things, when certainly others will say, "Don't be a baby," using the word in denigration; and that is a time which the school system certainly supports, where secondary rationalism, that process of thinking, becomes institutionalized by the educational system. But it was first invented, after all, as a way of protecting ourselves from animals, building fires, building shelter; it was, evolutionarily, necessary for our survival that we put away childish things, that we abandon, largely, primary process thinking and go into rationalism, plan ahead in order to survive. I'm talking now about millions of years, not hundreds of years in our society, but millions of years in our evolution. I think that poetry, which is a rather recent phenomenon in the history of man—poetry is only about three thousand years old or so, as far as we know—that poetry is a new step which is a synthesis of the earlier processes of thinking. In poetry we can go beyond the rationalism and include something of the earlier primitive world of thought that is recapitulated every time a child is born: add it on. That is what poetry does. I also think that is what other artists do, or participate in. It is obviously true that the majority of adult human beings are terrified of this irrational addition, cannot open themselves to it, are afraid of madness and failure if they do. And that is why the audience for poetry is small.

BELL: That's a terrific analysis!

KUNITZ: I'd like to try to comment on that question. I do think that there are two different traditions that we're concerned with in that question. There is an oral tradition, a popular tradition, and there is a literary tradition, an art tradition. And the challenge for the poet is to draw from the oral tradition whatever can enliven and enrich his art without diminishing it. If popularity is more important to him than excellence, he's lost. The reader he must write for is the best reader in himself. Ideally the popular tradition fortifies the literary tradition. With somebody like Bob Dylan, you see the process operating in reverse. He derives out of the literary tradition, of which he is a diluted version. But his voice is capable of reaching thousands, tens-of-thousands, of people. And that is what he rightly aims for in his role as entertainer. One of our consolations as poets is that our audiences will catch up with us in time—maybe! In fact, if we were given the choice between having a hundred thousand readers this year and a thousand readers a year for the next hundred years, is there a poet in the house who wouldn't settle for the latter?

HALL: The vertical audience and the horizontal audience.

KUNITZ: Right. Incidentally, in this respect, there is a publisher whom most of you probably don't know about, Broadside Press, run by Dudley Randall, himself a poet. It's a press for black poets. Dudley Randall says that it is not unusual for the books on his list to sell a hundred thousand copies. So there is that particular audience which is obviously hungry for the poetry addressed to it. The mass of the population doesn't seem to be that hungry.

HALL: That Broadside Press is . . . very rarely do you find a Broadside Press volume in a white bookstore.

KUNITZ: It has its own mail-order market.

HALL: Mail-order, and black bookstores, in Vaughan's in Detroit, and there's another in Chicago. Don Lee is going on toward two hundred thousand copies. And Etheridge Knight, Sonia Sanchez, thirty, forty, fifty thousand.

KUNITZ: True. And if you hear them read those poems aloud, you'll understand why.

AUDIENCE: Would you comment further about poetry becoming prose, perhaps using as an example the found poem read by Arthur Vogelsang on Monday night?

BELL: This can get very complicated, and I'll try to keep it very simple. I'll keep it simple by cheating. I'll make an assumption. And that is that you now feel (or will feel in ten years, as I do) that something rhythmic, musical if you will—something that has to do with rhythm and sound, which we might describe as musical—is going on and is itself of interest in all the poetry that we care to reread. Inexhaustibility for me is a test of good poetry. If I don't care to reread it, well . . . O.K., without going into detail, I think these rhythmic effects can be described. It is no good to prescribe them for people, that's not the point, but they can be described; one can be variously wise or ignorant of them. I think that one could look at the free verse of the century and one would find that, in fact, most of the good free verse has been written by people who knew a great deal about meter. They weren't necessarily writing the free verse out of any awareness of meter but an intuitive one;

but, as a matter of fact, they knew a great deal about it. We now come upon a generation of poets who do not know very much about meter, and who have some very forceful arguments against acquiring the knowledge. I'm not trying to take sides here for a moment, either. I think there are some effects available in prose rhythms which are not available in poetry rhythms. There are some effects available in a combination, but even to effect a combination successfully often requires knowledge of meter; it requires what we used to call a good ear. One could know nothing about meter and have a good ear, and everything would come out all right, I think. Auden used to like to make lists of what a young poet should do to become a good poet; and Auden would have the poet have a garden, and have an animal and learn how to cook a French dish or something . . . I don't know whether he had this on his list or not, I don't remember; but it might not be bad to require everyone to learn a musical instrument. I'm not sure you can help anyone's ears. I'm not sure it's necessary to know how to play a musical instrument, but the ear is crucial, the ear is crucial, and one does resort to misdirection when asked what is poetry and what is prose. You know, just as jazz people resort to misdirection when you ask them to define jazz: you'll know it when you hear it, right? O.K. You gotta ask the question, you'll never know the answer; all that sort of stuff. But as a matter of fact . . . boy, I don't know if I want to say this. I get into a fish-net here. But, generally speaking, prose has more unstressed syllables in it between stresses; and there comes a point at which there are so many unstressed syllables between stresses that there is nothing engaging about the rhythm any more. At that point something else might take over. There is prose poetry, Karl Shapiro published a book of prose poems called *The Bourgeois Poet* in the sixties? Fifties? Forties? Thirties? Sixties?

HALL: Sixties. Early.

BELL: And all those prose poems in that book take their definition in contradistinction to what we think of as not only poetry, but prose poetry. Prose poetry itself has in English been defined in contradistinction, in opposition to what we expected of a poem on a page. Here came prose poems which said: "You're not gonna get any of that. You thought you were gonna get lovely, lilting anapaestic rhythms; you thought you were gonna get lush images out of French poetry: you thought you were gonna get a concern with the inner recesses of the imagination, the deep psychology of perversion. You're not gonna get any of that. This is gonna be external, lumpy, angry, full of junk!" It was very interesting, and it effectively destroyed the prose poem, though a great many people are writing prose poems now. But there's some question as to what they're writing, whether it's . . .

KUNITZ: Could I add another to that?

BELL: Please. I'm tied up.

KUNITZ: I think that the boundaries of all the arts are dissolving. This is one of the conspicuous contemporary phenomena. The boundary between prose and poetry is certainly getting harder and harder to define. The boundary between dance and theatre, between painting and sculpture, between music and noise. These are all boundaries that are becoming more and more impalpable. It's part of that whole process we have been talking about; and, in a way, it's a reversion to those primitive feelings that we have mentioned before, those feelings we associate with childhood, with the synesthesia of childhood when all the senses are operating at once. In the modern arts there are few defenders left of the sacred purity of the forms.

HALL: Maybe somebody ought to say something about found poems. The found poem (I don't know Vogelsang's poem, so I'm not talking about that), the found poem is fairly common these days.

You take out a bit from an old advertisement or a piece from a newspaper, or something, you isolate it on the page, and call it a found poem. This is usually a form of camp. I would define "camp" in art as taking an object from its usual or intentional surroundings, and isolating it in another surrounding; to laugh at it, to find it comic or absurd or inappropriate. There are lots of magazines which print old drawings from mechanical books, or great hands pointing, and *so* on, and the illustrations are amusing and witty. The found poem, however: once it's been done it has been done. It's a form of conceptual art because it is an idea; that you remove something from its context, isolate it somewhere else. And, on the white page of the poetry book, or read aloud at the poetry reading, it takes on a new, very disparate, sort of life. Once it's been done it's been done; every time you do it again you are doing the same act of imagination over again, which is to say it's repetitive, though each particular incident may have its own amusement . . . I'm not terribly interested in the found poem or in other conceptual art, except for the first time.

BELL: How about the lost poem?

HALL: The lost poem. He's talking about the lost poem!

KUNITZ: I think it's more important to find yourself than to find a poem.

AUDIENCE: I'd like to correct that. Vogelsang's poem isn't a real found poem at all.

BELL: It turns out the found poem was a fake.

HALL: We have found a new genre, the fake found poem!

KUNITZ: The *poeme faux-naif.* Or something like that.

LOXTERMAN: We'll take one more question, I believe, since I don't think any other hands were up.

AUDIENCE: Do you think there is room for a one reality which exists somewhere outside the person perceiving the poem, as in the Platonic concept?

(We will never know, for at this prophetic moment the videotape recorder's own synesthesia of sound and image came to the end of its reel.)

Stanley Kunitz:
Action and Incantation

Harvey Gross / 1978

Antaeus 30/31 (1978), 283–95. Reprinted with permission.

Harvey Gross: I am speaking with Stanley Kunitz in the garden of his Greenwich Village house. Our particular subject is prosody; however, I expect that we shall be ranging over a wider area: the whole craft of writing poetry. To begin: a question on the use of the word *prosody.* Among theoreticians especially there is an ongoing dispute about the terminological implications of the word. The linguists seem to feel that the word refers to the vocalic elements in language: matters of voice, intonation, pitch, etc. Poets think of prosody as the science of metrics; the word still carries with it some implications of classical prosody based on quantitative principles. Do you feel that the word is still a viable one?

Stanley Kunitz: I don't know that there is any alternative, any really valid substitute for it. So that even though I think it's true that it means different things to different persons, it still seems to me the only term you can use effectively.

Gross: Ezra Pound says that prosody concerns itself with "the articulation of the total sound structure of a poem."

Kunitz: I tend to think of it as combining the elements you mention. It has to do with voice and the inflection of voice, the sound of the poem: the way it breathes. But it also has to do with the systematic reduction of it.

Gross: The meter itself?

Kunitz: The imposition of limits on the voice. I thus use prosody in both senses: as reconciliation between the constraint of meter and the freedom of the voice.

Gross: Let us move on to another rather troublesome set of terms: rhythm on the one hand, meter on the other. How do you think of these two words: their respective denotations and connotations?

Kunitz: Rhythm to me is the more general term and extends beyond poetry into the arts, into the life itself. Metrics is a specific application of rhythm; it's a system of measuring rhythm, actually, or defining it. Rhythm is the broad term, metrics is the limiting term.

Gross: Metrics is then the more technical term. Of course, you can say that a nonmetrical prosody has rhythm: free verse has rhythm.

Kunitz: Yes, prose has rhythm; it doesn't have meter unless it's highly organized, in which case it's moving toward the condition of the poem.

Gross: Whitehead makes the fascinating distinction that a diamond has too much pattern to have rhythm, a fog has too little pattern to have rhythm. I would like to turn toward the phenomenon of rhythm itself, and then perhaps we can work toward the more specific elements of meter and metrical form. Most of your poetry, as I read it, is metrical.

Kunitz: Or quasi-metrical.

Gross: Certainly your earlier verse is written in the metrical modes.

Kunitz: However, I must say that I don't think of my later poems as metrical at all.

Gross: In *The Testing-Tree*?

Kunitz: In *The Testing-Tree* and in the poems since *The Testing-Tree.*

Gross: I haven't seen those poems: is there a collection available?

Kunitz: No. I am publishing them next spring.

Gross: What will the title of your new volume be?

Kunitz: My complete *Collected Poems.*

Gross: In your prose collection, *A Kind of Order, A Kind of Folly,* you come up with this intriguing notion about rhythm: "Even before it is ready to change into language, a poem may begin to assert its buried life in the mind with wordless surges of rhythm and counter-rhythm. Gradually the rhythms attach themselves to objects and feelings." Would you care to elaborate on this activity of the poetic unconscious?

Kunitz: Because it *is* a preverbal activity, it is very hard to describe it in words! But I suspect that when one detects in oneself this surge of rhythm and counter-rhythm, really what you are locating is a complex of feelings.

Gross: Is rhythm, then, as the aestheticians say, "isomorphic" with feeling: a map or symbol of feeling?

Kunitz: It is a complex of thoughts and feelings looking for a language, seeking a language. It is like coming out of that fog you have just mentioned and beginning to shape itself. But the only way it can shape itself, in the beginning, is in wordless rhythms which gradually attach themselves to words. And then that fog becomes palpable.

Gross: Do you ever start out with a rhythm oscillating or vibrating in your unconscious, and then you have an experience and then you see that the rhythm and the experience are related? Or you recall an experience and then the poem becomes, in a sense, the rhythm of that experience?

Kunitz: Usually, what I find is that these rhythms are ancient. They have been buried in me a long time; they have roots in experiences that may be long forgotten.

Gross: Childhood experiences, perhaps?

Kunitz: Perhaps. Many times. Certainly, in recent poems that is true. Then something happens today that triggers that old wound, that old joy: whatever it may be. It begins to assert itself. It begins to find its way towards a language. And so you have the combination of something old with something new which then gives you that effect of cross-grain or cross-weave which is to me essential to the making of a poem.

Gross: Do some of these rhythms go back to nursery rhymes or children's poems or memories of particular childhood experiences, like going to the circus?

Kunitz: The events are often the property of childhood; the rhythms are not necessarily out of nursery rhymes. They tend, in my case, to be more complex rhythms because the feelings they are attached to are no longer simply the feelings of the child. They are the feelings of the child combined with the feelings of the man.

Gross: I find in all your poetry, metrical and quasi-metrical, the rhythmic elements richly stylized, heightened to the level of incantation.

Kunitz: Definitely so. This goes back to the way I write my poems, which is by speaking them. My voice, so I've been told by those who have overheard me, is definitely incantatory when I'm making a poem, and even, I think some of that remains after the poem is written and I read the poem aloud to an audience. There is an element of incantation present and this is the rhythm on which the poem rides and builds.

Gross: In your earlier work, when you were writing within the constraints of formal metric and stanza, did you find that these formal elements limited the incantatory freedom of your speaking voice?

Kunitz: That is, of course, the problem of writing in metrical forms. But the meter also offers opportunities: the tension created between the regularity of the ideal pattern and the irregularity of the actual syntax of the poem. Then it is possible to create something that does relate to the natural voice, and yet is a formalized version of it. I think that what happened to me through the years is that eventually I began to feel that the necessity for formalizing the rhythms and the inflections became an impediment; it prevented me from saying certain things that I wanted to say. I wanted, for example, to be able to write in a middle voice, not always in a high style. It was increasingly difficult for me to see how that could be done, so that a good part, I felt, of my experience was cut out of my poems: I couldn't reconcile them with the high style.

Gross: When we move from the *Selected Poems* to *The Testing-Tree*, we recognize the dramatic change from formalized meters to freer rhythmic forms. In the *Selected Poems* there seem to be two modes: the flexible iambics of such poems as "The Science of the Night," "Foreign Affairs," and the magnificent *guazzabuglio* of polemic, celebration, and Roman history, "The Thief"; and then there are the other poems composed in stanzas.

Kunitz: The iambic pieces, I feel, anticipate a good deal of later, freer work.

Gross: These poems are always moving against an iambic norm.

Kunitz: But not rigidly.

Gross: No, hardly, but in the way that much modern blank verse is written.

Kunitz: Even Shakespeare!

Gross: Yes, the Shakespeare of the later plays: *The Winter's Tale, The Tempest*.

Kunitz: Yes, I think that the late Shakespeare has a very modern sound.

Gross: Although there is a change of prosodic style in *The Testing-Tree*, I still hear the same voice. There is one poem, however, "Three Floors," which is written in ballad stanzas.

Kunitz: That is the earliest poem in *The Testing-Tree*, and it is closer to my older style.

Gross: I am very much moved by the use of free rhythms in your "Around Pastor Bonhoeffer," certainly one of the most profoundly expressive poems you have written.

Kunitz: That I couldn't possibly have written in a metrical mode.

Gross: You were adapting actual notebook material, records of conversation, and so on.

Kunitz: Yes, and some of it with very little variation from the original entries. But you understand that the voice you still recognize in *The Testing-Tree* as being fundamentally the same is, of course, a testimony to the persistence of the psyche—which is, after all, the motor behind the poetry.

Gross: Do you feel that the earlier discipline of the metrical verse gives you an advantage even in your freer verse: namely, that having learned to work in strict forms affords a greater expressive potential? Let me use the analogy of the composer who first learns the rules of harmony, counterpoint, and fugue—then goes on to free composition.

Kunitz: Oh, of course; I think that a poet who doesn't know anything about metrics, who hasn't really practiced the discipline of formal metrics, is at a great loss.

Gross: There are many poets who are operating today . . .

Kunitz: . . . who have never learned . . .

Gross: . . . or don't care about it.

Kunitz: But I think that what happens there is that their ear is never finely tuned. The great thing that you learn from the metric discipline is to recognize the beat and the evasion of the beat. That is the great lesson: you train your ear for that.

Gross: You have taught courses in the writing of poetry. Do you ask your students to write exercises in metrical forms, as a matter of ear training?

Kunitz: In my early years of teaching, when I was teaching undergraduates, yes, I worked very definitely with the metric forms; and found it very helpful to them. Then in the period of the sixties I discovered that the young writers were impatient.

Gross: They didn't want to hear about metrics.

Kunitz: They didn't want to hear about it. They were rejecting their parents, the social structure, and the metrical tradition. Poetry had to begin anew; it was born that year, that day. And so it was impossible really to do much of anything except surreptitiously about technique, about craft. Recently, a new thing has happened: there is a definite sense of return and an interest in the traditional forms. My students, who are graduate students, are supposed to know about metrical matters, and in the last few years I haven't worked with the metrical disciplines at all. One assumed that the students already had the advantage of that kind of training. But it was a false assumption in many cases. This year, for the first time, my students really asked for instruction in prosody.

Gross: This is fascinating because it brings up the whole question of the *Zeitgeist* and prosody in general. When Robert Lowell published *Lord Weary's Castle* in 1946, right after the war, he seemed to have set a prosodic fashion. His book set me to writing rhymed couplets, *terza rima*, sestinas, etc. Very often the impact of a major poet will establish the prosody of a creative age. Similarly, in 1959 when *Life Studies* appeared, we experienced a rerun of freer forms.

Kunitz: I don't think that Lowell, with *Lord Weary's Castle*, really set anything because he derived his style out of the Southern traditionalists: Ransom and Tate in particular. I don't think it was a novelty in that epoch.

Gross: Do you think the main influence during the fifties was Auden—who was a very conscious prosodist?

Kunitz: I think that Auden was the strongest influence through the thirties. Every decade has had a dominant voice which is related to prosody; for example, Eliot certainly was the "voice" of the twenties.

Gross: You can listen to the rhythm of a particular poem and date it.

Kunitz: I tell in my prose book (*A Kind of Order, A Kind of Folly*) the game that Roethke and I used to play. We would dig up the most obscure poem we could find out of the past, and try to date it just by reading it aloud to the other. We got to be so proficient in that game that we rarely missed by more than ten years.

Gross: Do you feel that a revision in our reading of cultural history is going on? We used to divide the nineteenth century into a Romantic, a Victorian, an Edwardian period; but in the twentieth century we speak of the twenties, thirties, forties, fifties, sixties.

Kunitz: That is the acceleration of the tempo. We experience a faster obsolescence which seems to be built into our society. History itself is turning faster.

Gross: Do you feel that as a threat to the whole enterprise of poetry or to your own practice in particular? Do you believe poets worry about being outmoded?

Kunitz: No, definitely not. The fact remains that if one is honest with self and with work, the fashions, in the end, don't count. One lives through the fashions. And what persists is your own identity. Naturally, there are periods in which the work is admired and periods in which it is unloved. One has to expect that if one lives long enough.

Gross: From about 1660 to the end of the eighteenth century, we had the dominance of a particular prosodic form, the heroic couplet. Then things seem to break up at the time of Wordsworth, and we see the emergence (or reemergence) of a great variety of metrical modes. We can, I believe, define the prosodic norms of the eighteenth and nineteenth centuries, even recognize the changing period styles. Do you believe we can discern a period style in twentieth-century prosody—more exactly, prosodies? Do you believe that nonmetrical verse will emerge as the "period style" for modern prosody, or do you feel that the very concept of "period style" simply does not apply to our age?

Kunitz: Nonmetrical verse has swept the field, so that there is no longer any real adversary from the metricians. The defining element of poetry is no longer whether it is metrical or nonmetrical: the defining element is something else. It is substantive; or it is defined by a certain inflection of the voice rather than in terms of a particular prosodic practice.

Gross: I think of some of the features of our most recent poetry—the use of surrealist images and radical metaphors; the persistent use of the end-stopped line—ultimately derived from Whitman. Do these usages define our current style?

Kunitz: I don't think that there is a defining element, right now; it seems to me that what we have is an open field. All possibilities are open, even including, I think, metrical verse.

Gross: I noticed in a recent issue of the *New Yorker* two new poems by Donald Justice. They are pointedly metrical, in rhymed quatrains.

Kunitz: I think it is perfectly possible these days to write metrically—if you do it well enough.

Gross: You don't feel that there is any necessity in the experience of the age that requires a particular kind of prosody, namely that we have to be free, therefore we must use nonmetrical verse?

Kunitz: I think that's nonsense. You can be free in heroic couplets. In completely unconfined, unrestrained verse, one is a prisoner of infinity: that is the worst kind of bondage because there is no escape from it. In a sense every artist is both a prisoner and a free man. As Goethe said, "Art exists in limits." We cannot deny that. It is better to be a prisoner of a form that you yourself have defined and that you know the limits of.

Gross: I would like to ask about your musical training. In your *A Kind of Order* you tell us: "I was with the Pierian Sodality at Harvard under Walter Piston . . . one day I read John Donne and locked my fiddle-case." You obviously have had considerable musical training.

Kunitz: Yes, many years. Music was my first art, really.

Gross: You don't speak very much about music except in that one passage. I am interested in your giving up one kind of music, the violin, and turning to another, that of John Donne.

Kunitz: I think the reason for my giving up music—which meant performing music—was that I was not satisfied playing somebody else's compositions. That was a sense of limitation that I didn't want; I wanted to write my own music.

Gross: Did you ever do any actual musical composition?

Kunitz: No. I didn't do any composition. I didn't want to play other people's music, that was basically it. In answer, I don't think I would have been a first-rate musician: although I was a good technician.

Gross: To play the violin well, you need a good ear.

Kunitz: My ear was very good, but I never felt that I was really a master of the instrument—even though I did give concerts.

Gross: Do you ever play the violin anymore?

Kunitz: No, I haven't played it for years.

Gross: I'd like to explore the matter of John Donne. On the one hand, Donne is often regarded as a very "unmusical" poet: he was sentenced to hanging by Ben Jonson for violating the metrical rules, and so on. On the other hand, some recent critics have heard in Donne's metrical irregularities a highly complex and idiosyncratic "music."

Kunitz: Yes, I think of him as being a musical poet. He is a musician of the passions. That was what I was seeking when I read him and first turned to his art. Those metrical variations, which he should have been hanged for, were really human inflections: exactly the same sort of thing that Hopkins later formalized in his sprung rhythm. Hopkins, by the way, has been a great influence on my prosody, although it isn't obvious.

Gross: It certainly is not obvious. In your earlier poetry, it seems to me, you do work as Donne worked by setting up an initial stanza which then becomes the pattern for the rest of the poem.

Kunitz: Oh yes, and I learned that from Donne. Donne was very much a master for me in that period.

Gross: I don't, however, hear in your poetry that characteristic grating quality that seems so typical of Donne.

Kunitz: Donne did not work with incantation; and I suppose, from the beginning, the incantatory element was for me the other approach to the whole question of prosody, to what I was seeking in poetry.

Gross: There are two poles, then. We have the conversational, then voice, and we have the incantatory.

Kunitz: That's right. And there's a delicate area where the two may meet, but it's a very difficult one to define.

Gross: I'm interested in another thing you say in *A Kind of Order:* "By and large I prefer the company of painters and sculptors to that of poets." Is that a matter of personalities, or do you feel that the company of painters and sculptors provides a better environment for the practice of your art?

Kunitz: To prove that I prefer the company of painters, I am married to one. I often envy painters and sculptors because there is so much physical release in the plastic arts—an expression, an assertion of the whole body. In the very kinetics, as it were . . . Poetry is supposedly the sedentary art—that's why I pace, I walk, I talk when I write. I am a physical being.

Gross: Have you ever tried composing into a recording machine?

Kunitz: No, I couldn't think of doing that. I have to see it also. I say it and then I put it down. I write it and then after I write it, after I get a block of it, I type it. I like to see it on the page. And that helps me. The visual element is very important to me, as much as the auditory, but in a different way. The visual element helps me understand the architecture, helps me achieve the architecture. Until I see it on the page, I don't quite know the ultimate shape of the poem. The shaping of the poem, the way it looks on the page, is important, too.

Gross: This seems more evident in *The Testing-Tree* than in the *Selected Poems*. We find in *The Testing-Tree* very intricately arranged poems like "The Magic Curtain," or "The Testing-Tree" itself with its use of triads.

Kunitz: I was just looking at the notebooks and worksheets for "The Testing-Tree" and I see that I started it with flush margins. And then it began sprawling: I didn't know where it was going. It could go on forever.

Gross: Do you use the typewriter when you compose?

Kunitz: I compose first by writing it out on the page. At a certain stage, when I feel I am in control of the rhythms, then I can go to the typewriter and proceed. I go to the typewriter after the poem has really taken charge of me; then I can trust the typewriter, but I have to find the poem on the written page.

Gross: Another matter of craft: did you ever have a teacher who set you exercises in the writing of verse, or did you work it all out for yourself when you were a young man?

Kunitz: I never really had any instruction that I felt benefited me at all. At Harvard I did take a course with Robert Hillyer, who was a very conventional poet. He did assign metrical exercises which I resented and resisted because his ear, I felt, was defensive, he wanted absolute regularity. When I wrote a poem with Donneish variations, he would slaughter it!

Gross: Did you study Latin and did you have instruction in classical prosody?

Kunitz: Yes, I studied Latin and the scansion of Latin verse.

Gross: Was this of any use to you?

Kunitz: Let me say that I think it had two influences on me. First, the interest in the roots of language, in the radicals. So that the effort has always been in my poems to *use* words in terms of their root sense as much as in terms of their current meaning. This is something I learned from Milton: to think of a word as belonging to a secret language, as always containing its root meanings. Second, the interest in quantity, in the lengths of the syllables. Quantity is a factor in my concept of prosody. I am very aware of the time sense: a line to me is very much a time unit. So I am often compensating for a swift passage with a slow passage; I also often work with sounds that are in opposition, for example, short syllables that are formed labially or dentally, and with deep syllables that are formed down in the throat. These are important elements in my concept of prosody: I see them as having to do with time and depth and surface. They are part of the tension of the prosody.

Gross: After you work on a poem, after you establish the lines of verse, do you ever go back and consciously adjust accents, lengths of syllables, metrical ictus?

Kunitz: Yes, revision is often exactly that. I will not be satisfied with the way a line moves. It doesn't interest me; it seems to have just a running sort of movement without enough variation. I want to slow it down, then get it started again; I will change the word with a different vowel sound or consonant until I achieve the right movement.

Gross: Ransom speaks somewhere—and he had a curious theory of meter as "a low grade musical material"—of poets who deliberately roughen up lines of smooth metrical verse for particular effects. Do you think that this was an idiosyncratic notion of Ransom's?

Kunitz: No. I think that it is very true, and I do it myself, I know in conversation with Lowell that he does that, too.

Gross: So Lowell follows the tradition of his teacher. In this connection, I think of Ransom's poem "Captain Carpenter." I wonder if the first line originally went: "Captain Decatur rose up in his prime" rather than "Captain Carpenter rose up in his prime." Obviously, you can't say "Captain Car-pen-ter . . . "

Kunitz: That reversed second foot . . . Hopkins said that the reversal of the second foot was the most violent of all the reversals.

Gross: In that celebrated and somewhat notorious line from your "Father and Son," "The night nailed like an orange to my brow," you reverse that sensitive second foot.

Kunitz: But it is after a caesura. It should be read with a heavy pause after "night": "The night||| nailed like | an or | ange to | my brow." It is easier to reverse the foot after a caesura.

Gross: That deliberate consciousness of metrical matters is, I feel, part of your approach to the writing of poetry.

Kunitz: Yes, and I still work very much in revision in those terms. But to go back to what I was saying about the way the sounds are formed: I don't think there has been an adequate study ever made of the location of the sounds and their relation to prosody. One of the deficiencies in so much of the poetry written by young people nowadays is their lack of awareness of these possibilities: all these influences on the process of the poem. They never think of the element of sound, of the location of sounds. Take a line like "Full fathom five thy father lies." The first three words are formed right in the front of the mouth; the next three completely different sounds are formed deep down in the throat. The kinetic force of certain poets is generated by making these jumps from front to back.

Gross: I wonder if any poetry has ever achieved the music of the Shakespearean song.

Kunitz: I wish we were closer to song than we are.

Gross: I often feel that poets ought to have musical training, prosodic training, linguistic training.

Kunitz: And life training.

Gross: Yes, and life training. As we look back at the prosodies of the various modernist movements, does it make sense to speak of the alternation of freedom and restraint? We have had periods in which the nonmetrical or quasi-metrical techniques have dominated followed by periods, notably the thirties and fifties, when we had a return to traditional syllable-stress norms.

Kunitz: Yes, historically that has certainly seemed to be true. We have been, of course, in a long free period. But I do think, as I said earlier, there is now some sense of a return to form. I also think that the whole concept of open form, which was around for a little while, out of Olson largely, the concept that the poem was infinitely open, with no possible closure, was anarchic and a denial of form. The whole concept of form depends on the setting of limits. There has to be a weave and a cross-weave in order to make the cloth. A straight line to infinity is not a poem; there has to be some sense of enclosure in order to complete the poem. There has to be at least an exhaustion of the impulse that began the poem. Aristotle said in his *Poetics* that a painting ten thousand miles long was an aesthetic impossibility.

Gross: You have published a volume of translations from the great Russian poet Anna Akhmatova. Were you partly attracted to her by her formal qualities? I note that in your translations you use a great many slant rhymes—where in the Russian, I suppose, they are perfect rhymes.

Kunitz: Yes, she is a very formal poet. But that isn't basically why I was attracted to her. I was attracted to her largely by her themes, and by the degree of feeling she managed to assert in her poems without breaking the mold. These poems are full of pain and terrible suffering and yet they retain their validity as poems. They don't crack up.

Gross: What is the metrical form of such a poem as her "Cleopatra"? Is the Russian line analogous to the English iambic?

Kunitz: Yes, the equivalent of an iambic line. But because Russian is such a different language, you cannot really adapt its metrics; it's so free in vowel sounds and rhyming possibilities—because of the inflectional endings there are thousands of rhyming possibilities. And you usually have feminine endings. When Brodsky attacked my translation of Akhmatova, he said that I had denied her formal virtues. But it isn't true; actually what I am resorting to is what I call functional stressing. The tetrameter lines are still tetrameter in my concept of functional stressing: a four-stressed line with any number of unstressed syllables. But Brodsky didn't hear that.

Gross: I have done some translating from the German, and in dealing with a highly formal poet like Stefan George you often discover yourself "stuffing" the line with polysyllabic adjectives. A German ten-syllable line, with its wealth of inflected forms, breaks down in English to a line of eight or sometimes seven or six syllables.

Kunitz: One of the main differences, I think, between modern poetry and the poetry of another age is in the linear unit. The pentameter line seemed to be natural to the Elizabethan speech pattern—which was highly rhetorical and inflected speech, full of adjectives and adverbs. What has happened is that we are gradually stripping down the language of its ornaments. In our poetry in particuiar, the movement has been towards a language that relies largely on nouns and verbs without qualifiers. That certainly has been the tendency in my poems; so I am getting down to a functional trimeter line. Three beats seems to be my natural speech pattern. If I were to write in a four-beat or five-beat line, I would have to qualify my nouns in order to fill out the line. But I don't want to do that; I like that stripped quality.

Gross: We have covered a wide sweep of territory in our talk, and I believe you have answered most of the questions I had in mind to ask.

Kunitz: I enjoyed that. This is the first time I have talked about prosody to anybody in a long, long time except to my students.

Gross: You still ask your students to think about prosody?

Kunitz: Even when I wasn't teaching, I was always, in my criticism, talking about what happens to this or that line: why doesn't it sound right, why has the energy leaked out of it? I once made the comment, "I like a poem that rides the beast of an action." That is very important to me, and that has a lot to do with my whole sense of prosody.

An Interview with Stanley Kunitz

University of Virginia Alumni News / 1980

University of Virginia Alumni News (July–August 1980), 9–10. Reprinted with permission.

The poetry festival honored Pulitzer Prize–winning poet Stanley Kunitz who, at age seventy-five, serves as adjunct professor of writing at the Columbia University Graduate School of the Arts, Consultant in Poetry to the Library of Congress, and editor of the Yale Series of Younger Poets. A Phi Beta Kappa graduate of Harvard University, Mr. Kunitz has been awarded both Guggenheim Fellowships and Ford Foundation grants. He is the author of ten volumes, including *Selected Poems 1928–1958*, *The Testing Tree, Poems of Akhmatova* (with Max Hayward), and *Selected Poems 1928–1978*. His poem "The Flight of Apollo" was printed in the *New York Times* on the day of the historic moon landing, and he recently read "The Lincoln Relics" at a White House gathering which included President Jimmy Carter.

The following remarks are taken from an interview in which Mr. Kunitz considered both the political dilemmas and personal joys of contemporary poets. "The Layers" was his concluding poem in a reading given to a crowd of more than three hundred at Minor Hall on March 30.

Q: Many poets seem torn between the struggle to survive of times past when neither social nor economic approbation was offered them and the recognition they can find today in universities. How can they keep the process and motive of their poetry pure?

A: The question has certainly concerned me. One of the differences between poetry today and poetry of another age is that it has become a profession instead of a vocation. In our country this is due partly to the whole democratic process—mass education that has come around within the last generation to teaching the writing of poetry at the academic level. We are turning out thousands of young people who think of themselves as practicing poets, in the same way they might be practicing lawyers or physicians. The result is that it becomes a trade like any other trade, and you try to figure out how you're going to live by it, instead of living for it.

Poets do now have opportunities they didn't have before, though poetry itself is worthless as commodity. It is possible to find teaching jobs and even poets who are not universally recognized manage to read at universities and get some return for it, and some modicum of fame.

Poetry still must be written in the dark. It is a secret and hermetic activity, and it is an abuse of the spirit of poetry for it to fall into the hands of the technicians. So much poetry that is being written and praised now is poetry that has simply learned a technical skill.

Q: Even beautiful images can be made by tricks?
A: Yes. You are taught how to manipulate language, to play verbal games. And since we have almost no critical standards in this country, since we are not a poetry-loving culture, this ersatz product is regarded more highly than anything else. It seems to fit into a social structure.

My feeling is that the poet must in the end return to the sense of himself as a vessel for a great tradition of language that has to do with the unfolding of the meanings of life, not only in relation to the self but in relation to the whole world around one. Poetry has to be passionate; it must have innerness. Of course it must also have verbal skill and a love for language, but without that substance out of the life, it is technique occupying a vacuum.

Q: Can you always tell the difference between someone who has either a great feeling for aesthetics or for his own gut and the occasional rare soul who has both in concert?
A: I value a poetry that has not only the kind of quality that I have spoken of, but has a moral passion. I'm thinking of moral not in the puritanical sense. For example, to find the right word, to speak something true, is a moral obligation on the part of the poet. If he neglects it, if he is too lazy, then he betrays his calling. And that to me is immoral.

One of my other thoughts about poetry is that it's a lonely activity. Poets don't travel in packs. When you set up cliques, coteries, or schools of poetry, you are trying to combine in order to gain some kind of power that in fact is destructive.

Q: Ultimately, does it make a difference whether salaries for poets are written in the economy? It might be hard to say, if you're hungry and have no time to write.

A: In my youth there were no encouragements of that kind for poets, and I know that many gifted young people simply dropped out of sight. It wasn't only that you didn't have any monetary encouragement—you didn't have grants, you didn't have jobs—but in fact poets were turned away from the academies. It was impossible to get a job on a faculty.

The deficiency that hurt me most as a young poet was that I could find no older poet to turn to. There was no communication; in fact none was wanted, between the senators of poetry and young poets.

Q: Who was the first poet who did give you response?
A: It certainly wasn't an older poet. My first friend in poetry was Theodore Roethke, and that was after I'd already written my first book.

One of the reasons I continue to teach and to work with young poets is that I am so mindful of what a grievance it was in my own life that I had no encouragement from the elders. Since I do believe in the perpetuation of a great tradition, I think we older poets have some kind of responsibility to poetry itself, to pass on the little we have learned in a lifetime, and give it to others.

Q: From reading your work it would seem that looking back on the loneliness of writing, you could never regret it. Yet many poets find decisions about security versus the continual risk of that loneliness very difficult. Did you go through balancing, too, and looking back now, what would you say to young poets about it?
A: I went through years of solitude, and sometimes I did say "too much." I lived for a good portion of my life in deep country without any contact with others like me, and it was a dark period in many respects. And yet I was writing. And some of the poets that still seem readable to me came out of that darkness.

I think one needs to sustain oneself as well as one can, perhaps in compensation for the solitude of that vocation. The great resources for me were love and the natural world. Those two, and poetry, are such consolations in themselves and such spiritual gifts, that if one is sustained by them, the life principle will not wither.

Stanley Kunitz on the Labyrinth of Forms and the Turning of Worms

Kathleen Weldon and Rose Slivka / 1981

From *Craft International* 1 (Fall 1981), 27–28.

When Rose Slivka invited me to do a series of interviews for *Craft International* which addresses the theme of tradition, value, and form, I chose people in the New York area who were familiar to me through our mutual involvement with books—poet Stanley Kunitz, with whom we proudly launch our series; papermaker Susan Gosin, and rare book and print dealer Lucien Goldschmidt, both of whom appear in the Spring 1982 issue. I met with Lucien Goldschmidt in his internationally known shop on Madison Avenue, in the dark back office crammed with rare books and prints. The interview with Susan Gosin took place after work hours in her papermaking mill "Dieu Donne," a fifth-floor loft in Soho. Rose and I went together to meet with Stanley Kunitz in his lovely Greenwich Village apartment, filled with books, objects of American folk art, and paintings by his wife Elise Asher and their wide circle of friends in the art world. —K. W.

Kathy Weldon: When I read your work, I had the feeling that something larger had been brought down to the essential parts, rather than expanded. And when I picked up the *Poems 1928–1979*, the first thing that hit *me* was

. . .

SK: Why aren't there ten thousand poems?

KW: And then it brought to mind Yeats, because it was so condensed, and the language has a song to it that underlies the action.
SK: Yeats was important to me in my youth, one of several poets from whom I learned about song and action and the possibilities of language. Yeats is there in that background, Hopkins is there, Keats and Blake are there, and

the metaphysical poets. They are ancestors, in the way grandparents are, invisibly coded into one's genes. The same family stamp, but the mix is different.

RS: You've said that a poem has a life before it is even a sign, a physical presence with its own history. It's something we'd like to know more about. How do you perceive this?

SK: There is a shaping faculty in the mind, but it isn't in control at every moment. The poem you seek lies hidden under layers of consciousness. You must trust intuition and memory to lead you there. I think of the process as, to some degree, archeological, like excavating a temple. But at the same time you're building it, out of your buried life, image by image, stone by stone.

RS: As you recognize the form that is there, you create it. In your act of recognition, do you invent new forms?

SK: I doubt it. My assumption is that the sense of form is inherent in the race, substantially the same from one generation to another. Our artistic inventions, from age to age, are really not much more than modifications of old forms or new applications of them. I tend to think of form as a constant in art, as opposed to techniques and materials, which are variables.

KW: When you use traditional forms, the results are never academic. It always seems the logical way for each poem to turn out.

SK: What fascinates me about the logic of the imagination is how unpredictable it is in practice, how full of surprises Blake's "crooked road," not the straight roads of science and philosophy.

RS: Stanley, what is form?

SK: I wish I had a neat, easy answer.

RS: I'm sure you have considered this question. It's always a question, and you always have to rethink it.

SK: OK, let's bat it around. We are born into a world of forms. We ourselves, in the symmetry of our bodies, in the rhythm of our heartbeats, in the seasons and cycles of our experience, are embodiments of form. Of course, we are flawed creatures, who can only yearn for the ideal, who can only imagine what it is to be whole and harmonious to every part of our flesh and spirit. Pragmatically, the function of form in art is the conservation of energy. A poem or a painting represents an effort to gather together, at least metaphorically, certain random bits of our universe in order to consolidate their power. A badly made thing falls apart. It takes only a few years for most of the energy to leak out of a defective work of art—anything slipshod, pretentious, full of lies. In the absence of form we confront waste and absurdity and recognize in them a sign of our condition. But we must not strive for too mechanical a perfection. The truly creative mind is always ready for the operations of chance. It wants to sweep into the constellation of the artwork as much as it can of the loose, floating matter that it encounters. If form were completely understood, it would be sterile, all preplanned, prefigured. What makes form adventurous and exciting is that we can never chart its course or define its limits. How much accident can the mind incorporate? How much of the unconscious life can it dredge up from the depths? Paul Tillich told us that "the self-affirmation of a being is stronger the more non-being it can take into itself." That to me is an aesthetic principle as well as a spiritual truth.

KW: I wish you'd illuminate the poet's use of the particular in the search for larger meanings.
SK: Coleridge has a magnificent passage in his *Biographia Literaria* in which he anticipates most of what we know today about the imaginative process. The work of the imagination, he says, is primarily in the balance or reconcilement of opposite or discordant qualities: of sameness with difference, of the idea with the image, of the general with concrete. A poem is a sum of contradictions, "a more than usual state of emotion with more than usual order." I like to think that it is the poet's love of particulars, the things of this world, that leads him to universals. The most poignant of all lyric tensions stems from the awareness that we are dying every minute we live. To embrace such knowledge and yet to remain whole—that is the consummation of the endeavor of art. The epithet that Coleridge coined, from the Greek, for the work of the imagination was "esemplastic," shaping-into-one.

KW: In my own experience poetry induces a physical response that seems to differentiate it from prose.
SK: That's because poetry is rooted in the wisdom of the body. It is not an abstract language. It speaks out of the same sensations of being alive. And it is full of sleeping gestures—gestures that stir themselves awake in the mind of the receiver.

KW: Poets give the impression of drawing from an inexhaustible reservoir of memories, often going back to their early years. Is this a determining characteristic?

SK: My feeling on that score is that anyone who forsakes the child he was is already too old for poetry. The poets of any culture inherit a common tradition, by which they are sustained and replenished. What makes them separate and distinctive is the use they make of their own past. I once wrote that memory is each man's poet-in-residence.

KW: How did you recognize at such an early age that you would be a poet?

SK: Curiously enough, it never occurred to me to be anything else.

KW: You read omnivorously when you were young?

SK: Yes, but I also wandered through the woods. In my hometown of Worcester, Massachusetts, I followed the Indian trails. I was fleet of foot, played baseball, and was a real demon on the tennis courts. No sedentary life for me! I still work in my garden on the Cape. That's my vision of bliss.

RS: You enjoy solitude?

SK: Oh, I like plants and grubbing in the earth and—yes, the opportunity for meditation.

RS: Your poetry has a tragic vision. I've always been struck by what I have called your gift for grief.

SK: I suppose the first grand concept I had was that of death, my death. Through the circumstances of my childhood I felt besieged by it, overwhelmed. I couldn't sleep, thinking about dying. And then I realized I had to live with this thought, this fear of annihilation, and make it creative instead of destructive.

RS: How long did that take you?

SK: Long enough. That theme has been with me from the beginning. I'm still struggling with it. One of my observations is that human pride is at the source of much of our anxiety. After all, we are only one link in the great chain of being. Most of us have lost touch with the natural order of things. We live in a narrow world of sympathies. Why is it so terrible to contemplate that the universe will roll on inexorably without any one of us, or even in the absence of all of us, our entire species? Last summer I went on whale searches off Cape Cod. I saw the mighty fin backs leaping out of the water, tremendous, awesome. They seemed to express something beyond our reach, in their nobility of form, their incorruptible beauty and power.

RS: Do you think we are a more imperfect form of expression?

SK: I have it from an unimpeachable source that we ate the apple of consciousness, and we know good and evil. Both glory and curse. We pride ourselves on being lords of the universe, but we pay the price—in guilt and dread.

RS: One of my prides is that I bear some responsibility for a poem—a suite of poems—that you wrote a few years ago.

SK: Indeed you do. It was *Words for the Unknown Makers*, one of the few occasional poems I've ever written. The occasion was an exhibit at the Whitney, that spectacular show called The Flowering of American Folk Art. They gave me *carte blanche* to do anything I wanted with it for magazine publication. Usually my poems simmer for a long time. Sometimes years pass between the conception and the birth. It was intuitive of you to guess how much American folk art meant to me. I must tell you a story that springs out of that storehouse of memory we were just talking about.

Back in the thirties, in the midst of the Depression, I fled the city and moved to a Connecticut farm. It was the period of my first marriage. We were living in an old gambrel house, built about 1740, on top of a hill called Wormwood Hill. I had bought the house together with more than a hundred acres of land for five hundred dollars down. It had no electricity, no heat, no running water and it was in bad repair, but it was a great, beautiful house. I spent most of three years, working with my hands, making it habitable. At that time early American art and furniture were practically being given away. Poor as we were, we managed to fill the house with priceless stuff. We were so far from the city and from all signs of progress that we might as well have been living in another age.

One spring there appeared on the road, climbing up the hill, a man in a patchwork suit, with a battered silk hat on his head. His trousers and swallow-tail coat had been mended so many times, with varicolored swatches, that when he approached us, over the brow of the hill, he looked like a crazy-quilt on stilts. He was an itinerant tinker, dried-out and old, thin as a scarecrow, with a high, cracked voice. He asked for pots and pans to repair, scissors and knives to sharpen. Outside on the lawn, in the shade of the sugar maples, he set up his shop and silently went to work on the articles I handed to him. When he was done, I offered him lunch in the kitchen. He would not sit down to eat, but accepted some food in a bag. "I have been in this house before," he said to me quietly. On our way out, while we were standing in the front hall at the foot of the staircase, he suddenly cried out, "I hear the worms rustling in this house." "What do you mean?" I asked. "I hear the worms, I hear the worms," he repeated. I took it as a bad omen, a fateful prophecy, about my house, my marriage. And so it turned out to be.

Sometime later I learned that my visitor was a legendary figure, known throughout the countryside as the Old Darned Man. He had been a brilliant divinity student at Yale, engaged to a childhood sweetheart, with the wedding set for the day after graduation. But on that very day, while he waited at the church, the news was brought to him that she had run off with his dearest friend. Ever since then he'd been wandering distractedly from village to village in his wedding clothes.

As for the worms, they had the source in local history. Late in the nineteenth century the housewives of the region, dreaming of a fortune to be made, had started a cottage industry in silkworm culture, importing the worms from China. The parlors of every farmhouse were lined with stacks of silkworm trays, in which the worms munched on mulberry leaves, making clicking and rustling noises. That was the sound heard in my hall. It's a story without a happy ending. The worms died, the dream of riches was blighted, I never saw The Old Darned Man again.

Why am I telling you all this? Blame yourself for bringing up the subject of American folk art. Maybe it's a little parable of sorts.

A Dialogue with Stanley Kunitz

Ayappa Paniker / 1982

Journal of Literature and Aesthetics 2 (January–March 1982), 13–24, 77–81. Reprinted with permission.

How does a poet like Stanley Kunitz, the strong gentle voice of American poetry, achieve that self-effacing quality which distinguishes him from several of his contemporaries? That was the main question in my mind, as I tried to seek an appointment with him after my arrival from India. The first time I contacted him from New Haven, he was away in Provincetown, and so we agreed to meet in his apartment in New York, on his return. The sober maturity of his voice as he answered the phone was an assurance of his friendliness as well as the lack of fussiness in his poetry. When we met at last in New York, therefore, we could carry on our dialogue with perfect ease. We talked about his own work, about the work of his contemporaries, especially Robert Lowell, who seemed to have been personally very close to him, and about the current situation in poetry as well as the criticism of poetry.

Paniker: Mr. Kunitz, there are three aspects of your work which I have found quite interesting and a little intriguing too. First your work as a poet, and then your work as a translator, and finally your work as an editor. I have read your interview with the Russian poet Andre Voznesensky, some of whose poems have been translated into my language, Malayalam.
Kunitz: How well do they translate into your language?

Paniker: We have published some, and the response from our readers was very good. I don't know much Russian, but I can just identify the combination of vowels and constants, and the phonetic structure of his poetry reminds one at times of his interest in architecture.
Kunitz: Has Andre been to India?

Paniker: I don't think he has. And when I was in Moscow, I couldn't meet him either.

Kunitz: Well, he, Andre, is an old friend of ours, and so we have an intimate relationship, which helped.

Paniker: Some of his poems I found rather difficult to translate—poems like "Antiworlds" with a pun on words like *Bukashkin.*

Kunitz: Sometimes they get very precious.

Paniker: But the poem "I'm Goya" has been very well done, and it had an immediate response when it was read aloud.

Kunitz: Well, as long as you are dealing with pure sounds, it's easier.

Paniker: But my main concern today is with your work as a poet.

Kunitz: I should think myself that everything else is incidental to that.

Paniker: So we might start by talking a little about that, though you must have talked a good deal about that to other interviewers . . . Although your 1930 volume—your first book came out the year I was born—is called *Intellectual Things*, I find that your poems are not that intellectual; they are, I think, strongly emotional. I was wondering what could have made you give it this rather unpromising title.

Kunitz: Well, you have to remember the year in which these poems were published—1930. There was a great wave of interest in the metaphysical poets, largely influenced by Eliot, and through Eliot by Donne, Marvell, Herbert, and the rest, so that they thought of poetry as a metaphysical process. It was certainly intriguing to a young man. I remember I was in my early twenties—I was writing these poems when I was twenty-two or twenty-three. And at the same time as being drawn to these poets, I was also reading William Blake. And there's a line of William Blake's which struck my fancy and it contained the phrase "an intellectual thing." That seemed very much what I wanted to say—that the emotive life and the rational or intellectual life are really synchronized and dovetailed—and that was the reason. Now, it was taken literally as though I was premising the superiority of the intellect over the heart. That is not true. That is exactly contrary to my intentions.

Paniker: Did you read a lot of Donne in those days? And where was it?

Kunitz: Yes. I went to Harvard. I didn't read them in any classroom. I read them on my own.

Paniker: They were not part of any course at the college.
Kunitz: No, in those days there were no courses in metaphysical poets. Remember that in the twenties when I was at Harvard, the Eliot school was considered to be outlandish and not taken seriously by the academics. When I proposed to write my thesis on the techniques of modernism and I used Eliot and Joyce and others as examples, going back to Hopkins, whom I started with, the head of the English department said this was not admissible, because none of these poets could be taken seriously. But I wrote my thesis anyhow on these authors.

Paniker: That probably was a good beginning. In Donne, apart from this fusion of intellect and emotion, was there anything in his religious attitude of his concept of God that influenced you?
Kunitz: I myself have had no religion and therefore can follow my religious feeling into my poetry that liberates those yearnings towards the divine in a way that may be less possible for one who practices an institutional religion—that is my theory about that. And there are certainly those religious feelings present in Donne, and I saw the connection between religious and sexual feelings did interest me, and that has always been one of my preoccupations.

Paniker: The kind of mystical element one finds in Vaughan and in Blake probably did not attract you so much.
Kunitz: Oh, yes, it did. I think, in the long run, I would say that maybe Herbert and Vaughan attracted me more than Donne, and then largely because of their transcendental feelings which appeared to me of primary importance in the whole concept of the poetic function. The great words for me in terms of the art of poetry are transformation and transcendence. And one of my disappointments with much of the poetry of our age is that it lacks those transcendental yearnings, that it is content with the perception of what is called reality, the quotidian.

Paniker: I have found that in some of your poems, you deal with simple things, very simple themes—small animals and everyday occurrences, but you are able to invest them with a kind of perception that is truly given to you.

Kunitz: Well, I'd like to begin with a particular reality, something observed, a perception out of the natural world, usually—and that is moving from the known towards the unknown, and then to have it go by association and reach out towards mysteries, rather than to be content with the mere grasping of the phenomenal world around you.

Paniker: I think that in that little poem "The Waltzer in the House" the concrete and the known moves towards the unknown and perhaps the unknowable, but the poem does not end there: it leaves reverberations.

Kunitz: I like a poem to end not with the slamming of a door, but with the opening of a window, so that we are moving out into space.

Paniker: And then perhaps we can go farther and farther, depending upon the reader. But do the last lines ever form a kind of closure?

Kunitz: To an extent, I think. More so in my early poems. I think my early poems wanted a much more definite closure than I really desire any more. I think my poems have opened up more than they did in the past. And I don't want them to close the way Yeats had a poem close for him.

Paniker: Yes, with a rhymed couplet or something of that sort. Maybe the influence of the seventeenth-century metaphysicals.

Kunitz: And also because I was working in much tighter prosody than I am now. I have moved away from strict metrical conventions and gone into much more open kind of verse, and so my ear is trying to hear the rhythms of a poem, and I say my poems when I am creating them rather than write them down. I write for the ear more than I do for the eye—well, the two do have to work together.

Paniker: You don't like to intend to slip into the uncertainties of what is called free verse?

Kunitz: Well, I don't know what free verse is. I don't think I could write free verse, because as I said, I was trained in the discipline of a metrical convention, the old tradition of prosody. And so even now when I don't count beats, for example, and certainly don't count syllables, I am seeking for certain rhythms, certain cadences, certain repetitions and variations that I learned during the period when I was working in the stricter metrical convention.

Paniker: What does "opening out" mean in metrical terms? Is it that you leave the older stricter forms, but stop short of what is called free verse? In what sense do your poems open out metrically?

Kunitz: I suppose the basis of my concept of prosody in my more recent work has been what I call functional stressing, which is in a way going back to old English poetry. Heavy stressing and a certain pattern of stressing: very heavy stressing and permitting any number of unstressed syllables. The advantage there is that there is the establishment of a rhythmic base, but at the same time all sorts of opportunities present themselves or complex rhythmic variations.

Paniker: But in Old English they used alliteration as a structuring device, too.

Kunitz: I use a lot of assonance and consonance—agreement of vowels and consonants. I don't rhyme any more.

Paniker: That could perhaps be illustrated with the reading of a few lines from one of your poems.

Kunitz: (Picking up a copy of the November 1981 issue of the *Atlantic Monthly*) This is from my most recently published poem called "The Wellfleet Whale" which is based on an encounter that I had with a drift whale, up in Cape Cod, where I spend a good part of my time.

Paniker: So it is based on actual personal experience?

Kunitz: Most of my poetry is based on actual experience. This happened fifteen years ago, in 1966. Well, I kept it submerged and every once in a while brought it up to the surface, and examined it again, and tried it through the years. But I wasn't able to, until this year.

Paniker: Probably the whale has a longer period of hibernation than any other animals.

Kunitz: Well, I believe in that kind of long marinating of the concept of a poem. I think that those images that stay deep in your unconscious life accrue strength and gather to themselves other images, other associations, and when you finally dredge them up, they are rich like a big mass of seaweed, a great tangle out of your whole buried life.

Paniker: That itself is a submarine image. Perhaps you believe that a poem transforms a piece of reality itself into something of a mythical nature, into a myth, but not a given myth.

Kunitz: A created myth. Well, I think that every poet has a set of key im-ages, these go back to childhood, to the most formative seminal experiences of life, sometimes traumatic experiences, but not necessarily so. Now, these are the images that really constitute the constellations of the self, and when one is writing at one's deepest level, one inevitably goes back to one or more of these key images, establishing a contact with your central self. Now, these key images also in themselves attached to your persona, reach out towards the great archetypes, which are common to all living creatures. I have said more than once that part of the task of a poet is to convert his life into a legend; and that legend reaches out to the whole mythology of creation it-self, and of all the great cultures, where you find all the central archetypal images, linked with the same kind of, let us say, the creation myth: you can find connections out of all cultures and with any other cultures.

Paniker: That brings up another idea: the writing of a poem as a kind of ritual.
Kunitz: Yes, very much. For me it is largely a kind of incantation in the say-ing of it so that there is almost a self-hypnosis induced, where the rhythms finally take on body almost, and they become powerful. You can ride on them like on a horse.

Paniker: In Indian poetics there is a view that a poem is a Mantra, that is something chanted, a magical formula-like thing, which is capable of creat-ing meaning by its incantatory effect.
Kunitz: I believe that.

Paniker: A poem like your "The Testing-Tree" is a good example, perhaps.
Kunitz: Oh yes, very much. Around me, working in my whole childhood, and then bringing it up into contemporary history, really. Well, let's go back to "The Wellfleet Whale." I'll read a few lines, the first episode, which is like a prologue, in which I address the whale. This is before the narrative element enters there.

> You have your language too,
>   an eerie medley of clicks
>   and hoots and trills,
> location-notes and love calls,
>   whistles and grunts, Occasionally,
>   it's like furniture being smashed,

or the creaking of a mossy door,
    sounds that all melt into a liquid
        song with the endless variations,
as if to compensate
    for the vast loneliness of the sea,
        sometimes a disembodied voice
breaks in, as if from distant reefs,
    and it's as much as one can bear
        to listen to its long mournful cry,
a sorrow without name, both more
    and less than human, it drags
        across the ear like a record
running down.

Paniker: I think it is a full demonstration of your poetics, both in content and in form.
Kunitz: I agree it is very much a characteristic poem.

Paniker: You use words like "clicks" and "hoots" and "trills" and "whistles" and "grunts."
Kunitz: Every word has a different vibration.

Paniker: Yes, and your earlier statement that sounds mean more than the sight itself, and that a poem is meant for the ear, is very well illustrated by this poem. And your reading seems to emphasize that. The run-on lines particularly seem to carry the wave of emotion . . . I was wondering if the sea plays any important role in your poetry.
Kunitz: Yes, rivers and oceans.

Paniker: Are there any special reasons for that? Some childhood association?
Kunitz: Well, I have in one of my poems, speaking in the third person:

He is an inlander
Who loves the margins of the sea

I was born inland, but I always wanted the open water.

Paniker: I find that you were a lecturer at Columbia University in the School of Arts, and a professor of qriting: does your work as a poet influence your work as a teacher, and vice versa?

Kunitz: I teach to young poets. And what I conduct is a poetry workshop, so that I am dealing with the very stuff of poetry in my class. And I find it a very satisfying occupation, for, in the first place, it keeps me in contact with the gifted young. And in talking with them, in discussing their poems with them, I clarify my own thinking about "this difficult art." Then, it is also replenishing. I give a lot to my students, but they give back a lot to me. I think of them as being closer to me than my own generation. The young are to me a living presence.

Paniker: But do you ever flinch from the feeling that you are influencing their thinking or imposing your poetics on them?

Kunitz: No, that I do not try to do. I tell them what my feeling is about poetry. I share with them my own aesthetics, and naturally I communicate to them my true praise or appraisal—what I feel about the work they produce. But I do not try to impose a style that is imitative of my own. In fact, I consider that to be a sin—for a teacher of the young to do that. What I try to do is to discover what they are capable of, and then let that emerge as wholly and clearly as it can.

Paniker: Does it mean that you have had some young writers who had a different "theory" from your own?

Kunitz: Yes. There must be about forty or fifty young poets in this country today, well-known published young poets, who are writing—each one is different.

Paniker: Do you remember the names of some of them—your better students?

Kunitz: Yes, I could name several of them. The students I have worked with, the recent ones are: Louise Glück—she is a fine writer; Gregory Orr is another of my students. Others there are, not always in the classroom. Robert Hass, Michael Ryan, and Carolyn Forche: they are all there. Let me add another point; when I was a young man, I had nobody to help me. There were no older poets who were in the least interested in working with young poets. And there were no poets in the university system. So there was no opportunity for any sort of contact. You spent years trying to work your way through your errors and misdirections. And I vowed that if I were in a position to be of any help to a younger generation, I would do my best to fulfill that responsibility. Because I believe the tradition of poetry is great and good, and that we are all servants of that tradition, poetry speaks through us; we are only the vessels of a great spirit.

Paniker: Perhaps the classroom situation helps to maintain that oral tradition too.
Kunitz: Yes, of course; we are always reading the poems and talking about them.

Paniker: When you turn to your later style as in *Passport to the War*, it was not merely a widening of interest, or a relaxation of form, but some changes in the themes also. You probably outgrew the metaphysical tradition. Or, do you think you are still close to those intellectual preoccupations?
Kunitz: In terms of the transcendental, yes; I have sort of veered from that, but I think my strategy for writing that has changed in that what I seem to find most congenial to me now is to work with some narrative element. By narrative I mean a dramatic element. I want to be a story-teller, the way the old poets in the beginning were story-tellers. After all, the origins of poetry belong there. And that is out of the oral tradition and there is a momentum established with a narrative which I find pushes the poem along, moving towards a climax. It gives me a little more space to work in and to fulfill my concept of the nature of form itself. I have been very much influenced, for example, by Greek tragedy, and I think if anyone really studied along these lines, he would have to start out being episodic; they will see that I am using Greek or classical materials, I think of the agon, the struggle, I think of the peripeteia or reversal or discovery, revelation and so forth; which is at the heart of the Greek concept. Not that I do it in the actual writing consciously, but since I am so stupid in that whole tradition, it in a way starts shaping the poem out of the unconscious rather than out of conscious direction.

Paniker: Do you still read the Greek and Latin works you studied at school?
Kunitz: My Greek is not that good. My Latin is better.

Paniker: Apart from the work of Voznesensky, you have also translated the poems of Anna Akhmatova, who is, I think, much more lyrical than perhaps Voznesensky.
Kunitz: Yes, Akhmatova's work is much closer to me than Voznesensky's.

Paniker: I have read a few of your translations including "I am Goya," "The

Skull Ballad," "Lament for Two Unborn Poems," and "Story under Full Sall." You have done other translations?

Kunitz: Yes, I have done some Mandelstam, Yevtushenko . . .

Paniker: Most of them are Russians?

Kunitz: I have also done translations from the classics. Then Baudelaire, Ungaretti; and I have done some Spanish translations, too.

Paniker: How will you characterize your approach to translation of poetry? Some say that poetry is what is lost in translation; nevertheless, I guess, we have to go on doing translation.

Kunitz: We all believe that, and yet we continue to translate because though something is lost, much is gained. And even if you agree that translation is only a sum of approximations, nevertheless that is the way another people is brought into touch with your own. It is the binding element of civilization, and it is tremendously important. I think we are living in a great age of translation. There are more translations than ever before. The world is becoming smaller and closer thereby. It is a counterforce against the whole militaristic passions of time. For every bomb, translate a poem!

Paniker: Quite apart from the value and necessity of translations, there is this agonizing problem of the technique and the feeling of inadequacy when we do not translate successfully. What are some of the devices that may prove helpful to the translator of poetry?

Kunitz: There are two different pressures really on the poet who is translating: one of them is to be as faithful as possible to the original text, and the other is to make it new, to make a new poem in the other language; and the two are violently in opposition of each other, so that the great principle is one of reconciliation between these two demands. Coleridge said this was the characteristic principle of the imagination, the reconciliation of opposites and contradictions. The very act of translation is an illustration of that principle, and so you know that you cannot be completely faithful to the original text, because no language can translate it literally. It has a different genius, a different word order, different metrics based on completely different prosodic principles. So how can you possibly say there are literal translations, which some academics think as possible? It is impossible. Since you know that you are a little freer to say, "Well, I'll try not to betray them, but I'll employ them to create a new poem that will keep the spirit of the original alive, and recreate it in another poem which is in that new language."

Paniker: Perhaps a greater difference than that between the languages is the one between personalities of the two poets.

Kunitz: Yes, but that, of course, is a value to the translator, because through entering the body of another person's imagination, you enlarge your own, you stretch its possibilities. You emerge out of that translation somehow strengthened and extended, because you are really touched in yourself, doing what you didn't think you could, or wanted to do.

Paniker: You are a poet in English, and now you translate another poet into English. There should be some difference between your own poems and these translations. Won't it become a problem sometimes when the translations look like your own poems?

Kunitz: That was the problem, I think, with Lowell's imitations. It was that in the end they were more Lowell than they were the original. And I think that is really in a way using the original text for your own ego, or your own advantage, so that actually you have to be more dedicated and more concentrated on the original text than Lowell was in those imitations. On the other hand you want to be as free as you possibly can be, and not become a prisoner of a given text, or a given meaning, so that you are always in a state of high tension during a work of translation.

Paniker: Since you have brought in the name of Lowell and I myself have done some work on him, and I know that you had some very generous things to say about him . . .

Kunitz: I think that Lowell will always be one of the finest poets in English. I think he will have his place. And as is usual, the period of a poet's death is a time for reevaluation, and usually it is a time of rejection, because a new generation wants to emancipate itself from its immediate predecessors. In the same way I wanted to write not like Eliot; I wanted to be counter to Eliot rather than merely a servant of his art so that there is a natural diminishing of reputation after a poet's death. In Lowell's case because he was a prolific poet and the work is uneven, there has to be a weeding out. But there will remain a substantial body of work that will stand. I have absolutely no doubt about it. There is a live intelligence in most poems, a tormented spirit, and a sense of history that makes his work rich in quality.

Paniker: If one thinks of the three periods in his career, the pre-Confessional, that is pre-*Life Studies* or the "Quaker Graveyard" period; then the Confessional or the *Life Studies* period; and finally the post-Confessional period, that of the *Notebooks* and *Day by Day*; is there any justification for thinking that there was a decline of poetic powers in the third period? Or, is there a new Lowell in the last works which seem to reveal an epic dimension, without perhaps the dramatic intensity of the second period or the lyrical fervor of the first?

Kunitz: I would suppose that the middle period is the greatest. It is purer in a way, less cluttered and less compulsively readable than the last period.

Paniker: You mean it is more pure Lowell than the other?

Kunitz: He was so deeply immersed in the destructive element of life itself then that it speaks with great clarity. Incidentally, have you ever come across the album of Lowell's readings that I edited for the Library of Congress? There is an essay of mine on the jacket; I wrote a long essay really, uncovering this subject.

Paniker: When was it done?

Kunitz: That was done right after his death, and you hear Lowell's voice, and I picked the reading where he talked about his poems and clarified many of these points; and then I wrote this essay, which is on the jacket of the recording.

Paniker: Professor Kunitz, you have always been very generous in your estimate of contemporaries, particularly younger writers. For instance, of Roethke you said: "The poet of my generation who meant most to me in his person and in his art was Theodore Roethke." That was in 1963.

Kunitz: He was the first poet of my generation I met, who became a friend; and in our early years we really nurtured each other, because we had no audience except each other. So that is also important.

Paniker: Do you think Roethke finally got the audience and the reputation he deserved after his death?

Kunitz: Yes, after his death, mainly. But he had some fame before he died—not as much. He means a great deal to young poets today. Everywhere I go, inevitably when there is a question period after my reading, somebody in the audience asks about Roethke, and many poets have learned from him, imitated him.

Paniker: Does that include the New York School of poets, too?

Kunitz: Well, some of them. There are some very good poets very profoundly influenced by him. There is an interesting book on Roethke recently published by the University of Massachusetts: it is by Jay Parini, and there is a chapter there about our relationship, with quotations from letters.

Paniker: Like you, he also did not found any school . . . You were sort of individualists.
Kunitz: We were never a school. I don't believe that poets run in packs. I believe in the individuals.

Paniker: All the same, this was also a period of little movements, like the Black Mountain Poets.
Kunitz: But Roethke and I always stood apart from any of these groups. We were always working alone.

Paniker: Who would you consider to be the most promising of the writers under forty?
Kunitz: That is a hard question. I named some of them when I mentioned the ones I have directly known. Certainly that group is as good a group as one could find.

Paniker: They also do not form a group, I suppose.
Kunitz: No, they are very individual, very individual.

Paniker: It is important for a creative artist to be himself, and not to surrender his personal vision to any kind of manifesto is that what you mean?
Kunitz: There is no manifesto. A couple of years ago at the University of Virginia, all these young poets who had worked with me held a festival in my honor; it was a three-day festival, and it was a beautiful thing from beginning to end. What impressed everybody who attended the festival was how each poet was different, sang with a different voice, and they were all there in a way as friends and more or less attached to me in one way or another. The fact remains they were different poets and could not be lumped as a school at all.

Paniker: Is that somehow connected with your earlier view that a poet is a seer or a prophet rather than a functionary like a journalist or journeyman?
Kunitz: The great threat, I think, in the world of poetry today is that we are breeding a whole generation of technicians. And though technique is important, it is not the end of poetry; and the technician without a soul and

without a sense of vocation, prophetic destiny can be the death of poetry be-cause you will be like any other trade, every other craft, if you only represent a skill, and that is not enough.

Paniker: Living in New York and in the age of science and technology, do you find a place for poets in the new set-up, where he has to compete with the computer, and not only make a living, but make his voice heard? How can the Word be uttered and heard in this cacophony which is New York?
Kunitz: Yes. Well, it can be done. It can be done out of one's need and out of one's absolute, unwavering devotion to the old great principle of poetry, which is beyond the moment, beyond history, beyond time, beyond nation, beyond church.

Paniker: A unique aspect of your career, Professor Kunitz, which distin-guishes you from most other writers I have met here, is that either as editor or as Consultant in Poetry in the Library of Congress—and by editor I mean not only editing books like *Living Authors*, informative books, but also the Yale Series of Younger Poets—you have displayed a kind of open-minded-ness, absolutely free from all trace of envy for senior writers or contem-poraries or younger writers, an evenness of vision, a certain large-hearted comprehensiveness. An ordinary poet would have considered it a waste of time to edit books like *Twentieth Century Authors* or *Living Authors*; he would rather leave it to pure academics, because they are good at that.
Kunitz: Of course, when I started that whole series of literary biographies and reference works, there was no such work in existence, and I had, I sup-pose, two motivations: one, I had to earn a living—and this was one way of earning a living—at the same time I was performing a service to the writers of your age. So I could do it without a guilty conscience, because it was not a dishonorable thing to do, even though I did it for money and had to do it. During the period I was actively editing those reference works, I had a con-nection with the H. W. Wilson Company, which is largely a publisher of ref-erence works and that was the first job I got when I came to New York, but then I left. I was really attached to the office of that company as an employee for only about two years or so. But I founded the *Wilson Library Bulletin*, it is called—and so I started the series and then detached myself and moved to the country. When I lived in the country and did my editorial work by mail, because I wanted to be free, I really didn't feel I could live at that time in the city—at a time when I needed to be solitary and to work out my own destiny, when I knew I could never do it in the middle of New York—that would be

impossible. So for over twenty-five years, I lived in the country and did my work there apart from literary circles. That was no problem.

Paniker: And yet, you appear to be quite free from the kind regionalism that we find in some of the writers living in the country. You have opened out to international perspectives; and it is interesting for a person like me coming from India.

Kunitz: But I have always had very strong political convictions—of the left—and I have been opposed to most of the behavior of our own government and its influence on the other peoples when it engages in military imperialism of any sort. And the poet has a role to play as an adversary of the state, and part of his function is never to become a creature of the ruling institutions; always he has to have a free voice and use it.

Paniker: But I suppose the question is: how does he do it? There are difficult times when the media are everywhere around us . . .

Kunitz: The answer is that he cannot do it by becoming a polemicist. Poetry isn't a vessel for argument about political issues. But in the pursuit of the true and the noble and the good, you stand in a way as a model of hope, a counter-possibility, a contrary culture, really. You keep that alive. You must not let it die. If you surrender and become a tool of the ruling powers, you kill your art, and in the end you destroy yourself.

Paniker: But at the same time, if you merely write a few poems, what effect is it going to have on the community as a whole?

Kunitz: Well, you cannot write for immediate success. You cannot create a storm overnight. You could only build slowly this monument which you really hope will abide, which will stay, and which will speak for you, and which will be heard by some in every generation. That is the long view. But cheap effects and cheap sensationalism—tirades and rant—aren't going to do good either for poetry or for the cause. Others are better equipped to do that than the poets.

Paniker: It's perhaps like the Statue of Liberty, which only stands there. But it has only to stand there, silently beckoning man to what it stands for. The function of the statue is to stand there where it is placed, but always a beacon. Well, I must thank you for the insights you provided during our conversation. It has been a rewarding experience for me.

Kunitz: When you have passionate convictions, you can only speak of them passionately. But if you don't have them, what can you say? Again, I think there is a tendency to forget the bond between the poetry and the character of the poet. The two are absolutely inseparable.

So I left him with that integrating vision. That was perhaps the secret of his self-effacement: the perfect fusion of the poet and his work. Not to talk like a disembodied voice: we see the prophet not in his gesticulations, but in the texture of the prophecy. In the end personal and the impersonal are one.

Interview: Stanley Kunitz

Madeleine Beckman / 1982

From *Minetta Review* (New York University Literary Magazine) [1982]: 13–18. Reprinted by permission of Madeleine Beckman.

Stanley Kunitz, a Pulitzer Prize–winning poet, is a tall, thin, white-haired gentleman. This summer he will turn seventy-seven. The following interview was conducted in his Greenwich Village apartment, on a sunny Saturday afternoon, surrounded by his paintings, antiques, and plants.

MB: You were Poetry Consultant for two years. What does the Poetry Consultant to the Library of Congress do?

SK: The consultant's duties are not clearly defined. He's a presence in the library, he or she as the case may be. Duties are pretty much what the consultant decides on his own. There's a series of readings at the Library that the consultant arranges. There's also an archive of poetry recordings, the most comprehensive in existence, to which he is empowered to make additions. He invites poets for readings and recordings. He also has a good deal of contact with poets all over the country who want information about grants, publishing, copyright, that sort of thing. He has an office there, with a permanent staff. In the capital he is the national representative of the world of literature. There he is, on tap, whenever anything goes on in Washington that requires an official poet (*laugh*). It's a busy place. The consultant finds out, after wondering how on earth to fill the hours, that he has almost no time for his own work. The chores pile up. Visiting writers, especially from abroad, are immediately shuttled to the Library to be received by the consultant. A sort of papal blessing.

MB: When was the last year you held that post?

SK: I think 1976.

MB: Did they elect you for a third time?

SK: Two years are generally considered enough. One year is the term of the original appointment. If you are asked to stay on, you haven't obviously disgraced yourself.

MB: Have there been other posts similar to Poetry Consultant which you have been elected to?

SK: That post is unique. But I'm also one of the twelve chancellors of the Academy of American Poets and one of the fifty members of the Academy of Arts and Letters, which is modeled on the Académie française. I succeeded to the chair of John Crowe Ransom on his death. These are honors, to be sure, but nobody in this country pays attention to them. Rightly so, I suppose.

MB: Do you feel your academic involvements have contributed to your poetry?

SK: Actually, I have less academic involvement than most American poets. I didn't become a teacher of poetry until twenty years after I left Harvard and weathered the Depression. I did newspaper and editorial work, freelanced, and lived on farms in Connecticut and Pennsylvania. When I fell into teaching, it was not with any desire to become a permanent member of the academic community. To this day I have never accepted tenure.

MB: Why?

SK: Poetry requires some sense of discontentment, insecurity, danger. It's been said that poetry is the language of crisis. I think of it as an adversary enterprise with respect to the mainstream of our culture. A poet's image of himself is of first importance. If one thinks of oneself as essentially a professor of English, producing verses on the side, the work is bound to suffer. We seem to be breeding a generation of poets who have developed a specialized linguistic skill, but not much else. I look for poets who are connected with the long line of visionaries and prophets, who are more than verbal technicians.

MB: When did your image of the poet materialize?

SK: It was an image I had from the beginning. Nobody taught it to me. It came out of my love for poetry, my early reading. I still can't think of a greater vocation, a richer life.

MB: Do you think that technique can interfere with content or freedom?
SK: The more command you have of your medium, the more liberated you are in your expressive possibilities. But you must not consider technique as an end in itself, separated from content.

MB: What do you think about the poetry being written today?
SK: Any age, in the entire history of mankind, that produced a half-dozen poets who had something important to say, is exceptional. Our own age excels in the quantity of poetic accomplishment, not in the emergence of isolated genius.

MB: Why do you think that's so?
SK: Perhaps it's the inevitable outcome of a democratic and permissive society. Emerson looked around him and noted that persons descend to meet. No other country that I know of cultivates "creative writing" to the extent that we do as an academic subject. Young poets today if they have a modicum of talent can hardly escape being showered with fellowships and grants and prizes. It's beautiful!—but it has its consequences.

MB: Was it a turning point when Professor Gay encouraged you to write poetry at Harvard?
SK: I doubt that it changed my life, but of course I feel grateful. There were also teachers in high school to whom I feel permanently indebted. I wasn't born into a literary environment, and I had no personal help from established writers.

MB: Before that time had you thought of becoming a poet?
SK: I knew that I was going to be a writer, even in grade school. I was lucky to come into literature on the great wave of the twenties, a marvelous period for both fiction and poetry. Joyce and Lawrence were my first heroes of the novelistic imagination, followed a few years later by Kafka. As for poets, I discovered Hopkins in the stacks of Widener Library, and that was a great thrill to me. There too I came across the seventeenth-century metaphysical poets and Yeats, my first contemporary master, and Eliot, from whom I learned a good deal, but whose doctrines and politics I resisted.

MB: Your childhood figures largely in your poetry. Are you still writing poems drawn from your experience in Worcester, Massachusetts?
SK: Right now I'm working on a poem that goes back to that period, even

earlier than others. It's an inexhaustible source. I don't doubt that one's psychic energy is rooted in the traumas of childhood.

MB: Did you become a poet because of your childhood?

SK: If I had a different childhood, I would be writing other poems, or none at all. The lost father, the loneliness, the Indian-haunted woods, the stony New England landscape—these are the sources from which I spring in every act of the imagination. Everything conspired to make me introspective—not that I sat and moped all the time. In fact, I rather prided myself on my athletic ability. I always played to win. Poetry was the other game in which I wanted to excel.

MB: Did you ever feel that there was a conflict between your introspective and your outward self?

SK: I love the fullness of life in all its phases. I can truthfully say that I've never known what it is to be bored. There's always so much to do, so much to think about, how can one ever be bored? I was such a shy child, painfully shy. One of the first tasks I set for myself was to grow outward as well as inward. When I started playing tennis by banging a ball against a barn door, I knew I wouldn't be happy until I won the city championship—which I did. That didn't stop me from writing or thinking about poetry, but it did give me some pride of self, a tangible evidence of accomplishment.

MB: When was that?

SK: Jr. Champion of Worcester circa 1920.

MB: What sorts of activity do you enjoy now other than poetry and gardening?

SK: I had to give up tennis a couple of years ago because of an arthritic condition. Gardening is still a passion, to which I devote my summers on the Cape. I'm always happy when I work with my hands. Given a little different push, I suppose I could have become an artist. Painters are my favorite people. Indeed, I eventually married into art. Whenever I have the chance, I make something. I'm always making something.

MB: What sort of things do you make?

SK: Sculpture, wire mobiles, boxes, assemblages, collages—that sort of thing—for diversion only. Woodworking is another specialty. Over the years I've renovated and refinished several old houses.

MB: That you've lived in?

SK: Yes, four or five of them, beginning in 1930 in Connecticut. Old farmhouses mostly. But even here, in the city apartment, I did the floors, scraping and staining them, and built shelves in my library. Whenever I grow impatient with the sedentary life, I take a piece of wood and do something with it. I love to glue things; repair cracked china, lighting fixtures, plumbing, anything.

MB: Do you write more poetry in the country or the city?

SK: My main productive season is the fall. I've ordered my life so that I spend the fall alone at the Cape. That's where I've written most of my recent poems.

MB: Where was "The Testing-Tree" written?

> On my way home from school
>   up tribal Providence Hill
>   past the Academy ballpark
> where I could never hope to play
>   I scuffed in the drainage ditch
>   among the sudden seethe of leaves
> hunting for perfect stones
>   rolled out of glacial time
>   into my pitcher's hand.

SK: It was written over a period. Provincetown, New York, and the final passage in New Haven. At that time I was editing the Yale Series of Younger Poets and staying with an old friend from my Bennington days. I had a reading scheduled that evening. As we were leaving the house, we heard on TV that Martin Luther King, whom I had worked with in the civil liberties movement, had been assassinated. I sat down and wrote the ending of my poem, the lines that start, "In a murderous time/ the heart breaks and breaks/ and lives by breaking."

MB: Do you feel that you have any poems that are as childlike in their rhythm and content as that poem?

SK: Childlike? The poem draws on my childhood, but its awarenesses are not those of a child. An innocence of eye and heart, combined with maturity of understanding—that's what one strives for in one's writing—to be open and vulnerable and yet not to be deceived. I like a poem that works on several different levels, alternating states of awareness, including that of the child one was and hopes to be.

MB: You have said that a poem is a combination of experience and passion. What decides for you what experience and what passion are going to be turned into a poem, have to be a poem?

SK: I wish I knew . . . .there's no way of telling. I suspect that if one stayed with anything long enough, the most trivial episode, the most insignificant, one would ultimately arrive at an overwhelming conclusion. No thought or feeling or image is creatively important in itself, but only in its connections with the nerve-work of a life. The tracking of those connections is the deep labor of the imagination. So many poems I read seem to be woven out of a single thread when what I am looking for is the crossweave. I want a certain density of texture, a grid of particulars and correspondence, a layering.

MB: Does your poetry reflect the environment where you've written, for instance, the City or the Cape?

SK: I'm not an urban poet. Even when I'm here I'm likely to be working with events that are linked with the natural world one way or another.

MB: What sorts of events?

SK: Poems start in different ways. Some of my poems begin with nothing more than a rhythm I hear in my head that I try to give flesh to. Or a phrase. Or most often something that happened to me, usually years ago, something that keeps returning, rejecting its isolation, yearning to link itself with other emotions or perceptions, to make an image-cluster.

MB: How long have you been working on the current poem taken from your childhood?

SK: Oh, I've been thinking about it for maybe thirty years! I knew it would eventually work out—it kept popping up in my notebooks. But not until this week did I suddenly find an opening into it and a right connection.

MB: Was Aba Stolzenberg's poem "Bolsheviks" easier for you to translate than the work of Anna Akhmatova?

The motorcycles spring out of nowhere.

A blast from the roaring White Guards!
Of Trotsky's soldiers nothing remains here
But some sad little mounds near the woods.

SK: The voice seemed curiously my own. Stolzenberg was a poet I had never heard of, an obscure Polish immigrant who died young. His poem was given to me by Irving Howe, who was editing an anthology of Yiddish poetry. I don't read Yiddish and so had to rely on Irving's English paraphrase. It a dramatic lyric, a genre that I favor. I like the hard details, the physicality of the poem and the velocity of its movement.

MB: The poem "After the Last Dynasty" has a voice that suggests a turn in your writing; is that so?

Reading in Li Po
How "the peach blossom follows the water"
I keep thinking of you
Because you were so much like
Chairman Mao,
Naturally with the sex transplanted
And the figure slighter.

SK: I'd been reading a lot of Chinese poetry, admiring its intimacy, its modesty, its historical plangency. I thought it was just the right voice for a nostalgic love-song. By and large my work doesn't resemble Chinese poetry at all. I'm a Westerner, but there are moments when I feel Chinese, plus I like Chinese food.

MB: What are the most important themes in your work?
SK: Yeats believed that sex and death were the only themes worth the attention of a serious mind. I tend to agree, except I would add nature to the list. In fact, nature may be the one universal theme, since it includes both sex and death.

MB: At some point did you see patterns in your work and go with them, or did you allow yourself new themes as they arose?
SK: One would always like to expand the boundaries of one's work. The psyche is a trap from which it's hard to escape. One way is to change your

life but that requires heroic determination. An alternative is the act of translation. By deliberately entering another person's imagination you liberate yourself from your self-made prison-house. Everything new that happens in your life changes you.

MB: You have said, "Let life happen to you." Have you followed your own precept?

SK: So much has happened to me. But it's never enough. You have to be prepared for surprises—even at my age. That's the way destiny works. A favorite motto of mine is one I borrowed from Louis Pasteur: "Chance favors the ready mind."

MB: How do you see yourself today?

SK: I look and sometimes feel older, I know more, and my inner life is very much the same. The will to live and do is just as fierce as ever.

MB: You've said, "Mobility!—and damn the cost!" What does this mean to you?

SK: It means not becoming a stuffy and cantankerous old codger. It means keeping the mind open and curious and companionable, especially in relation to the young. On the physical level it means getting around, traveling. In that sense I'm at the peak of my mobility. Recently I've been in England, Israel, Egypt; before then I visited Russia, Yugoslavia, Austria, Italy, Africa. Not just as a tourist, but to read my poems, to lecture, to learn about other people, other cultures. I try not to stagnate.

MB: What are you working on now?

SK: I'm writing new poems, thinking about a new book, teaching some young poets, and wondering what I can do to help avert nuclear catastrophe.

An Interview with Stanley Kunitz

Peter Stitt / 1990

Gettysburg Review 5 (1992), 193–209. Reprinted with permission.

Stanley Kunitz, who will turn eighty-seven on July 29, 1992, is the reigning dean of American poets. Not only is he still writing, but he is writing as well today as he ever has, as is evident from poems he has published recently.

With his wife Elise Asher, Stanley Kunitz spends his winters in New York City and his summers in Provincetown; his flower garden is both one of his great passions and one of the primary attractions of Cape Cod. He visited Gettysburg College on the twelfth and thirteenth of March 1990, to read his poems and to visit classes in creative writing and contemporary American poetry. The interview was conducted in his apartment in New York on the third of May 1990.

Interviewer: What sort of childhood did you have?
Kunitz: As I look back on it, my main impression is of how lonely I was. Aside from school, where of course I did have a degree of companionship, it was a childhood without much company outside the household itself, largely because, for so much of that time, we were living far out at the edge of the city without any neighbors. My main refuge was the woods that lay behind the house, where I wandered every day. That is where I invented the game I write about in "The Testing-Tree." I would throw three rocks at the tree, and the results would determine my fate. In retrospect I realize that those three throws of the stone against the patriarchal oak reveal much of the meaning of my life, at that point and in the future. If I hit the target with only one stone, somebody would love me. If I hit it twice, I should be a poet. And if I hit it three times, I should never die. That was the game, and I think it expresses my deepest yearnings.

Interviewer: How old were you at that time?
Kunitz: I must have been in my early teens. Thirteen or fourteen.

Interviewer: It is interesting that you should have wished to be a poet at that age. When were you first conscious that this was your desire?

Kunitz: It is hard for me to define exactly. I was writing from the very beginning, from the moment I went to school. Writing was what gave me the most gratification. I was also reading omnivorously. Every week I would walk to the public library, about three and a half miles from where we lived, and I would pick out this great bundle of books. The librarian would say, "Now, Stanley, you are permitted to take only five books, no more. That's the limit." So I would wrestle with the problem of which five books out of this big bundle I should take. The regulation was that you could do this only once a week; I do not know why there was such a limitation. But I would always be back a day or two later, wanting five more books. So eventually she consented to bend the rules and let me have those extra books. Then I would trudge all the way home and devour them. My taste was indiscriminate. I did not know what I was reading! I just grabbed anything that caught my eye.

Interviewer: I take it this was going on even before you were twelve.

Kunitz: Yes, it started early. I still have—on yellow sheets of sketch paper—a collection of short stories I wrote at the age of eleven, recounting my adventures in the far north. All of them are very detailed, very tragic and desperate. They are about survival. I am mushing through snow and ice with my team of huskies. We are lost in this terrible storm, and one by one they start dropping off, dying of the cold. Finally, there is just one left and we sort of keep each other warm. No doubt I was influenced by Jack London.

Interviewer: That is a lonely story, a story without companions, and it reminds me of another great loneliness in your life. A moment ago you referred to the "testing-tree" as a "patriarchal" tree. I am aware that you grew up in a single-parent home. How aware were you as a child of the absence of your father? How aware were you of how he left you?

Kunitz: I do not remember exactly how or when I learned that he had committed suicide a few weeks before I was born. There must have been a prior state of innocence, but I cannot recall it. It is as though I had plucked the knowledge of his death out of the air.

My most vivid memories are of stumbling by accident on a few bits of information. In my tenth or eleventh year, I was rummaging in the attic among old garments and trunks and some odd pieces of furniture. In one of the trunks I found my father's Masonic robes—apparently he was a thirty-second degree Mason—and some documents pertaining to his member-ship in that order. I have written about this discovery—which I kept secret then—in my poem "Three Floors."

On another occasion, something far more dramatic happened. Rummag-ing again in the attic, I came across a pastel portrait that I knew immedi-ately, intuitively, was a portrait of my father. I brought it down to show to my mother. Her instant reaction was to slap me and tear the likeness into shreds. This was out of anger, I am sure, but not anger directed at me. My mother wanted to erase my father out of her memory. She never referred to him, never spoke the slightest word of him. And that one gesture was the only manifestation of her emotion about him that I ever saw. I never dared question her, dreading the consequence. This of course made him all the more mysterious and important to me. I was compelled to create a mythical father to replace the real father I never had. This mythical being is the one who has dominated my imagination and my poems through all the years.

Interviewer: Did anybody else in the family ever mention him?

Kunitz: The only person I could talk to was my older sister. She was only six when he disappeared, so her memories were limited. I tried to pump her for information, but she had little to offer. The detail that I remember most clearly relates to my father's funeral. At the cemetery, when my mother became hysterical and tried to leap into the grave, our family physician—whose name was Dr. Nightingale, all so mythic—restrained her and said, "Be quiet! Don't forget, you have a lot to do with this." Now that is my sister's story, I do not know how accurate. Late in my mother's life, actually forty-six years after my father's death, I persuaded her to write an informal memoir. She was able to describe her life, in exact detail, up to the moment of her marriage, but at that point she froze. She could not write another word.

Interviewer: Let me go back to what you were saying about your early read-ing and writing. Was Worcester the sort of community that would support that kind of activity on the part of a very young man?

Kunitz: It was hardly an ideal environment. The Worcester that I knew was largely an immigrant city. It was built on seven hills, like ancient Rome—as the town fathers liked to boast—and each hill was inhabited by a differ-ent ethnic group: Irish, Swedes, Armenians, Italians, Jews, etc. Each group was isolated from the others. In fact, you were apt to encounter animosity and even some violence if you strayed into the wrong neighborhood. I bit-terly resented the all-too-visible signs of parochialism and sectarianism and vowed to make my escape at the first opportunity. Sherwood Anderson's *Winesburg, Ohio*, with its depressing picture of the frustrations of small-town existence, was a book that reinforced my determination.

In high school, I founded a literary magazine called *The Argus*, in which I published early poems and other writings. In the old WASP section of Worcester, there was a group called the Browning Society, staunch survivors of what had once been a flourishing network of chapters. I have no idea how it came about, but as a young poet and editor I was granted the privilege of joining them. The elderly ladies of the society, in their prim hats and long dresses, drank tea and discussed the poetry of Robert Browning in reverential terms. That was my first taste of the literary life, that invitation to the Browning Society.

Let me add that despite the reservations I have expressed about the Worcester environment, I remain forever grateful for the quality and breadth of instruction I received in the local schools, particularly at Classical High, a sort of magnet school, though the term hadn't been invented yet. I still treasure the hand-inscribed copy of *Bartlett's Familiar Quotations* that the faculty presented to me at graduation. No prize since then has meant as much to me. Those teachers, I believe, were superior to almost any you would find today in the public school system. I'm not even sure you could find their equivalent in the private sector.

Interviewer: Was there a special teacher at Classical High School who encouraged your poetry?

Kunitz: One such teacher was Perry Howe, the coach of the debating and declamation teams. In those days debating and declaiming were taken very seriously—there were interschool competitions in both categories, and silver cups were given to the winning teams. I was chosen captain of teams that successfully defended Classical's championship record. These were big events, held in the main auditorium of the city, with overflow audiences of students and parents in attendance. One of our first debates was on the subject of granting suffrage to women; fortunately, we drew the right side. Perry Howe helped me to overcome my native shyness and taught me how to project my voice.

I am indebted most of all to Martin Post, whom students joked about because of his love of poetry. One day he tossed aside the textbook from which he was reading to us a set of soporific quatrains—you know, the kind of didactic verse they fed to youngsters then—and reached into his pocket, saying, "I want you to hear some real poetry." That was my introduction to

Robert Herrick: "Get up! get up for shame! . . . / Get up, sweet slug-a-bed and see / The dew-bespangling herb and tree." And those other unforgettable lines: "Whereas in silks my Julia goes,/ Then, then, methinks, how sweetly flows/ That liquefaction of her clothes." I had never heard such delightful music. Right after school I dashed to the public library on Elm Street and took home Herrick's poems. I have been smitten with them ever since.

In another session of his class, Martin Post went over to the piano, struck a sequence of bass notes, and asked us, "What color did you hear?" In the midst of the snickers, when I saw that nobody else was tempted to respond, I raised my hand. The bottom notes, I said, were black, but a bit higher in the scale they moved toward the purple. Then Mr. Post put me to the test with the high, tinkling notes at the other end of the keyboard. I told him the topmost notes sounded white or crystal, moving downward toward the yellow. He turned to me and said, "Stanley, you're going to be a poet." Years later I read about the new findings by psychologists in their study of sensory perception. At birth all our five senses are fused; their differentiation is a developmental process. So that synaesthesia, the translation of one sense into the language of another, is tantamount to a return to a state of innocence. It is one of the great metaphorical resources of the poetic imagination. What was it Emily Dickinson wrote? "To the bugle, every color is red." I don't know where Martin Post got his information.

Interviewer: Tell me something more about the magazine you founded, *The Argus*. How long did that go on and how much writing did you do for it?
Kunitz: I must have been a sophomore when I started it. Publication continued for a good many years after my departure. Eventually the school shut down: classical education was no longer considered to be essential. Somewhere I have a file of *The Argus* tucked away. Among my contributions, I can recall, were parodies of Poe's "Raven" and Longfellow's "Excelsior." I suppose that parody was my way of learning metrics, as effective a discipline as any I know of. Perhaps, too, I was already beginning to distance myself from the nineteenth-century worthies who dominated the literary landscape.

Interviewer: How did you happen to go to Harvard after high school?
Kunitz: This was the period in which there were heavy restrictions on the number of Jews in the colleges. Even as valedictorian of my class, I had no assurance of being admitted to the college of my choice, especially since I needed financial assistance. The principal of Classical High School, Kenneth Porter, had his heart set on my going to Amherst, but failed to persuade

his alma mater to accept me. Fortunately, Harvard—which I scarcely dared dream of—came through with the grant of a handsome scholarship. This despite its notorious two percent quota.

Interviewer: I recall that you were an English major at Harvard. Did you receive any encouragement there as a writer?

Kunitz: In my second year I took a course in composition with visiting professor Robert Gay. His requirement was the submission of a one-page typed manuscript every day, Monday to Friday, on any topic of our choice—an heroic assignment, since he read and commented on every paper. After a month or so, he wrote on one of my papers, "You are a poet—Be one!" That was an even clearer signal than Martin Post had given me, and I tried, as best I could, to apply myself accordingly. In my senior year I was awarded the Garrison Medal in Poetry. During my graduate year, 1927, I took a course in versification with Robert Hillyer, but not with any appreciable benefit, since I resisted the mechanics of his approach to prosody.

Alfred North Whitehead came to Harvard, from England, while I was still an undergraduate. I knew his work and was eager to study with him, but his only offering was in advanced mathematical theory and philosophy. When I inquired about auditing his lectures, I was told that as an English major with inadequate scientific background I did not qualify. So I went to Whitehead himself. He examined my record and asked, "Why do you want to study with me?" I replied, in the firmest tones I could command, "Because I admire your work extravagantly and because I hope to be a poet." He looked at me in some astonishment and said, "You're in."

But I ended up bearing no great love for Harvard. This is an old story now, but I don't want it forgotten. After graduating *summa cum laude*, I assumed I would be asked to stay on as a teaching assistant. When I inquired of my counselor why I had not been approached, he said that he had wondered about it himself and would discuss the matter with the head of the department, Professor John Livingston Lowes, who was famous for his book on Coleridge and his course on the Romanic poets. He came back, looking embarrassed, and delivered his message, carefully giving each syllable equal weight: "What I've been told is simply this—'Our Anglo-Saxon students would resent being taught English by a Jew.'" That really shocked me. I felt crushed and angry. At that point I abandoned all thought of an academic career. How could I foresee then that eventually I would thank heaven for having been deflected from that course? After I received my master's, I left Harvard for good. During the previous summers I had been working as a cub reporter on the *Worcester Telegram*. Now I returned to Worcester as a full-fledged member of the staff and a few months later became assistant Sunday feature editor.

Interviewer: How did all that come about?

Kunitz: At Harvard, since I needed to supplement my scholarship income, I applied to Captain Roland Andrews, editor of the *Worcester Telegram*, for summer employment. It did not strike me as absurd that, in order to impress him with my qualifications for a job as cub reporter, I enclosed an essay I had written on James Joyce. This must have been in 1924, shortly after the publication in Paris of *Ulysses*, a book judged then and for an entire decade to be obscene and unfit for American consumption. I still wonder what an old-school conservative New Englander could have made of my panegyric. Nevertheless, I got a letter back from Captain Andrews saying, "You certainly can write. There's a job waiting for you. Come in whenever you are ready."

My major assignment on the *Telegram* was to report on the last-ditch effort to save Nicola Sacco and Bartolemeo Vanzetti from the electric chair. Like tens of thousands of others, I passionately believed that this pair of Italian immigrants had been condemned to die, not because they were proven guilty of murder during the course of a payroll robbery in South Braintree, Massachusetts, but because of their radical politics. Their case became the cause of a whole generation of writers and artists, who joined the demonstrations in the streets. Edna St. Vincent Millay wrote a poem of outrage whose title, "Justice Denied in Massachusetts," was picked up as a battle cry. I was sent to interview the judge of the trial, Judge Webster Thayer, a mean, little, frightened man who hated what he called "these anarchistic bastards." In the end, all the efforts to reverse the conviction or to secure clemency failed. Sacco and Vanzetti were executed in August 1927. It seemed to me the closing of a chapter. After consulting with members of the defense organization, the Committee for Justice, I decided to leave my job and go to New York in the hope of finding a publisher for Vanzetti's proud and eloquent letters, the ones he wrote in prison. A few months later I arrived in Manhattan and made the rounds, beating on every publisher's door. But my mission was a failure. Because of the Red scare, nobody would touch so controversial a project. Besides, I was young and unknown, just the wrong person to enlist support for this risky enterprise. The letters needed and, luckily, found a better advocate in the person of Felix Frankfurter, whose sponsorship insured that a dead man's voice, his poignant broken English, would yet be heard. As for me, I had to face the hard reality that I was jobless in a strange city, without friends or prospects.

Interviewer: As I recall, you ended up working for the H. W. Wilson Company, the great library publisher.

Kunitz: It was not what I had hoped for, but it was my last resort. That was 1928, and the Depression was coming on. I tried every literary publisher and newspaper in New York. The letters from my editor in Worcester to the editors of the *Times* and the *Herald Tribune* did not get me past the reception desk. Finally, when I was virtually penniless and did not know how I could survive, I spotted a blind ad in the *Times* for a "correspondent"—whatever that might mean—at a publishing house. That led me eventually to the sprawling plant of the H. W. Wilson Company, uptown in the Washington Heights area, near the Yankee Stadium. The Wilson Company is the leading publisher of reference works for the library profession, *The Reader's Guide to Periodical Literature*, *The Cumulative Book Index*, and countless other invaluable tools. The founder and president, an entrepreneurial Scotsman, who had started the business in the back room of his Minneapolis bookstore, was still in charge, running the show like a family shop. Halsey W. Wilson was obviously impressed with my credentials and indicated I might be the right person for the job. I asked what the job involved, and he said writing letters. When I expressed some diffidence about this prospect, he commented, "Well, maybe we can find something better for you. I'll let you know in a week." True to his word, he called to offer me the job, for twenty-eight dollars a week. I had been earning forty in Worcester, so I did not think this was great progress. Nevertheless, I told him I would report for work the following Monday. In the meantime, Alfred Knopf called me up—I had been to see him, and he had not been very encouraging. But now he said, "I think, on later consideration, that we can use you." I said, I'm sorry, but I've given my word." Maybe that was a great mistake. Who knows what might have happened if I had gone to the great house of Knopf?

Interviewer: So were you a correspondent, did you work at home?

Kunitz: I was given a desk in a vast loft with people sitting at open desks; there were no enclosures of any kind. It was like going back to the nineteenth century, to a Dickensian world. Even the president—well, he had some filing cabinets stacked around him, but otherwise nothing separated him from his staff of several hundred employees, most of them doing indexing of various kinds. When I came in for work on the first day, one of the editors approached me and asked who I was. I told her my name and introduced myself as a new employee. She said, "You'll have to punch in on the time clock." I recoiled in absolute horror: "Oh no, I can't do that." She said, "Everybody punches the time clock." I stood my ground: "Nobody told me." She said, "Well, you'll have to see Mr. Wilson."

"What is the trouble?" he asked. When I told him, he said, "Everybody does it. Nobody has ever complained." I asked him, "Do you punch a time clock?" He replied, "No, but I'm the president!" I said, "Well, I'm only me, but it goes against my grain." We looked at each other for a few minutes. At last he said, "If I make an exception for you, it would not be good for my relations with other people in the office. But I'll tell you what: suppose somebody else punches the time clock for you, and you don't have anything to do with it." I said, "That suits me." Looking back, I can only marvel at his tolerance and patience.

Then I sat at my solid oak desk for three long days, and nothing happened. Nobody gave me any work to do, not even a single letter to answer. I was a correspondent who didn't seem to exist. Was this a test of some sort? When Kafka appeared in translation some years later, I had a sense of *déjà vu* reading him. It was embarrassing for me to have to go back to Mr. Wilson to complain how useless I felt, but he gave no sign of being vexed or surprised. "What would you like to do?" he asked. I had been studying the firm's operations and did not have to hunt for a reply. My first suggestion was the publication of a library periodical that—without repeating the details now—would be livelier and more literary than the trade competition. My other proposal went something like this: "It's amazing that there's no standard reference work available in this country, or anywhere for that matter, on contemporary world authors. I visualize an illustrated series of books on writers, presenting biographical, critical, and bibliographical information for ready reference, in encyclopedic format." "Go ahead," said Mr. Wilson. "Let's see what you can do." So that was how the *Wilson Library Bulletin*, *Twentieth-Century Authors*, and the whole multivolumed Wilson Author Series got their start. They are still flourishing, but of course I am no longer connected with them. That's ancient history.

Interviewer: I take it that you were also working on your poetry at this time?

Kunitz: I was working on the poems that constituted my first book, writing them at night and feeling good when they began to appear in various magazines, including *Poetry*, *The Nation*, *The Dial*, *Commonweal*, and *The*

New Republic. Early in 1929 I put my poems together and sent them in the mail to the biggest publishing house in the country then: Doubleday, Doran. Only a few weeks later I had a telephone call from an editor who identified himself as Ogden Nash; he had read my poems with pleasure and wanted to congratulate me on the acceptance of my manuscript. Would I please come in to talk things over? So that is how I got my first book published. I felt that I was fortune's child. By the time *Intellectual Things* came out, in the spring of 1930, I was abroad.

Interviewer: What was Ogden Nash like?
Kunitz: Soft-spoken and amiable, keeping his witty persona under wraps—but I never got to know him well. I should explain that my foreign adventure was made possible by a free-lance arrangement with Mr. Wilson. Living abroad then was extraordinarily cheap. I remained in France and Italy for about a year.

Interviewer: Did you return then to The H. W. Wilson Company?
Kunitz: Yes, but not for long. My taste of freedom had spoiled me for office routine. I decided to move to a run-down farm in outer Connecticut that could be acquired for a pittance. "I suppose this will be goodbye," I said to Mr. Wilson. He paused for a moment before replying: "Not necessarily. There is always the U.S. mail. We can send manuscripts and other materials, and you can continue to do your work in the country, just as you did in Europe." But then he added, "Of course, you'll have to take a cut in salary." I was back, financially, where I had started. Nevertheless, I felt enormously relieved.

Interviewer: You mentioned your sense of isolation from any kind of literary community in your early days. Was that isolation absolute?
Kunitz: Not by this time. But keep in mind that in those days there were no creative writing programs, no poetry readings, few arts organizations or fellowships. Poets tended to work in isolation unless they were motivated to meet by a convergence of political passions. The old established writers were, as a rule, indifferent or hostile to the new upstart generation. If I have spent so much of my life trying to build a sense of community among writers and artists, it is largely because I know from experience how much the lack of it means. And yet I realize as well that I have been luckier through the years than most and am accordingly grateful for the many acts of friendship

and generosity and hospitality that have eased my journey. In 1928, when I still thought of myself as a stranger in New York, I was invited, out of the blue, to be a guest at Yaddo. This was shortly after it had opened its doors as an artists' colony. I was one of the first to enjoy its lavish hospitality.

Interviewer: Really? How did that come about?

Kunitz: I suppose that without realizing it, I was beginning to acquire some sort of underground reputation. More to the point, I was seeing a girl who knew Lewis Mumford, and I believe she told him about me and showed him some of my poems. He and Alfred Kreymborg were editing a publication called *The American Caravan*, which collected the new writing of the day. They asked me to contribute to it, and they also recommended me to Yaddo.

Interviewer: What was Yaddo like then?

Kunitz: It was still shaping itself, and there were not many people there. The guests included Kreymborg himself—rather an avuncular figure in contemporary poetry at that time, editor of an avant-garde magazine called *Others*. One special attraction to me was a poet in her thirties, Helen Pearce, a great beauty, whom I courted and later married, disastrously. Then there was the playwright Hatcher Hughes and a painter named Carl Schmitt. Only two others, I think. I was by far the youngest there. It was a fateful visit, though it lasted only two or three weeks, when I had my encounter with a ghost, an incident that has become part of the Yaddo legend.

Interviewer: A ghost?

Kunitz: Yes. Here's what happened. Yaddo is a big, baronial estate, and the great house, with its old-world stone architecture, built for the ages, could be the setting for a Gothic novel. My bedroom was upstairs in the spacious tower room. One night, while I was lying in bed reading, I heard something scratching at the casement window. It must be the scraping of a branch, I thought, and went back to my book. The scratching continued. I rose, went over to the window, and looked out on the silent landscape. There was nothing suspicious in sight. I went back to bed and turned off the light. It was well after midnight. The moment I stretched out, the scratching began again, growing louder and louder. I got up again and again found nothing. I used all my willpower to ignore what was happening, even putting a pillow over my head, but the noise sifted through, clawing at my ears. I gave up trying to sleep and sat up straight in bed.

Suddenly, the wall I was facing became eerily luminous, and a mottled shape appeared on it—a winged creature, suspended from a pendulum, which kept swinging back and forth in a wide arc. The tempo of the scratching on the casement accelerated, the pendant bird swung faster and faster, and the glowing wall began to pulse. I was spellbound, terrified.

And then I heard the glass shatter! Everything went wild.

In panic I turned on the bedside light. The wall showed me its usual blank face; the closed casement was perfectly intact. I crept out of bed and fled downstairs. I lay down on the sofa in front of the enormous stone fireplace and spent the rest of the night there.

In the morning I went back to my room, where everything looked serene. I was too shaken to reveal my story. Then at breakfast, Elizabeth Ames, the founding director of Yaddo, said to me, "Stanley, wouldn't you like to make a tour of the painting gallery? You'll be interested, I'm sure, in the family treasures." Like everything else at Yaddo, the paintings—mostly nineteenth- and early twentieth-century portraits—belonged to the estate of Spencer and Katrina Trask. The tour consisted largely of anecdotes about the subjects of the portraits, several of them illustrious or wealthy friends of the Trasks. I was only half-listening when at one point I found myself standing mesmerized—I did not know why—in front of a portrait of a delicate young girl. "Who is that?" I asked. "The daughter of the Trasks," said Mrs. Ames. "She was at the center of the great tragedy of their marriage." And she continued: "One summer evening this lovely child disappeared. She was last seen walking down the path to the pond at the foot of the rose garden. When they instigated a search for her, they found her floating among the lilies; she had fallen in and drowned." I had a premonition of the answer, but I asked the question, "Can you tell me where she slept?" Mrs. Ames said, "Yes, in your room." I thanked her, packed my bags, and left Yaddo.

Interviewer: How did you happen to meet Theodore Roethke?

Kunitz: In the late thirties, when I was living in Bucks County, Pennsylvania—this was after the breakup of my marriage with Helen Pearce—Ted drove down in his jalopy from Lafayette College, where he was teaching, and knocked at my door. He was wearing a voluminous raccoon coat, and he had my book, *Intellectual Things*—much of which he knew by heart—under his arm.

He was very large, very formidable, and he stood on the doorstep reciting lines out of my poems. Then he said, "May I come in? I'd like to talk with you." With an introduction like that, he was more than welcome. Of course, he had also brought his own poems with him in manuscript. He was working on the poems that were to constitute his first volume; which I titled for him, *Open House*. It was clear to me from the start that Ted was a force of nature, a real poet. The poems he was writing then were by no means great—they were quite formal, somewhat imitative, and restricted in range. But there were signs everywhere of his ultimate destiny.

He was the first poet I had met whose passion for poetry was like mine—who had the same rather terrifying immersion in the poetic medium and who had read everybody. Through the years we learned a lot from each other, though I, being a little older and having already published, was certainly at first in the position of being more his mentor than he was mine. Later he was to open doors of the imagination for me, particularly during the period when he erupted into the poems of *The Lost Son*. To me those were the most important poems written by anyone in my generation.

Interviewer: I would like to turn more toward talking about your own poetry. You have said something elsewhere that intrigues me. I think this might have to do with poetry, but maybe not. Apparently you played the violin as a child, and then you gave it up—because you resisted playing other people's music.

Kunitz: That's right.

Interviewer: Would you have kept it up if you could have played your own music?

Kunitz: I doubt it. My deep, sensuous delight in language made me feel that this was the art I was born for. Once I became absorbed in poetry, I lost interest in playing the violin.

Interviewer: Perhaps the connection would be between the way a violinist can physically feel the music and the way you feel about language.

Kunitz: All the arts, in varying degree, are somehow connected with the human body. The violin tucked under the chin—what an intimate and comforting sensation! I must tell you about my teacher, Margaret MacQuade, who invested so much hope in me. She had been a favorite pupil of the famous Belgian virtuoso Eugene Ysaye, and he had presented her with one of his violins, saying, "Pass it on some day to your best student." I still have that violin—a beautiful, old Italian instrument—and I feel guilty about its lying there in my closet, abandoned and unused. Perhaps I have made amends by trying to pass on to some of the gifted young poets who have worked with me the sense of having inherited, if only metaphorically, the equivalent of Ysaye's violin.

Interviewer: You once said, "The language of the poem must do more than convey experience, it must embody it." Does that mean for you the physicality of language?

Kunitz: Definitely. The poems that mean most to me are the ones to which I respond physically as well as intellectually or aesthetically. When we say that we are moved or stirred or shaken by a poem we are describing a kinaesthetic response to fields of verbal energy. In the dynamics of poetry, all the sounds are actions. It is as though some intrinsic gesture of the soul itself were being expressed through the resonances of language. In that context the marriage of sense with sound seems to me to be a deep metaphysical action.

Interviewer: Is this why you love the metaphysical poets so much, and why your own work has been grouped with that of the new metaphysical poets?

Kunitz: I don't care much for these groupings. Through the various stages of my work, I've been put into some rather strange company. But seriously, I'm inclined to think of myself less as a metaphysical than as an existential poet. To me, the struggle of words to be born, to arrive at the level of consciousness, is like the struggle of the self to become a person. I think that what the poet is trying to do is to bring words out from the darkness of the self into the light of the world. That is like the primordial act of creation, what Coleridge meant when he spoke of the repetition in the finite mind of the infinite I AM.

Interviewer: As you were talking about the physicality of the language, which would seem to imply the necessity of a rich verbal texture, it occurred to me to ask if you have that same feeling about your more recent poems, those beginning with *The Testing-Tree*.

Kunitz: Some years ago, in commenting on my later work, I said I was trying to write poems with a surface so simple and transparent that you could look through them and see the world. I didn't mean to suggest that I had lost interest in the orchestration of the world within. Texture is more than a superficial phenomenon and is not to be confused with the maintenance of a high style. My main concern is with psychic texture, which is a deeper and more complex thing.

Interviewer: When you compose your poems, is there that same sense of actual physical engagement?

Kunitz: I have never known how to compose poems except by saying them. The problem always has been to discover a rhythm on which I can ride. When that happens, I am on my way. A poem springs to life when its energy begins to flow from one's deepest wells.

Interviewer: In my interview with him, James Wright quoted you as having said to him when he was a young poet: "You've got to get down into the pit of the self, the real pit, and then you have to find your own way to climb out of it. And it can't be anybody else's way. It has to be yours."

Kunitz: Very sound advice!

Interviewer: Do you write regularly, say a little bit every day?

Kunitz: No.

Interviewer: How do you know when it is time to write a new poem?

Kunitz: I have never been able to sit down and write a poem as an act of will. My poems seem to have wills of their own. They keep their own schedules secret, and they don't answer the phone. They usually come to me at night with a phrase or image that starts troubling my sleep, gradually hooking up with other words and images, often counter-images, searching—as I've already indicated—for a controlling rhythm. It's a slow process.

Interviewer: Have you ever had poems come to you ready-made, a kind of spontaneous perfect composition?

Kunitz: Miracles happen now and then, but not if you count on them.

Interviewer: I am going to name a few poems and see if you have anything to say about the story behind the poem or its genesis: "End of Summer."

Kunitz: That's one I happen to have written about. It dates back to the time I was living in Bucks County. I was hoeing in the corn field when I heard a clamor in the sky—it was the season for the wild Canadian geese to be flying south. Great V-shapes, constellations of them. Something in that calling of the birds disturbed me. I dropped my hoe, ran into the house, and started to write. After the geese delivered their message to me, they flew out of the poem. They told me to make an important decision, to change my life, and I did. It is a poem about migration.

Interviewer: How about the poem "No Word"?

Kunitz: That's simple. I don't believe anyone has ever asked me about it before. I was waiting for a telephone call from someone who meant a lot to me, and the call did not come. Well, it did finally come, but too late.

Interviewer: How about "Open the Gates"?—Jim Wright's favorite of your poems.

Kunitz: "Open the Gates" originated in a dream. The landscape suggests the cities of the plain, Sodom and Gomorrah, from which I am fleeing—at least that was my interpretation on waking. In the climactic action, the monumental door I knock on is the door of revelation. Many of my poems speak of a quest, the search for the transcendent, a movement from darkness into light, from the kingdom of the profane into the kingdom of the sacred. As a rule, I don't feel I'm done with a poem until it passes from one realm of experience to another.

Interviewer: Your interest in politics is profound, as we see in your devotion to poets who have lived under totalitarian governments. But your poems are never overtly political.

Kunitz: Well, almost never. I maintain that to live as a poet in this society is to make a definite political statement. The politics is inherent in the practice of the art, as well as in the life. At the same time I feel that poetry resists being used as a tool. The truth is that we are suffering from an excess of political rhetoric and a dearth of the compassionate imagination.

Stanley Kunitz: An Interview

Leslie Kelen / 1991

From *American Poetry Review* 27 (March–April 1998), 48–54. Reprinted with permission.

The following interview with Stanley Kunitz is the outcome of two conversations taped at his New York City apartment. The first took place on the afternoon of November 26, 1991, the second on the evening of March 24, 1993. The first session focused almost entirely on the poet's early years: The aim here was to identify and describe the personal and social contexts that influenced the poems and to place the poet's earliest efforts in their atmosphere. The second interview concentrated on the dramatic transformation that marks Kunitz's recent, mature work. It attempted to locate and articulate the connections between radical stylistic change and altered psychological or personal awareness.

Leslie Kelen: Stanley, I'm wondering if you could give me a sense of the community or world in which you were raised. How do you recall its particular cultural and religious atmosphere?

Stanley Kunitz: My birthplace early in the century was Worcester, a sprawling industrial city in central Massachusetts. The city fathers liked to boast that Worcester, like Rome, was built on seven hills, a romantic parallel that intrigued me. But the curious and, to me, invidious circumstance was that each hill was occupied by a single ethnic group. It was a divided city, with little conversation between the hills. The Jewish community, occupying the Providence Hill section, was one of the largest immigrant groups and the one most isolated from the others. We lived in a middle-class neighborhood, consisting largely of shopkeepers and small-scale merchants, with a sprinkling of younger professionals, the first sons of their respective families to go to college. Daughters, of course, stayed home, waiting for a husband to show up, while the more adventurous worked as clerks or secretaries. The terms of existence on Providence Hill made me restless and melancholy. I was curious about the world of possibilities beyond those other alien hills, and glad there were roads that ran out of town. I felt that when the time came I must be ready to leave.

LK: Were there friends who contributed to your resolve to leave or was it primarily your decision?
Kunitz: Entirely mine. But of course I was influenced by my reading. I read anything I could lay my hands on. And I knew there was a great free world outside and that I would need to find it and prove myself worthy of it. The imagination would show me the way.

LK: In *Next-to-Last Things*, you included an autobiographical sketch your mother wrote describing her life before coming to America. In it, she states that the twenty-four years she spent in Lithuania were "wasted." Though she doesn't specify, was she indicting the Jewish culture and community she came out of? And was that indictment part of the atmosphere in which you were raised?
Kunitz: I never heard her speak ill of her family or the Jewish tradition. What she rejected was provincialism, poverty, ignorance, bigotry, oppression, all of which she identified with her birthplace, "the Godforsaken village," as she called it, of Yashwen in the province of Kovno. She was determined to escape from it, and she did. She must have been an exceptional child in that village of three hundred families. It was in Yashwen, at the age of twelve, that she read Spinoza and lost her God. In her later years she used to say that there was too much suffering, too much evil, in the world for her to believe in the existence of a God who cared.

LK: Was there a sense in your household that traditional Jewish religious values were being rejected?
Kunitz: The stress was on cultural and ethical values rather than on ritual practices. I grew up with a feeling of detachment from organized religion, but with a deep-rooted pride in my heritage and a steady flow of religious impulses and yearnings. At thirteen I went through the form of a bar mitzvah at the local "German" shul, the smaller and more liberal of the two Worcester synagogues, the other being the brick temple of the Ashkenazim. The rabbi gave me a speech to read and told me I was a descendant of the priestly house of Levi.

LK: What kind of an education did you receive? I mean, as you look back and try to assess it, what were its outstanding positive and negative attributes?

Kunitz: How lucky I was! I could not have hoped for a better education than the one provided by the public schools of Worcester at that time. From the beginning I was given special attention and encouragement. There were always teachers, most of them Irish in elementary school, who took me under their wing. The only exception I can recall was Miss Ryan in sixth grade, who railed against "dirty foreigners" in general and "dirty Jews" in particular and who threw pieces of chalk at those of us who offended her sensibilities. Actually, I had no sense of belonging to an immigrant family. I did not realize that in 1905, when I was born, my mother had been in this country only fifteen years and had come out of the sweatshops of New York City to marry my father. I was raised to be an American. Nothing but English was ever spoken in our household, as a consequence of which I have no Yiddish, unlike others of the same background in my generation.

Of the three high schools in the city, Classical High had the top scholastic reputation. It offered a curriculum that paid homage to the classical tradition, the kind of education no longer available in the public school systems of this country. There I felt in my element, and after the passage of more than seven decades I still think of the school and its dedicated faculty—all vanished, including the school itself—with a glow of gratitude and affection. I was chosen captain of the debating team, which won the contest for the city championship—a big event in those days—and founded a literary magazine, *The Argus*, for which, in my capacity as editor, I shamelessly accepted the first poem of mine to appear in print, a parody of Longfellow's "Excelsior." When I graduated as valedictorian of my class, the faculty presented me with an inscribed copy of *Bartlett's Familiar Quotations*, which is still in my possession.

When I informed my high school principal, Arnold Porter, that I hoped to go to Harvard, he pointed out the advantages of a small college and spoke enthusiastically of Amherst, his alma mater. In fact, he volunteered to write about me to the president of Amherst and to sound out my chances for admission as a scholarship student. When his overture failed, he delicately explained to me what he had only hinted at in our discussions: Jews weren't exactly welcome in certain groves of academe. Luckily, despite my fears, Harvard did accept me, with a four-year scholarship to boot. I would have been even more anxious if I had known beforehand that Harvard at this time secretly maintained a two percent quota for Jews.

LK: Which meant two percent of their student body could be Jewish?
Kunitz: No more. In practice, probably less. The chosen few were huddled together in the dorms. At Harvard, in the early twenties, a minority student could not avoid experiencing a degree of social discomfort. Race, religion, and money clearly defined a class structure.

LK: At Harvard, you had a brilliant scholastic record, made Phi Beta Kappa, and won the Garrison Prize for Poetry. After graduating *summa cum laude*, in 1926, you stayed on for a year to earn your master's degree. Obviously you were preparing for an academic career. But when you inquired about remaining as a teaching assistant, you were told—so the story goes—that "our Anglo-Saxon students would resent being taught English literature by a Jew." How did that affect you?
Kunitz: It shattered me. I had not assumed that the prejudice ran so deep. Those few words of rejection told me that I must leave the shelter of the academy and find a different way of survival.

LK: Over the years you've consistently characterized yourself as an "outsider" in relation to the poetry establishment and the university system. What is the connection between that sense of yourself as an outsider and the experience of being a Jew?
Kunitz: I once remarked, somewhat facetiously, that to be a poet in this country is to be a kind of Jew. Most of the poets I know, regardless of their origins, tend to see themselves as marginal to the mainstream of twentieth-century American culture. It's a compliment, I think, that in certain quarters poetry is viewed as a subversive activity.

LK: After your rejection by Harvard, what did you do in terms of livelihood? What course did your life take?
Kunitz: I had been working during the summers as a reporter on the *Worcester Telegram*. Since I had no other choice, I decided to return, though I took it badly, as a defeat and a surrender. One of my local assignments brought me into contact with Webster Thayer, the infamous judge of the Sacco-Vanzetti case, whose conduct of the proceedings had led to worldwide protests and demonstrations. What I heard from him convinced me, if I needed any convincing, that this frightened and vindictive old man could not conceiv-

ably have given a fair trial to a pair of poor Italian immigrants, who may or may not have been involved in a payroll robbery and murder—the evidence against them was confusing and some of it fabricated—but who were presumptively guilty of the crime of being "anarchistic bastards," to borrow Judge Thayer's terminology. I became passionately involved in the effort to save Sacco and Vanzetti from a miscarriage of justice. But it was a doomed fight. In August 1927 they died in the electric chair. Their execution was for me the closing of a chapter. I gave up my job at the *Telegram* and with the blessing of the Committee for Justice for Sacco and Vanzetti I left for New York, intent on finding a publisher for Vanzetti's eloquent death-row letters. But without any influence or reputation and in the midst of the Red hysteria of the period, I had to concede the failure of my mission. For many months I was equally unsuccessful in my search for employment. Finally, on the eve of the Great Depression, when I was penniless and desperate, I replied to a blind ad in the *New York Times* for "correspondent"—meaning a low clerical job—and got myself hired in that capacity by the H. W. Wilson Company, reference publishers to the library world. That was the inauspicious beginning of a long and fruitful association.

LK: Commenting on your beginnings as a poet, you once remarked that you suppose you "willed yourself to be a hermetic poet." Considering the difficult emotional background you came out of—your father's suicide a few weeks before you were born and your mother's disinclination to talk about it—do you think there might be a connection between your mother's attitude and your hermeticism?
Kunitz: Possibly so. There was a secret locked within that household that I could not penetrate. Yet I had the sense that the secret was the source of my emotional life and even perhaps of whatever strength I had. So it is not at all inconceivable that I translated that experience into my concept of the poetic imagination, something secret and magical and dark like the emotional life locked within me.

LK: The atmosphere of your home seems to have had a profound and long lasting impact on your work. Would you mind describing it?
Kunitz: I was brought up in a household of women, consisting of my mother and my two older sisters. We were different from other households in that my mother was the breadwinner and dominant figure in our family. She left us each morning for her factory loft downtown, where she conducted her business as a designer and manufacturer of children's dresses, supervising

long rows of operators at their sewing machines. In those days that was an extraordinary exercise of authority for a woman. In her absence I was often alone and learned how to be self-reliant. In my thirteenth year we moved into a new house at the edge of town. My favorite room was the comfortable library—probably the only room of its kind in the neighborhood—where I could curl up in the Morris chair after dinner and read till I fell asleep. The book that I kept returning to, though it frightened me, was a folio edition of Dante, in H. F. Cary's translation, embellished with Gustave Dore's fantastic illustrations. I had dreams about my father in his grave and the torments of Hell.

LK: At the beginning of your writing life, you were drawn to writing about dreams. Some of your more successful early efforts, in fact, had dream content in them. I'm wondering if you could explain what allowed you to trust in dream content at that point? What made you so open to that?

Kunitz: Freud had something to do with it. I was much affected by his whole theory of dreams. Incidentally, do you know of Freud's association with Worcester? In 1909—I think that was the year—he came to Clark University for an extended visit at the invitation of the psychologist G. Stanley Hall. Carl Jung came at the same time. Their lectures and disputes are part of the history of psychoanalysis. I've always been attracted to dream activity. I love its illogic, its intimations, its fluidity, its hint of revelation. The dream life still feeds my imagination.

LK: Reading *Intellectual Things* and *Passport to the War*, I sensed that one of the great struggles you had as a young poet was opening yourself to your own pain and inner chaos, submitting yourself to the very experiences that obsessed you at the time. Would you agree with that observation?

Kunitz: My problem was not whether to acknowledge my losses and frustrations but how to transform them from a destructive experience into a creative one. I still remember the very first of my father poems, "For the Word Is Flesh." It opens with an invocation, "O ruined father dead, long sweetly rotten/ Under the dial, the time-dissolving urn," and it closes with a summing-up couplet, "Let sons learn from their lipless fathers how/ Man enters hell without a golden bough." That's in *Intellectual Things*. At twenty-three my poems tended to be dense and formal, written in the metaphysical mode. The pain is there, but you have to penetrate the high style to get at it.

LK: Would you try to describe the person you were at that time, your personality, your inclinations?

Kunitz: I guess I was a rather complicated young man—moody, shy, troubled, ambitious, hoping to find, as I say somewhere, "the language that saves." I've never been able to separate the mastery of the medium from the mastery of the self.

LK: Did your early inclination toward the hermetic make it difficult for you to establish friendships with other poets? Was it something you struggled against?

Kunitz: The only times I haven't had strong bonds with other poets has been when there weren't other poets around. One of my earliest drives was to find a community or else to create one. And, in practice, I have tried to do just that. The two organizations or cultural entities that I have been most intimately involved with as founder and counselor through the years are the Fine Arts Work Center, in Provincetown, and Poets House, in New York, and both of them are premised on the need for a community. I do not think that poetry can flourish in an indifferent or hostile environment unless poets take pride in their vocation and heritage and connect with one another, establish that sense of belonging one to another. The poet, as I gradually perceived, is a social being and intimately tied to the political life of his time. My poetry and my politics drink from the same well. Consequently, I haven't isolated the politics in the poetry from the rest of the experiences I deal with. They belong together.

LK: To find "the language that saves" sounds urgent, momentous. What was it you were hoping to save yourself from?

Kunitz: Mediocrity, the death of the heart, annihilation. The original working title for *Intellectual Things* was *Against Destruction.*

LK: What was the destruction you feared?

Kunitz: The destruction of the self, the loss of identity, becoming nameless. In my vocabulary, "self" and "name" have persisted to this day as pivotal words. While still in college I learned from Coleridge that the distinguishing attribute of the imagination is its power to reconcile contradictions, and I came to believe that the way to become whole was through the exercise of that healing power. In those early poems I am trying to reconcile flesh with spirit, time with eternity. Blake gave me my title with his unifying pronouncement that "the tear is an intellectual thing," and from him, too, I received the comforting assurance that "Eternity is in love with the productions of time."

LK: While completing the poems in the first manuscript, how conscious were you of the effort to identify and reconcile these conflicts within yourself?

Kunitz: I'll let a passage I can still recall speak for me. It's from "Vita Nuova," the closing poem of *Intellectual Things*:

> Now I will peel that vision from my brain
> Of numbers wrangling in a common place,
> And I will go unburdened, on the quiet lane
> Of my eternal kind, till shadowless
> With inner light I wear my father's face.

The young man whose voice I hear in that poem is telling me of his discontent and his determination to change his circumstances and himself. He knows that he must test his resolve in the crucible of experience. At the same time he realizes that he cannot escape from his sources: in his end is his beginning. Much has been made of the difference between my early and later work. I am more interested in what I perceive to be the persistence of the self through all my changes. In "The Layers," a poem written in my sixties, I begin with a statement of that perception:

> I have walked through many lives,
> some of them my own,
> and I am not who I was,
> though some principle of being abides,
> from which I struggle not to stray.

LK: Comparing your early and later work, I observed that in your first two books you tended to use long lines, end-stopped rhymes, and little enjambment. Then in your third and fourth books, a dramatic stylistic change occurred. The poems started using short lines, a great deal of enjambment, and they began moving quickly, almost furiously down the page. Since rhythms are tied to or are an indication of emotional life, I'm wondering what caused this change?

Kunitz: I like to think there was a change in me corresponding with the change that you detect in the rhythms; that I became a freer, more open person, as I evolved. You cannot separate the word from the maker of the word. That's why I have insisted in my teaching that the first crucial act of the imagination is to create the person who will write the poems.

LK: It seems to me that creating the person who'll write the poems cannot be done just once.

Kunitz: My reference was to the young, who haven't yet established an identity. It's true that, in the passage of time, they may face the need of reinventing themselves. At every stage in life we need to create a self that we can bear to live and die with.

LK: The idea of person-making in that context had not occurred to me, but I understand what you are saying. The poetry you wrote in the *Selected Poems* prefigures much of the strong writing that follows. You seem to have emerged out of some sort of personal crisis. I'm wondering if you could comment on it.

Kunitz: That was a period of revolution for me, a time of breaking and rebuilding. In the middle of my life, I earned my keep as a kind of peripatetic bard, traveling from one college to another, each year at a different school. Academic tenure, I must say, was a kind of security I felt obliged to resist, as I did to the end of my teaching career. But during those difficult, restless years, I became, I think, much more outgoing, involved, and outspoken, deeply involved in the civil rights movement and, in the next decade, the opposition to the war in Vietnam. Although I am not overtly a political poet, my convictions are an active element in the subtext of my poems.

LK: Speaking of subtexts, I get the impression that even in the arrangement of poems in a collection you are following a psychological track toward some point of resolution. Is this a deliberate procedure?

Kunitz: I certainly don't preplot my poems to fit into a pattern. But I do give serious thought to their order of presentation, so as to convey the sense of an unfolding drama, a movement toward illumination or climax, possibly toward catharsis. Ideally, the book as a whole incorporates the same organic principle of development as its constituent poems. A random collection of poems makes me think of a random collection of flowering plants: It is not to be confused with a garden.

LK: A note I made while reading "The Thing That Eats the Heart" was that at a certain stage—in mid-career—you had arrived at a concept of poetry as inner theater.

Kunitz: The drama of the life has always been at the center of my investigations, and I gradually realized that the dramatic lyric was a natural medium for me, especially true in a time of stress and turmoil. I found my best mentors in a combination of the late Yeats with the Hopkins of the terrible sonnets. An even earlier source, a poem that shook me in my first encounter in my twenties, was George Herbert's "The Collar."

LK: I'm fascinated by the psychological developments that occur in your poems. It seems as if your poems move from dualities and impasses to paradox and balance. Somewhere along the line, you had to realize that the struggle in yourself, the war, did not have to be won, that what you had to do was contain the energy in a new way, find a new form. Did such a reckoning occur for you?

Kunitz: Certainly the old dualism that dominated my thought in the beginning has long since evaporated. I am no longer conditioned to celebrate the triumph of reason. I turn more and more to the old self, the buried self, the one that's "wild with years" when I am in need of understanding. Often in the workings of a poem the body and one's trust in the wisdom of the body supervenes, and one recognizes that reason itself is not the ultimate gift of humanity. Certainly it is one of the instruments of civilization; but body, spirit, the reason beyond reason, are the instruments of transcendence.

LK: Reading through your books one becomes aware of symmetries between early and late work. For instance, in your first two books, myth and the poem itself are often used to defend against the nightmarish aspects of personal life. Whereas in later poems, in particular in "The Testing-Tree" and "The Layers," little overt use of myth occurs. The poem has become a vehicle through which to embrace the very things you initially distanced.

Kunitz: Poetry, I have insisted, is ultimately mythology, the telling of the soul's adventure in time and history. This conviction of mine does not necessarily require the reconstruction of classical mythology, but sometimes it becomes unavoidable, even as recently as in "Proteus." This is a poem based on the desperate transformations of the self and there is no way to deal with it subjectively. But as Proteus I can write it because I am delivered into the body of the myth. And this is what is so painful and so difficult about poetry: trying to penetrate through all the states of one's being back to its state of innocence.

LK: In the poem "Around Pastor Bonhoeffer," in *The Testing-Tree*, you write about the Holocaust. You, in a sense, are engaged in fighting the Holocaust, but from a Christian perspective, through Christian eyes. It struck me as somewhat ironic. Why did you use that vehicle?

Kunitz: It wasn't a deliberate choice. And I must tell you that I didn't feel at all alien to Christian eyes. Maybe I felt it was impossible to write of that monstrous event unless I reduced it in scale and focused it on an individual, an active adversary to Hitler, rather than a multitude of helpless victims. I could do it through Bonhoeffer. The one great and immortal poem to come out of the death camps is Paul Celan's "Todes Fuge" (Fugue of Death). As you know, he was a survivor, who spoke the unspeakable, and eventually committed suicide.

LK: While reading the Bonhoeffer poem, I equated his search for a way to actively oppose Nazism with what may have been your inner conflict as a pacifist during World War II. Did you make that connection, too?

Kunitz: Of course! That was my struggle. Here I was a committed pacifist and yet part of me would welcome the assassination of Hitler. So there was a real confusion, which I recognized. That's why I accepted service in the army.

LK: Stanley, you've consistently described yourself as being in exile. How do you reconcile your sense of exile with the recognition and honors you have received as a poet?

Kunitz: It's a paradox no doubt. I expect to die in exile because my feeling of metaphysical loneliness, something I experienced even as a child, is so deeply ingrained. Yet I have that other countervailing tribal sense, that has let me into the world. Through the years, as I look back, my search for a community has been one of my most urgent motivations. My association with other writers and artists, particularly younger poets, remains to this day one of the happiest chapters in my story. So here I am, with these con-flicting states of being. But I don't mind contending with paradoxes. That's a condition of the life.

LK: The father quest, a central theme in your writing, appears to take place on numerous levels. For instance, it is a search for a biological father, a spiri-tual father, and, even possibly, a father-God, out in the universe somewhere.

Kunitz: I put that in the form of a paradox, too. In one of my journal notes I say, "The God in whom I believe does not exist."

LK: Could you expand on that?

Kunitz: I can't reject either assumption, so I hold them both in suspension. I don't pretend to have resolved any of the main existential conflicts within me. Maybe that's why I am still ticking.

LK: A distinguishing aspect of your recent work is its focus on the past. The older you get the more, it seems, you need to or are able to dive back into your roots. *The Testing-Tree*, where such poems first appeared, also has a strong feeling of personal liberation or illumination running throughout it. Did you have such an experience while writing those poems?

Kunitz: Definitely! That book was my emancipation proclamation. Writing the title poem itself both attached me to my origins and liberated me from them. That was the first poem in which I wrote about my childhood, not symbolically, not mythologically, but realistically—surrealistically maybe— but certainly with a lot of minute particulars. All of them true to the experience and all, in a way, legendary. And this is what I feel a poet has to do with his life: not expose it, not confess it, not present it literally, but convert it into legend. And from this vantage my story seems to be as legendary as the ancient tales and the creation myths. It has an aspect of having become, in a way, an act of the imagination as well as something lived and experienced. I can't separate the two anymore.

LK: In his illuminating work on your poetry, Gregory Orr observed that your poems often comment upon each other, even pun on each other. For instance, the stone you toss against the oak in "The Testing-Tree" for a "score" returns in a later poem, "The Knot," which is "scored in the lintel" of your door.

Kunitz: I hadn't thought of that connection myself. But that's the way with one's key images: They have a surprising way of reasserting themselves. My conviction is that each poet has a set of key images that are the clue to one's deepest identity. And the key images never change. So, in a way, all the poems dissolve into one poem, the poem you spend your life writing.

LK: Is the threshold you refer to throughout your work the threshold between the ego and the id?

Kunitz: When you cross that threshold you are in dangerous country. Terra Incognita. Beware the wild dogs!

LK: I believe it took you half your life to begin to forgive your mother for what she withheld from you when you were growing up? What led you to finally reconcile with her?

Kunitz: You have to understand that there was a good deal of denial that was associated with my childhood. I felt deprived of a father and deprived of a soft, maternal presence. And since she was so strong-willed and capable, I had to fight for my own survival, my own will, my own power. That was the contest of our early years. She loved me and encouraged me in every way. But she was unable to demonstrate affection. She had lost that capacity through all the tragic circumstances of her life. It was only after her death that I began to rethink my feelings about her and to realize what an extraordinary human being she was and what she had done for me in other than obvious ways. So, gradually, my image of her changed. It's a complicated portrait I now have of her. It isn't that I was completely mistaken about her. It was that I have recreated her now in terms of a new understanding. She has become part of my legend.

LK: It's interesting to note, too, that in your later poems powerful, combative women suddenly appear. In addition, in the poem "King of the River," sexuality is fused with spirituality in a new way: The speaker of that poem suddenly has a new kind of power or authority. Do you recognize that?

Kunitz: One of my friends said that the surprising thing about that poem is that you can't tell which is the salmon and which is me. I think there is that absolute fusion. And I remember feeling that I was really fighting upstream all the way through that poem, that I was inhabiting that flesh, battering the dam.

LK: I made a list of the insects and animals you've brought into your poems since you started publishing. You began with worms and dragonflies, then went to rodents, birds, a raccoon, and finally a whale. Looking at the list (which could be considered a kind of bestiary), I felt that as you moved closer to yourself, the animals became larger and more complex, too.

Kunitz: I suppose I am closer to women and animals than I am to any other category of living creature. I was brought up in a household of women. There wasn't a male presence around and it seems to run through a whole life pattern. Come to think of it, I have, through my marriages, one daughter who is the mother of two daughters. My wife, Elise, through another marriage, has one daughter and three granddaughters. We are a family of women.

LK: The animals, though, seem to offer you a way to access your unconscious. And the remarkable thing is that as you develop and become more complex the animals you select do, too. They reflect your development.

Kunitz: In a way that's what happens in "The Raccoon Journal." At the end of that poem, I recognize that these threatening creatures are coming home. They're coming home to me. Their wilderness is mine.

LK: Appraising your work, I was struck by the spirit, I believe, of intense formality that was there in the beginning. In later work, however, the speaker becomes more open, vulnerable to experience. The poems with animals are an example. In them or through them, you are given remarkable clues to the nature of your existence.

Kunitz: They give me access, I think, to the netherworld like those snakes in my garden.

LK: "The Snakes of September" is a remarkable poem, too, because it is full of praise. That happens only in your most recent work. You see the garden through fresh eyes.

Kunitz: A lot of real love has gone into that garden.

LK: Tell me a little bit about how you started gardening and, in particular, when you started this garden.

Kunitz: I've always been a gardener. I started this garden in 1962. It was a barren sand hill fronting on the bay, on Cape Cod, with not even a blade of grass growing. It was pure sand on a steep declivity. And I began leveling it, brick by brick, into terraces. It's the only way I could contain the sand. Then I started reconstituting the soil with infusions of seaweed, compost, and peat moss. So much of my spirit and love have gone into that plot of ground that I don't separate it from my poems. I think of it as being just one more aspect of my creative life. And every other summer a hurricane just simply devastates it. I don't know what's going to come back next spring. So I have to start over again. And though it really crushes me, in a way, I experience a kind of joy in thinking: Now I am free to make it better. I'll rebuild it, I'll start again. I'll put in more beautiful plants, more beautiful shrubs and trees. This time it will be absolutely right. And I think that's what one's involvement with the natural world teaches one, a belief in the possibility of renewal, that resurrection principle, that faith that all ends can lead to beginnings.

LK: In previous interviews you've said that the garden has sustained you. How has it sustained you?

Kunitz: That plot of land with which I have such a profound connection and those creatures that inhabit it are, in a sense, the Eden I have made. I'm not a nature poet, but I am a poet of the natural world. And I consider my human affinities as part of that natural world. There's no point at which I say: At this point my garden ends, then my human relations begin. To me it's all one continuous flow of reciprocity. You know, the relationship with the land is a mystical thing. I think this is part of the Jewish experience, too. Historically, through the Diaspora, the Jews left the land and became urban dwellers, but the return to the land in modern times is a manifestation, I think, of a resurrection principle. It has changed the character of the Jewish people. Does that make any sense to you?

LK: Yes, it does. In my bones.

Kunitz: My only visit to Israel was in 1980 and I spent a month there at Mishkenot Sha ananim—that's the name of the lodgings the government provided. And I was overwhelmed by the beauty of the land, and by a sense of this glorious heritage. It didn't make me a Zionist or a nationalist, but it gave me another metaphor for the sense of the layering of history and of the imagination. All those archeological layers, all that digging into the soil on the hills of Jerusalem where Solomon erected his temple, this to me was exactly the way one digs into one's own past in order to find the truth about one's self that's buried there.

LK: Late in life, Stanley, it seems, you've become an elegiac poet.

Kunitz: That's my natural voice, I think.

LK: It's become your voice. It wasn't at the onset.

Kunitz: Well, a young man cannot be elegiac.

LK: What has to occur in one before one can lament?

Kunitz: I think that above all one has to understand that this is a ritual occasion: the lamentation is not for a specific loss. It is for yourself and for all the generations. Every act of mourning is like the saying of a prayer that generation after generation repeats. Every act of mourning is the same act and will be repeated *ad infinitum* as long as there are persons on earth who live and grieve. So it becomes part of racial memory: We grieve for all our ancestors and for ourselves at the same time. And that embrace, that cosmic embrace, is really what in one's youth one cannot possibly understand. As Virgil said, "lacrimae rerum," the tears of things.

LK: In his explication of "River Road," a later poem, Gregory Orr remarked that after many readings a key stanza in the poem refused to fully unfold its meaning and remained, in his words, "clear and cryptic." I was struck by that phrase and thought it might characterize a significant aspect of your recent work. For instance, you started out writing elaborate, oblique, hard to penetrate poems; poems that were more cryptic than clear. But in recent years, you've swung the other way. Your poems now have clear, accessible surfaces. It is only on closer examination, as Orr shows, that they reveal their elusive, many-layered selves. Is it fair then to describe your poems as clear and cryptic?

Kunitz: I would hope that's true. Certainly, my aspiration is to write poems that seem to be immediately accessible, yet when you go back, you find that there are levels that you hadn't first understood: It isn't the same poem you read the first time. So I say, "This is a very simple poem. Why don't you understand it?" Well, the truth is I don't even understand it myself, because often when I go back to my poems, I discover allusions, little linkages, that I had absolutely no awareness of at the time of writing the poem. I like to go beyond my own conscious awareness in search of materials that haven't yet revealed themselves to me. And the work of the imagination is to compel them to reveal their meaning, to seduce them so they become part of your awareness instead of part of your dark underself.

LK: The father quest started for you in futility. You searched for a father who would provide help in your pursuit of an identity, but the father you found in "Father and Son" couldn't respond. In a later poem, "Quinnapoxet," the father does respond. Not with practical advice, but with personal recognition. Where are you now in the father quest? Can you say?

Kunitz: In a way I have become the father. How that recognition resolves itself imaginatively, I don't know. Isn't that one of the challenges of poetry? You write your poems in order to find out what you mean, who you are. You're always working out of a cloud of unknowing in the hope of moving into a little area of light. I can't tell how many poems are left in me, but I'm aware of a blind stirring that leads me on. The curious thing, when I consider the course of my life, is that I have begun at this age to think of myself as a reasonably happy person. I wonder if I could ever have said that before.

Stanley Kunitz: "The Gifts of the Heart Are Always Added to Our Store"

Christopher Busa / 1992

Provincetown Arts 6 (1992), 6–14. Reprinted with permission of Christopher Busa.

Christopher Busa: After going to two of your readings in the last few months, in Provincetown and New York, I noticed that both times you read "An Old Cracked Tune." Is that poem now part of your repertoire?
Stanley Kunitz: Yes.

CB: "Solomon Levi" was a name that echoed in a distant time, in the teens of this century when you also were in your teens. He was a figure in an offensive street song that mocked a little Jewish tailor, depicted as a scoundrel. You remembered the tune and some of the words. When you wrote the poem, in the early seventies, you appropriated the first line of the song, "My name is Solomon Levi." Why?
SK: It's an extraordinary coincidence. My father's name was Solomon, and he was a Levite, a member of the long line of the priestly house of Levi. In Jewish tradition the given name and lineage are passed on from father to son. Why I should have remembered the name of Solomon Levi and virtually nothing else from the song, except its tone, its nasty tone, is of some significance. It's taken me years to understand why I had to write that poem.

CB: The connection occurred to me when I was reading the interview Bill Moyers did with you for public television. For some reason, I checked on your father's name, which is never mentioned in any of the poems you have written over the years about your father, who killed himself a few weeks before you were born. In "An Old Cracked Tune" you align yourself very clearly with the marginal figure, the outcast, yet define some enduring value which transcends marginality. The poem is as condensed as a stone.

SK: That's why I've been opening my readings with it.

CB: To the question, "Who are you?" the poem replies, "I am this person." But a decade passed before you began to claim it as a key poem.
SK: Sometimes you don't know at the time of writing how central a poem is. The effort, above all, is to discover, step by step, the spirit that answers to your name, to discover it and reveal it. In the workings of time you gradually fasten on a dozen or so poems, a small cluster bonded to one another and to your most secret self.

CB: In "The Long Boat" you say of the drifting voyager: "As if it didn't matter . . . as if he didn't know." You emphasize the *as if* condition of knowledge about dying.
SK: The danger was in sounding sententious, rhetorical. What I was saying had to be qualified, so that it would fit more easily into the flow of the passage, not produce the effect of someone hammering a point, trying to nail it down. To say, "he loved the earth so much/ he wanted to stay forever" is very different from saying "as if he didn't know/ he loved the earth so much/ he wanted to stay forever." It's more muted, more delicate and suggestive.

CB: It allows you to represent two states of consciousness within the poem. The dying figure is contained by another imagination which conceives of its existence.
SK: It tends to separate the author of the poem from the subject of the poem. It creates aesthetic distance. The poet as writer doesn't want to be identified completely with the self as subject. The poem is, after all, an aesthetic object. Some separation is necessary between poem and self.

CB: Which is why you have always resented some critical descriptions of your later poetry as "confessional."
SK: If you are fully a confessional poet, the chances are you're writing bad poems. Even in the church that ordains the confession of sins, it is a private and formal practice.

CB: In that uncanny love poem called "The Abduction," I marvel at how a legend is constructed organically from the seed of an "event" that may have been a hallucination, a rape, or a UFO abduction. You say, "Between us, through the years,/ from bits, from broken clues/ we pieced enough together/ to make the story real." You hold this woman in your arms while she sleeps, then you wake to a flood of memory from your own dreams. The two selves, at once intimate and alien to each other, merge in a common cry, "What do we know/ beyond the rapture and the dread?"

SK: The poem, even for me, has its mysteries. The speaker is trying to understand the enigma of his beloved's existence. She is the one who has been spirited away. She may be the soul of the poet. Like Eurydice or Proserpine, she has been to a kind of hell. How can you ever quite reconcile yourself to the other; the lover who has exists behind the veil of absence, separation, and, presumably, experience of evil?

CB: A new poem, "In a Dark House," has an epigraph by Primo Levi, whom you have referred to as "survivor of Auschwitz, eternal witness, presumptive suicide." Without the epigraph, one might never think it was about the Holocaust, as well as about Orpheus and Eurydice.

SK: The myth illuminates the modern instance, just as the modern instance illuminates the myth. Having lived in hell, how can one return to humanity? Orpheus went down into hell to bring his beloved back. In the familiar myth, after Orpheus played his lyre for Pluto, pouring out his grief and yearning, Eurydice was restored to him. On one condition: she would follow him towards earth, out of hell, but he must not look back. In my version, as she nears deliverance, trailing behind him, she realizes that she has already been destroyed. Therefore she cries out to him. Naturally, Orpheus looks back, and she is immediately whisked away, lost forever.

CB: She was the one who provoked Orpheus?

SK: Because she knew that she could not return to the land of the living. Orpheus, too, has been to hell, and the dark house that he occupies, waiting his doom, is his hell on earth. The poem has a complicated structure, but you don't need an interpreter to understand it. You follow the action, that's all.

CB: For you the essence is that when Orpheus goes back to earth, it is as if the present he encounters, such as it is, constitutes not life, but an afterlife.

SK: That's right. To me, this myth, like all myths, has to be examined at its core to understand its implications. All the myths that perpetuate themselves take on new meanings with the evolution of history. History adds to their significance. What the Nazi death camps signify for us is that human beings have an infinite capacity for evil. You don't have to go underground to find hell. It is here. As Christopher Marlowe wrote four centuries ago, "Where we are is hell."

CB: In our culture's thinking about hell you go there because you've done bad things. Whereas we are talking about victims. They were punished not for what they did, but for who they were.

SK: *Some* of those who survived could not rid themselves of an intolerable sense of shame for having been spared the common lot. Had they done unholy things to save their skins? Perhaps they had sought to become invisible when others were being herded into the gas chambers; or, even worse, had tried to ingratiate themselves with their tormentors, instead of spitting in their faces. Their guilt feelings were a way of coming to terms with an abomination that neither reason nor faith could explain or justify.

CB: A horrible psychological impasse. This situation of being taken from life to hell replicates the situation in "The Abduction," where the beloved is haunted over a lifetime by a horror greater than the story created to remember it.

SK: All one's poems have linkages.

CB: The legendary "dark period" in your life occurred between 1930 and 1944, the fourteen years that spanned the publication of your first and second books of poetry.

SK: In 1930 I was twenty-five, trying to survive in the midst of the Depression on a hundred-acre farm in Connecticut that I had bought for three thousand dollars, with a five hundred–dollar down payment—a fair price then, considering the condition of the property and the state of the economy. With a yoke of white oxen I cultivated the stony fields on top of Wormwood Hill, raising food and forage for domestic use and herbs for the market. Freelancing helped me pay the mortgage; but it was a struggle. Although my first collection of poems had been favorably reviewed on publication, I was cut off from the literary world. And I was going through the trials of a first marriage that was doomed to fail.

CB: You left that hundred-acre farm after the 1938 hurricane destroyed all your sugar maples, moving to a fifteen-acre property in Bucks County, Pennsylvania. Your present garden, in Provincetown, is a mere quarter-acre.

SK: I have always enjoyed grubbing in the dirt, organizing a portion of this whirling planet. It's true, as you indicate, that I began big and gradually dwindled. Contrary to the general impression, space in a garden simplifies your task. You can allocate areas to lie fallow, as the season progresses. A smaller garden is a much more intensive affair: it must be designed so that every section of it, going through its changes, gives continual pleasure. But any garden is a testing-ground, a metaphor for survival.

CB: Some plants, like poems, must be pruned, others removed.

SK: As you imply, neither gardeners nor poets can afford to be sentimentalists. A garden is more than a show of gaudy plants. It's a work of the imagination, whose ultimate beauty lies in its total design. And yet—this is a nice paradox—the design must not be so rigidly formal as to reduce the landscape to a state of conspicuous artifice. I like a garden that speaks of caring hands and that hints at the presence of a master plan but still looks free, adventurous, improvisational. Somehow that takes me back to the seventeenth century and "Delight in Disorder," one of the very first lyrics to excite me; maybe because of its erotic underpinning. No combination of qualities tempts me more—in gardens, poems, people, even ideas—than what Robert Herrick termed a "wild civility?" He was a country vicar, by the way, who wrote some wonderfully naughty verses.

CB: Do you have any advice on how the poet may operate ideologically, politically in the world?

SK: If the objective is how to prosper, no advice from me is likely to prove helpful. The truth is that poets in this country have lost connection with the dominant myth, the mystique of success and power. Whether or not we find it comfortable, our significant identification is with the American subculture and the disenfranchised of this earth. I don't know what stronger political statement we can make than to choose to live from day to day as vessels of the compassionate imagination, telling as honestly as we can how it feels to be alive in our time.

CB: When you were a young man, fresh out of college and needing to work for a living, you conceived and began compiling a famous set of biographical reference works, the Wilson Author Series. There was nothing like it in existence. Writing and editing these literary biographies, one or two thousand words each, must have taught you essential lessons about how a whole life can be contained in a short compass. Sometimes I think poetry, like biography, is a type of nonfiction writing.

SK: All creative writing is fiction, a distillation and transformation of reality. That's what makes it a work of art.

CB: Periodically, since the beginning of your career, some of your best poems have concerned themselves with the father and son relationship. When you were twenty-four you pledged to go "unburdened, on the quiet lane," until "shadowless/ With inner light I wear my father's face." What prompted you, sixty years later, to write your essay, "The Quest for the Father"?

SK: Naturally, it was something I'd been thinking about for a long time. When Jason Shinder's *Divided Light*, an anthology of son poems, appeared several years ago, I attempted to clarify my thinking on the subject.

CB: The Freudians may not agree with you when you argue that the son is not after his father's scalp.

SK: Since they accept the theory of the Oedipus complex as gospel, they think it's natural for the son to want to kill his father.

CB: The circumstances of your father's suicide, which occurred after you were conceived but before you were born, may have spared you from patricidal desires. There was no father to kill. But in your essay you said the situation of the lost father was common to a significant number of twentieth-century poets.

SK: As I pointed out in that piece, "lost" can have several different meanings. It can be death, abandonment, divorce. It can be spiritual separation. Remember, this is an era of great wars. More people have been killed in the twentieth century than at any other time in the history of the race. The killing still goes on. In the aftermath of the Industrial Revolution, parents are detached from the dwelling place and doomed to spend their days in the marketplace. The child is left alone or in the custody of strangers. So isolation, separation, loneliness, and deprivation are multiplied. In that extended sense, the lost father has been one of the dominant themes of modern art and literature, something intimately connected with the nature of the creative impulse itself. How can we make ourselves whole when we are separated from our source? The imagination sets out in search of the father in order to heal a psychic wound. Ideally, the quest ends in an embrace.

CB: When Dante and Beatrice rise to the Heaven of the Moon, they enter a pearl-like substance which encloses them "Within itself, as water of a well/ Receives, remaining whole, a ray of light." Here light is not divided from its substance. How did you become conscious that the burden of your past was a source of enormous wealth to you?

SK: It didn't happen all at once. A door opened, and there was always another door behind it. I learned through my poems what my dreams were trying to tell me.

CB: In your poem "The Illumination" you refer remorsefully to "the parent I denied." Which parent did you have in mind?

SK: It could only have been my mother since she was a living symbol of the ties of blood that chafed me, the possessiveness and constraints inherent in the family structure, whereas my father had escaped into the wilderness of mythology. The words of mine you quote should not be taken literally. They relate to a symbol more than to a person. Intuitively I knew that a soul has to leave its nest before it can fly free. My mother had known that, too, when she fled the Old World in her youth, to seek a new life on these shores. At seventeen, when I read, in *Portrait of the Artist as a Young Man*, Stephen Dedalus's impassioned disavowal of family and church and state—"I will not serve that in which I do not believe"—my heart sang with the recognition that he was speaking for me. But as Joyce himself discovered, there is a law of return written in our destiny. Sooner or later we need to go back and reclaim the abandoned territory of our heritage.

CB: An early poem, "The Words of the Preacher," argues that man is doomed by piecemeal living. In a dream the youthful preacher, living "all my life at once" has a vision of the future in which he will "vie with God for His eternity." A later poem, the magnificent "King of the River," sheds the direct statement of this extravagant ambition. Instead, through the weave of the strange logic of a carefully controlled conditional syntax, with its suspensions circling between the salmon's instinct to spawn and die and the poet's effort to identify himself with the subject, this poem enacts in its language the very trajectory of the fish's life cycle.

SK: A major difference between that early poem and the later one is that the former is spun out of air, whereas "King of the River" is immersed in the body. That suspended, circling rhythm took hold of me and made me its vehicle, everything flowing out of the one word "if." The poem is all in the process.

CB: The poem opens, "If the water were clear enough,/ if the water were still,/ but the water is not clear/ the water is not still." The fish cannot see how he is changing, but somebody does.

SK: A certain ambiguity in the point of view is an intrinsic element of the poem's architecture. Poet and fish are linked to each in the same biological chain of being. As I perceive them, they share a common destiny and in the fulfillment of it, appear as interchangeable protagonists. Perhaps the salmon battering upstream to spawn and die is the real poet in "King of the River."

CB: Over the years your prosody has removed the old shoes of its metrical feet. It has metamorphosed into an organic stressing that follows footsteps made by the breath unit.

SK: Part of the secret of musicality *is* the fluctuation of the movement of the breath units, the variability of pitch and tempo playing against the hard beats. I try to let my poems find their own rhythm in response to internal pressures of thought and feeling. The sound of a poem is the first clue to its validity. I can tell if a poem of mine is really rolling when I begin to hear the syllables calling to one another as birds do at dawn.

CB: It is interesting that after having spent a lifetime turning your life into poetic legend, you now seem to be deliberately turning to classic myths for the source of poems.

SK: I don't think of it as a radical conversion. Myth has always fascinated me, as is evident in a number of my poems dating as far back as my first collection. Yeats once said, "All that is personal soon rots; it must be packed in ice or salt. Ancient salt is best packing." The difference between legend and myth is one of scale: myth is a larger vision and sheds a grander light. Implicit in my poems is a recognition that the self being explored is not the same as a daily self, but a deeper and truer self, a distillation of all one ever was and hopes to be. Art is a transformational process. The self one seeks in poems is one's own archetype.

CB: The human being who has developed the relation of his individual self to his archetypal self may have the humanity required for cooperation between nations. Do you think we'll ever have a world government?

SK: Certainly not in my lifetime, or yours. The institutions that run this world are not in business for the greater good of mankind, and they have no intention of dissolving peacefully. Despite rumors to the contrary, there is still an imperialism of great powers over the weak, of the rich over the poor, of soulless bureaucracies over individual freedoms. Tremendous social and political changes seem more or less inevitable in the century ahead of us, but we won't get the beautiful world we dream of without a revolution of the spirit.

CB: Some people feel that the Gulf War demonstrated the possibility of international cooperation, through the United Nations, to achieve peace and justice.

SK: In my opinion the Gulf War was one of the most dangerous episodes in American history and a bad omen for the future. It was an unholy alliance based on greed and lies, fought mainly for oil, in the interest of oligarchies that mock every democratic principle. The administration controlled the press and hoodwinked the American people. We are told it was a sanitary war because only 150 or so Americans were lost, as if the hundreds of thousands of dead Iraqi soldiers and civilians, including defenseless women and children—who knows exactly how many?—don't really count. And the irony is that the monster we secretly helped to create and then pledged to destroy because he was "worse than Hitler" is still head of state, presiding over the ruins.

CB: You don't have an optimistic point of view for the immediate future. What will be the artist's role in the sort of world you foresee?

SK: Precisely what it has always been: to suffer history and to bear witness. And to keep alive the vision of human possibility.

CB: In the intellectual climate of your formative years, T. S. Eliot prevailed with his theory that the poem is the product of the mind that creates, not of the man who suffers.

SK: Eliot's premise, that there was no significant connection between the life of the poet and the work of his imagination, was treated as literary gospel. It became a cornerstone of the New Criticism. Overnight, subjective poetry fell out of fashion. I couldn't understand why a theory so obviously false could be taken so seriously. My own conjecture was that Eliot's effort to depersonalize the artist must have been motivated by a desire to defend his private life from scrutiny. Now that we know the circumstances of his domestic situation, we can see why he was so self-protective. I haven't heard any talk about depersonalization in years.

CB: It is peculiar that the two most influential theories of literary criticism in your lifetime, the New Criticism and Deconstruction, deny the life of the artist by asserting the primacy of the text. That invites an institutionalized, academic control over the text, because control over the life of the artist is impossible. Aside from your work as an editor, which you did largely freelance, you made no bonding alliances with institutions.

SK: I tend to distrust institutions and the institutional character of so much modern art. Academic critics don't know what to do with me, since I don't fit easily into any familiar category, any recognizable school of poets. I don't follow the fashions. I'm not even part of the establishment that, to a degree, has taken me in. At this age nothing is going to dislodge me from my observation post on the edge of the road.

CB: A position you have incorporated into your aesthetic. Worse than to be shunned maybe to be embraced by the insiders!
SK: Marginality suits me.

CB: In Provincetown, we have the Fine Arts Work Center, a residency program for the support and fostering of new talents among artists and writers. You had much to do with its founding and have remained a guiding spirit. There's an institution created by and for individuals.
SK: Respect for the individual is what keeps it alive. That's the secret of the Work Center. It has to be fought for. Like every other arts organization in the country these days, it is having its fiscal problems. The real danger for an institution of any kind, as it matures, is in losing its original freshness and initiative, its sense of joyous adventure—that is, acquiring a bureaucratic mindset, becoming, in short, institutional. As we enter our twenty-fifth year, I am confident of the Work Center's capacity for renewal and survival. It won't be permitted to languish or fail, simply because it means too much.

CB: You are a father figure to many fine poets, male and female, especially to those who have taken your various poetry workshops over the years since you first began teaching. The obvious thing to say is that, fatherless yourself, you compensated by becoming a father for another generation.
SK: Student poets who fall into a master-disciple relationship should beware of Cronus, who devoured his young. I don't really think of the ones you referred to as my children, and certainly not as my disciples or imitators. They are my friends and companions, part of my world of affection and discovery, and I do not doubt that I have learned as much from them as they may have learned from me.

CB: Although giving of the self may not involve a lot of time, many artists have been known to be monsters of pride and selfishness.
SK: Unfortunately, some people think of life as a zero-sum game: whatever we give, we lose. Whereas, in truth, the gifts of the heart are always added to our store.

An Interview with Stanley Kunitz

Donald G. Parker and Joan I. Siegel / 1993

An abridged version of the following interview appeared in *Wordsmith: A Journal of Poetry and Art* (1994): 2–5. The longer version below is a based on a typescript of the more complete interview, reprinted with the permission of Donald G. Parker.

On November 22, 1993, Stanley Kunitz visited Orange County Community College, Middletown, New York. During the afternoon he conducted a question and answer session with students and later presented a formal reading to the college community. Earlier that day the editors conducted an interview with Kunitz.

Q: In the epigraph to your first book, *Intellectual Things*, you quoted Blake's line "For the tear is an intellectual thing," implying the inseparability of passions and the intellect. How was that received by the critics?

SK: That title was completely misunderstood. They thought I was separating poetry from emotion, whereas I meant to identify that the two coalesce.

Q: In regard to a separation that you condone, you have advised young poets *not* to teach right away. What did you mean exactly?

SK: I feel rather strongly that one of the problems with contemporary poetry is that it has become relegated to the academy. And most poets feel quite content with that situation, but I think it exacts a considerable cost. I look for a poetry that is more involved with the world at large and that doesn't require an academic mediator to understand it, to interpret it, as is so often the case. It's unfortunate that so many of the gifted young, once they enter into the academic stream, never leave it. They go through college and they go to graduate school to get their MFA degree; then they become teaching assistants and become again involved for their subsistence with the academy. They become academic dependents. And it is inevitable that the academy assumes priority in their intellectual life, which to a great extent explains why the mass of our population feels that poetry, contemporary poetry, has so little to say to them. Such poets don't feel as involved with the masses' struggle to understand who they are, how to survive in the modern world, how to react to the tragedies of existence and to all the questions of injustice, bigotry, and intolerance in every form. Unfairness in the economic system, for example. You would think that none of these problems exists if you read most of the poetry that is published today. And not that I think that poetry has to become partisan and political in its theme, but there should be an awareness in the poet of what goes on in the world and some reaction to it, and that experience will color the work and give it that quality of the compassionate imagination that I think is the essence of true poetry.

Q: You have said that because William Carlos Williams existed outside the academic realm, he was never fully recognized despite his compassionate imagination.
SK: True. That explains why during his lifetime, though he had many admirers among his contemporaries in the world of poetry, he was dismissed from academic programs and criticism.

Q: One problem with the American audience is that since it is turned off by academic poetry, it turns to popular culture instead and gets its values and sense of beauty from that source, unfortunately.
SK: Of course, I think that is not to be completely dismissed. Popular culture has its place in the whole complex of the arts. And if there is no popular culture, there is no culture. So that it is to me somewhat of an encouraging sign that there is so much proliferation, for example, of poetry on the fringe . . . cafe poetry, such things as poetry slams, that sort of thing . . . the upsurge of ethnic poetry. All this is to be encouraged, and the absence of it from traditional poetry makes it important. Eventually this fringe is training an audience—just as popular song does—that at least has a rudimentary recognition of the pleasure of verse, of something that isn't quite like prose even though it is not high poetry at all. And eventually . . . well, if all things turn out well, some of the values inherent in that fringe poetry will enter into the mainstream, just as, for example, in the early history of English poetry, in the fourteenth, fifteenth, and sixteenth centuries, the ballads were an influential popular medium. They belonged to the oral tradition just as so much of the fringe poetry of our time belongs to the oral tradition. Such poetry was dismissed as being vulgar and in a sense a product of the ignorant and the lower classes, but it eventually entered the whole stream of poetry and

was largely responsible for the great poems that came out of the Romantic movement, which were fed by the ballads, so there is an interesting historical reference there.

Nobody spends a life in poetry in order to say nothing. The *desperate* effort is to find an audience, and the hope is that there will be a meeting, one of these days, where the mass of American society will respond to poetry as larger communities did in the past where you had a more homogeneous society. One of the problems today is the fracturing of our society, the distance between people of different educational backgrounds, different ethnic backgrounds, different opportunities for education, and so forth. We live in a much more varied and difficult and multiple society than any people on earth ever did before, and we have to keep that in mind when we approach the modern arts.

Q: So perhaps rap music is providing part of the foundation for our future.
SK: Who knows? Nobody can ever predict these things. It's certainly not going to replace the poetry of the great tradition, but it may very well charge it with some new energy. High art needs, let's say, low art (I don't mean that in a dismissive way) to reinvigorate it, to make it closer to common speech, to the common need for an expressive voice of ordinary lives. This is what poetry, even in so-called higher art, *can* do and *must* do if it is going to survive, and one way of doing so is to assimilate low art, fringe art, and to become more available, more accessible and, at the same time, not to degrade the art itself. It is possible to write poetry that touches the human heart and not to betray the high destiny of art. I believe that firmly, and in my own practices have tried to do exactly that. But it is difficult to do so and it is certainly not what one generally thinks of as being the fashionable art of the day, but forget about fashion.

My remark about the cafe poets was not to compare them with Shakespeare and Milton and Keats or anyone else. They are part of the whole stream of poetry that flows through our time, that flows through the ages, and eventually it becomes one stream. In the end they feed into the mainstream. They themselves will not be remembered, but they are parts of the whole activity of poetry, and they are, in a way, like the foot soldiers in the military. We need them too; you cannot win the war without the widespread conviction that there is something attractive, delightful, pleasurable in language itself—at any level, but especially when language is used at its best, with precision, which is what Blake meant when he said, "Grandeur of ideas is founded on precision of speech; art and science cannot exist but in minutely organized particulars." We are told that the devil is in the details, but God is in the details too.

Q: In your essay "Poet and State," you spoke about the poet as opposed to the prose writer, the novelist, the playwright, and you mentioned the sculptor and other artists who, unlike these three, were not creating for profit and were committed to the art and thus freer in that sense.

SK: The very fact that poetry is a noncommercial product makes it feasible for the poet to insist on perfection—purity—in other words, to look for the ideal rather than for the marketable.

Q: In the mid-1970s you wrote that, in contrast to your early work, you were aiming for a style characterized by organic form and immediate feeling. Is that still your ideal? How did you come to this determination? At what point in your career did you decide that a change of style was necessary?

SK: It was a slowly evolving concept. Gradually I became dissatisfied with the complication, artifice, and formalism of the high style. I wanted a more direct line of communication with the rest of humanity. The idea of a hermetic art no longer attracted me. In a passage later than the one you've cited I speculated on the possibility, beyond simplicity, of an art so transparent that one could look through it and see the world. I look back at certain early poems and see that I was already exploring that terrain in the late 1920s.

Q: To pursue this point about the ideal poem, the characteristics quoted do seem to describe the best poems in *The Testing-Tree* and the volumes that followed that.

SK: I hope so.

Q: That seems to be a way of looking at those. The rigorousness is there in form, yet there is this other way of approaching the subject.

SK: I think also that explains the difference between the poetry of my youth and the poetry of more recent years, in that it is not only a change in form and in mode of address. But it is, I hope, a more direct access to my inner voice that is not confused by too much reliance on the academic tradition. What I seek is direct access to my most interior thoughts and feelings.

Q: They don't seem to be compromised at all by the academic tradition.

SK: That's the hope. Naturally there are successes and failures, but that is certainly the aspiration. One of my dear friends among the poets, now alas

gone, Robert Lowell, said to me once, "Stanley, I don't so much write poems, I rewrite them." Well, that's true of me too. A poem rests on several
psychological, psychic textures, different levels. For example, my poem "The
Wellfleet Whale" seems to be a narrative of a whale that is beached on the
shore of Cape Cod, but if you go back to that poem, you'll find that much
else is going on. Though it can be read solely at that narrative level, it still
has a drama to convey. Let me give you some idea of how that poem came
into being. In 1966 a friend of mine called me up from Wellfleet, on the Cape
(I live part of the year in Provincetown), and said, "There's a tremendous
whale on the beach here—you'll want to see it." I immediately got into the
car and drove there. The whale was lying on the beach, and over the course
of that day and the next, it slowly died. When I got home, I made an entry
in my journal describing exactly how I had stroked the whale and how I had
felt the life inside as it was lying there. And I knew that there was a poem
there for me, but it took me fifteen years before I could write that poem. I
had to find not only a language, but I had to find a form that would express
all the thoughts that I had kept taking notes on through the years, yet I
couldn't find an entrance into that poem until one day it occurred to me
that this was a narrative structure that lent itself absolutely directly to the
tenets of Greek tragedy—the whole architecture of the Greek tragic poets
and dramatists (Sophocles, in particular). I could construct this narrative
in terms of Greek tragedy, but few readers would ever guess, since I give no
indication, that this is what I'm doing. But this is my whole breakup of that
poem, into the different parts of Greek tragedy. Once I had that intuition
about the formal nature of the poem, I was able to begin writing. But you
don't have to know anything about that; that's of no interest to you unless
you happen to be a student of drama or a poet, but for the reader, what is in
that poem is what strikes home to you and you get as much out of it as you
can. If there are mysteries, there should be mysteries. One of my thoughts
about poetry is that a poem must hold on to its secrets; it must never be
completely exposed, laid out on the table like a hunk of beef. It is something
that you need to explore, and it is the tension between what is revealed on
the surface and what is beneath the surface that keeps that energy flowing
out of the work itself.

Q: John Unterecker, in the mid-1980s, commented on your thrifty production, and you say somewhere that you envy prolific poets.
SK: Naturally! But with my mode of production it would be inconceivable
that I could be a highly prolific poet. A poem is a result of not only hours,

but days, weeks, months, sometimes years of reflection—in an effort to get at the essence, "the terrible crystal," a phrase I like about the heart of the poem that lies buried often, too often, under the artifice of the linguistic construction.

Q: Well, Unterecker wasn't being critical; he much admired the end result.
SK: I didn't take it as a negative comment. The fortunate aspect of that mode, as far as I'm concerned, is that I've lived long enough to turn out a rather respectable quantity of poems. One of my remarks on that subject is that my whole sense of a life in poetry is that it isn't a sprint but a marathon.

Different poets have different ways of writing. Some poets write out of the moment's impulse. Some poets put down the words that come to them and never touch the poem again. They're the lucky ones. I don't belong to that group; I have to dig for my poems. It's a long process, as I indicated about "The Wellfleet Whale." I am concerned with establishing connections between what goes on in the world and what goes on inside me. In other words, making that reconciliation between self and cosmos. I'm a poet who will sit ten to twelve hours at my desk and produce one line maybe, or perhaps not even that. I'm a poet who cannot write a poem before midnight. All my poems are written between midnight and dawn. I need the world to be quiet; I need to be completely immersed in the inner self, the consuming element. And the first draft of my poems, I deplore; they have intimations of what I am striving for, but only intimations. Then I must go back again and go through that whole process of finding. I am not so good at writing occasional poems or little verses. A few times in my life a poem has come to me completely, and that's like receiving a blessing from the divine being; you don't expect it and you shouldn't expect it. If you keep waiting for it, you'll never write another poem.

Q: You also make a distinction somewhere in your essays between poetry as a career and as a life. One of your "unshakable convictions" is that writing poetry has to be one's life, not a vocation. When did you know that you were committed to that extent?
SK: By my early teens I was already involved with reading poetry, reading and scribbling, but not daring to dream of more. At that age, I certainly had very little discrimination as to what I read. I read everything and gradually established a standard of value and began to separate what could be important to me from what was merely attractive versification. Another one of my very earliest poets that I learned by heart was Robert Service, of all people.

So, I think this revelation may have some lesson in terms of instruction to the young: not to be too managerial in one's approach to reading. Let them forage for themselves and find out who speaks to them, and if they become involved, gradually they will establish a certain set of values. They will be able to discriminate between the inferior and the superior in terms of their own lives.

Q: Were you already reading Keats as a teenager?

SK: Yes. When I was thirteen, a friend of the family gave me the complete works of Wordsworth and I became very attached to that book. It meant a great deal to me. Then I gradually took on all the rest of the Romantic poets, and Keats I began to read maybe a year or two later, but he did not become important to me until my early twenties, I would say. I went on to college in 1922; I was seventeen, and the teaching of poetry at Harvard then was certainly limited by academic taste. The last poet to be studied in the course in English poetry was Kipling, my twelve-year-old favorite, and the last American in the course on American poetry was Amy Lowell. There were no poets after that.

Q: That was the year "The Waste Land" was published. Were you aware of that poem in 1922?

SK: I was certainly was. I acquired that issue of *The Dial*, in which it first appeared in this country, and in fact I wrote, against the wishes and against the objections of the Harvard English faculty, I wrote my honors thesis on the techniques of modern poetry and included Eliot, Pound, William Carlos Williams, Joyce, Proust, and Gerard Manley Hopkins. They were aghast!

Q: As an academic exercise that must have been a good one.

SK: I've been looking for that piece, but I haven't been able to find it. I have such an accumulation of documents that I haven't come across it. Several have asked to see it and to publish it now after all those years. I still wonder what I actually said, but I think that my approach would not have changed much in all those years.

Q: Did you have any remarkable teachers of poetry at Harvard?

SK: No. But I suppose that may be too uncharitable because I did have John Livingston Lowes, who was excellent on the Romantic poets and especially on Coleridge; he wrote the great first book on Coleridge's imagination. But I think that really was the only teacher I had who in any way affected me. The poets I discovered I found in the stacks of the Widener Library. I can still re-member the day I discovered Hopkins, the first edition of his poems, which had never been taken out. That *really* changed my whole feeling about po-etry, the possibility of poetry in the modern age and though I had and have no religion, the intensity of his conviction, the intensity of his spiritual life, shook my world.

Q: How about your peers at Harvard? Did you meet poets at Harvard during that time?

SK: There were no poets at Harvard during my undergraduate days. I can-not think of anyone. I had one friend, Daniel Catton Rich, who became an artist or curator, who did have a feeling for poetry. Then in my graduate year there was Countee Cullen, but he was already an established poet and he certainly didn't seem to represent the modern writer at that point in history. Cummings, of course, was not around. He belonged to Eliot's generation. And the faculty dismissed Cummings and Eliot as traitors to the tradition. It now seems very strange.

Q: Did you write for the *Crimson* at all?

SK: No, I did not write for the *Crimson*, or the *Advocate*, the *Lampoon*. I felt very much on the margins of that Harvard world at that point. Remember this was a period when there was a two percent quota for Jews at Harvard. One felt (especially a scholarship student, which I was) that to be both poor and Jewish at Harvard was to be outside the pale.

Q: You have written that you were even discouraged from applying for a teaching post because you were Jewish. They didn't want a Jew teaching Anglo-Saxons.

SK: Yes. On the basis of my academic record, having graduated *summa cum laude*, I more or less expected to be invited and to stay on and teach.

Q: That was the custom?

SK: Yes, some of my friends among the students, whose records were not quite comparable, were invited, but I wasn't—and when I inquired, I was told, "Our Anglo-Saxon students would resent being taught English by a Jew."

Q: You mentioned you are soon going back to give a reading at Harvard.

SK: Oh, after many years, I'm reading there next week. Their Morris Grey special reading. I have no animosity against current-day Harvard, a different world, a different institution. But it took *years*. And that wound is still positive—it's covered over by scar tissue.

Q: Like the resounding slap in the face in your poem "The Portrait."
SK: And one can never forget it. I know when I'm reading there that will be in the back of my mind.

Q: Apropos of that experience, you wrote that "No bolder challenge confronts the modern artist than to stay healthy in a sick world."
SK: By staying healthy I mean healthy in character and in belief and in love. I suppose that to me is health.

Q: Was *The Dial* magazine the magazine for you in those days?
SK: It was the only magazine—that and *Poetry* magazine. Plus, one of the first magazines that published me, the Catholic magazine *Commonweal*. Also the *New Republic* and the *Nation*, those were where I first began publishing.

Q: Did you know Malcolm Cowley in those days?
SK: Yes, I didn't know him personally, but I did later. I was so much younger than the people around me then who were publishing that I thought these seniors, "senators," were completely out of my realm; they belonged to a different world. I would never have thought of approaching an older poet to ask for criticism or suggestions or anything else—they to me were unapproachable. It was such a different era. Remember there was no way, unless you happened to be a social friend, there was no way in that period of encountering an older poet, say, Edwin Arlington Robinson. One wouldn't dare to because they belonged to a completely different world. One of the greatest advantages that the young poet has today is access to the older generation of poets and then the benefit of communication about the work. That's the value; the danger is the incestuous quality of that relationship as it has been, more or less, structured by the academy.

Q: Later on you taught "creative writing," a term you don't care for.
SK: It was twenty years after I left college before I even dared to think of returning to the academy, but then I did it on my own terms, which was never to accept tenure, always to be on an annual contract, so I could feel I wasn't completely . . . that I was still an outsider. I remained that way until the end.

Q: Would you comment on your approach to teaching creative writing in terms of, say, the basic ways that you thought you could actually help someone?

SK: Once I began to teach, my first post was at Bennington, in the late 1940s after I got out of the army. I soon discovered that I loved to teach and that it was a precious opportunity for me to explore the nature of the medium and to improve, in the hope of perfecting, my own efforts at writing poetry. But as far as methodology, what I gradually evolved was a very relaxed classroom situation. No great insistence on drills, for example, and no persistent exercise in technique. My feeling has been that technique cannot be separated from the poetic voice as the basis of poetry itself. What I've always insisted on is that though poetry requires craft—and it is impossible to write poetry of first "quality," let's use that word, without some knowledge of the craft—the danger is in thinking that craft is poetry. The basis of poetry is essentially the desire to communicate one's deepest thoughts and feelings, to bear spiritual witness to what it feels like to be alive, and in that effort certainly one calls on one's craft in order to make it possible to convey that voice. But, the important thing is what one is bearing witness to. And without that, craft is merely an unexploited tool.

Q: One of the primary events you have borne witness to is your father's suicide. In his introduction to your poetry, Gregory Orr refers to "father" as a "primary pole" of your imagination. Has writing about your father brought you a sense of acceptance or reconciliation?

SK: There are certain traumatic episodes in life that, if you don't confront them, will overpower and destroy you. Jung said in one of his essays that it is necessary to confront one's childhood in order to mature and in order to become an adult human being. Those of us who have suffered tragic encounters or experiences in our childhood—if we don't confront them in one way or another—will in the end be damaged irreparably. I suppose the greatest trauma of my childhood was the suicide of my father, and that was something that could have either destroyed me or at least have left me crippled in a way if I had not attempted through art to not so much be reconciled to it as to incorporate it into my view of the meaning of my own existence and that of others—in other words, to deal with the whole question of what it is, what it means to us to realize that we are mortal, and most of us, I think, deny that thought. We try to exclude it as though it were somehow dangerous, destructive, impossible to incorporate into our sense of life. It is the task of art to make us confront the worst, the worst conceivable that enters into our thoughts, our dreams, and out of that to compose something that's whole and wholesome, healthy in that it doesn't flinch. Here we are and we have faced this and we stand here and we survive. Art can do that in a way that formerly belonged to religion. I think religion at one time, faith, is what people turned to in order to reconcile themselves to their existence, in order to face the misfortunes of life, and religion still exists for a large portion of the population. But for those who lack a conviction about organized religion or who have a tenuous degree of faith (there are degrees of it), art is the answer to most of the questions that perplex the human mind and inflict themselves on the human heart. So, I would say that poetry is one way of bearing witness, not only to the history of one's time, but also to the history of oneself. And that is its noblest function.

Q: You talked about working between midnight and dawn. What is it that sustains you when you immerse yourself in that destructive/constructive medium you talked about? So that you feel that you can come back out?
SK: Spirit perhaps. I think there is a soul that inhabits the human organism; that soul is, however you define it, present when all the lights are burning. Mind, body, soul—they are not separable activities.

Q: What inspires you to write?
SK: I think I am inspired to write poetry because I love language, I suppose . . . because I love life, I suppose . . . because I don't want to die, I suppose.

Q: What poets inspired you to write? Are there any particular poets that motivated you to pursue a career in poetry?
SK: The poets who have moved me and whom I think of as my ancestors are a varied group. I suppose the first poets . . . when I was still in college, in the stacks at the Widener Library, I encountered four poets who have remained my companions through all these many years. Those four are George Herbert, a seventeenth-century churchman; William Blake, who was a great rebel, a religious poet who said that the reason that Milton wrote badly when he wrote of God and the angels but wrote well of Lucifer, was because like all poets, he was of the devil's party. There is an element of truth in that. The other two are Keats and Gerard Manley Hopkins, a great Jesuit poet of the nineteenth century, who invented a new language and a new rhythm. Then, of course, the moderns came in, while I was still writing my first publishable poems, even before then. They didn't necessarily have to be poets; Joyce was a strong influence on me, as was Kafka. Yeats, among

the Irish Poets. Whitman, later in my life. And Eliot. They certainly made me think about how to write a poem. They are companions, and I go back to them all the time. I think of them as part of my family.

Q: You have from time to time involved yourself in translating poems, especially those of Russian poets. What interests and joys did you discover in those moments?

SK: One of the problems of being a poet for a lifetime is that one tends to get trapped in one's own skin, and one becomes a prisoner of one's own history. In a sense, one becomes a prisoner of all the poems you've written up to that time. Sometimes you have to think that poetry is the enemy of the poem and, to a degree, that's true. The great joy in translation is inhabiting some other poet's skin and perceiving the possibilities of another kind of imagination. I've translated mainly the Russian poets, and each time I come back from doing so it is like coming back from a long voyage, coming back transformed because one stretched one's skin in that process of entering another person's imagination. It isn't so much that you have simply translated word by word the poem in another language: you can do that—all you get then is words. Poems are not merely words. Poems are beyond language, beyond meter. Poetry is part of the human vision, the experience of life. So when I have translated poetry, for example, in my translations of Anna Ahkmatova, a Russian poet who lived through the Stalin era and went through enormous tragic humiliations of every conceivable description—I have changed due to that experience, feeling that I was no longer detached from history. I was involved with it every day and felt part of my dedication must be to interpret the historic process itself . . . in so far as it affected my own generation.

Q: Earlier you briefly mentioned being in the Clinton White House this fall, receiving the National Medal of the Arts, and spending three days in a gala situation. Would you tell about that?

SK: Those three days in Washington ended a continuous round of festivities—rather grand occasions—beginning with a congressional reception. Then on a Wednesday (in early October) there were thirteen recipients of the National Medal of the Arts. The other two writers happened to be old friends: Arthur Miller and William Styron. So they were a big help to me getting through. The ceremonies were on the South Lawn of the White House, and there was a band there and about 750 people. Both Hillary and Bill Clinton did the ceremonial thing. We were back in the White House talking a little while before we went out, and Hillary sort of took care of us on the platform. Among the other recipients were Ray Charles and Cab Calloway. There was a cross-section of the whole creative and performing communities. In any case, Bill Clinton introduced himself as being a frustrated musician and said that he felt that the arts are terribly important, that a democracy cannot exist if the arts aren't encouraged, that the arts are necessary for the health of the nation, and I believe that firmly. Of course, the climax of the day was a state dinner at the White House where my companion at the table was Tipper Gore, who turned out to be very lively. There was a fiddler at each table. It was done very elegantly, the whole thing. In the middle of it, one of the guests rose and began singing spontaneously, and it turned out to be Leontyne Price. Afterwards, there was dancing, and the first couple on the floor were the Clintons. And even I joined in, which indicates either that the liquor was very good or that I was swept away.

An Interview with Stanley Kunitz

Gary Pacernick / 1995

From *Meaning and Memory: Interviews with Fourteen Jewish Poets* (Columbus: Ohio State UP, 2001), 38–47. Reprinted with permission of Ohio State University Press.

Like William Blake, Stanley Kunitz glorifies the role of the poet in the modern world. In our interview, I began by quoting his statement to Bill Moyers that "poetry is the most difficult, the most solitary, and the most life-enhancing thing that one can do in the world." When I asked him to elaborate, he replied, "The experience of love and the creative act are the supreme expressions of the life force. They do more than express it; they refresh and renew it and give it back, magnified."

It is a testimony to the lights of love and poetry that Stanley Kunitz is so energetic, vibrant, and creative in his nineties. In my time with him, I began to feel that every word he used in speech or in writing is meticulously forged and crafted to be the best word possible. Nothing less would do. Our interview went through at least three drafts over several years. The finished document is very different from the original.

Small wonder that Kunitz is not a prolific poet. In our interview, he said that the hardest thing about being a poet is writing the poem and "making it right, in sound and sense; making it whole and true." For many years he was one of the finest practitioners of complex, intricately wrought formal verse. However, with *The Testing Tree* (1971), the reader senses a new, more open and free approach.

For Kunitz, form is not "an end in itself, only a means. Only a means to gain control over language, to make it more sensitive to the modulations of one's thoughts and feelings, to improve its precision so that one won't have to tell lies." Having been schooled in traditional rhyme and meter, he has turned to the sharply chiseled language of common speech to speak directly of his passionate responses to life and death.

The poetry of Stanley Kunitz is Jewish in only a tangential way. In fact, his Jewishness can hardly be separated from other cultural forces behind his verse. Yet it is tempting to link Kunitz's sense of loneliness and of being the stranger, an outcast upon the earth, with his Jewish heritage.

He begins his poem "The Flight of Apollo" with the memorable line "Earth was my home, but even there I was a stranger." The space voyage only increases his earthly alienation, which he equates with the Jewish Diaspora:

> I was a stranger on earth.
> Stepping on the moon, I begin
> the gay pilgrimage to new
> Jerusalems
> in foreign galaxies.

For Kunitz, Jewishness provides neither the poem's subject nor its theme, but it may be an underpinning that is essential to the poet's inner life that lies behind the poem.

Part of the poet's implicit tie to Jewishness is in his imaginary quest to rediscover his father. In "Father and Son," he longs to know the "Gemara" of his father's "gentleness" that fate had taken from him. In "An Old Cracked Tune," he lays claim to his Jewish heritage through his father's name. "My name is Solomon Levi," he declares, and "the desert is my home." Once again he links himself with the Jews' exodus and the long and lonely search for a homeland. While he too is a stranger, who has no father, he is also a survivor, who has learned from his mythic past and dances "for the joy of surviving."

On Tuesday, December 5, 1995, I interviewed Stanley Kunitz in his spacious Greenwich Village apartment crammed with books and plants and works of art. Although he is short and frail, Kunitz has large, brilliant eyes, speaks forcefully, and moves around gracefully. One quickly forgets his chronological age. He had just returned from a reading in Cambridge but had found time while on the train to write some answers to my questions, and he referred to these texts during the interview. In the spring of 1997 we had a follow-up discussion that led to a number of revisions and additions.

GP: Stanley, you have said to Bill Moyers that "poetry is the most difficult, the most solitary, and the most life-enhancing thing that one can do in the world." Can you elaborate, especially about what makes it such a life-enhancing activity?

SK: The experience of love and the creative act are the supreme expressions of the life force. They do more than express it; they refresh and renew it and give it back, magnified.

GP: What have you found the hardest thing about being a poet? You're obviously saying that it's extremely important and beneficial, but I'm sure there are hard things about it.
SK: Being a poet is more or less easy, but writing poems is difficult.

GP: Are you talking about the formal challenge? Are you talking about finding just the right word?
SK: Making it right, in sound and sense; making it whole and true.

GP: Are you the person who determines that? Do you feel that you, finally, are the person who knows whether the poem works?
SK: In the long run I do. I try very hard not to be self-deceived.

GP: What is the most enjoyable thing about being a poet for you?
SK: The knowledge that there is nothing else I would rather do or be.

GP: Here we are, almost at the end of the twentieth century with all these incredible technological changes, most significantly in the modes and process of communication. Is there any future for poetry in the new age?
SK: The relevance of poetry is to the history of civilization, not to the progress of technology. Poets today can hope to do precisely what poets have always done, that is, tell the story of the human adventure, express what it feels like to be alive in this particular time, this particular place.

GP: What does a poet need to know about craft, and are rhyme and meter still important enough to be part of a young poet's training?
SK: I am never satisfied that I know enough about craft. I am still learning. But I think that it's important to stress that craft is not an end in itself, only a means. Only a means to gain control over language, to make it more sensitive to the modulations of one's thoughts and feelings, to improve its precision so that one won't have to tell lies.

GP: You are someone who has written poetry of note, both in traditional forms and in free verse. Do you think free verse can be taught, and is there anything coherent and plausible that one can say about writing free-verse poetry?

SK: In the first place, I don't think free verse is free. It has rather indeterminate principles, but at the least it must connect and cohere and establish a defining rhythmic pulse. As to whether traditional form is still essential, all I can say, out of my own experience, is that my early discipline in metrics and rhyme has been invaluable to me, even though I no longer tend to write in strict metrical patterns and prefer subtler internal harmonies to the click of rhyme. Incidentally, there were no graduate writing programs in my youth. I learned my craft by studying the poets around and before me.

GP: What do you think inspired you to be a poet, and as part of that, were there poets who made you want to write poetry?
SK: When Henry James, toward the end of his life, reflected on his long creative voyage, he identified his point of embarkation as the port of his loneliness. That is true of most of the poets I know. "A poem is solitary and on its way," said Paul Celan, the poet of the Holocaust. What sets it on its way is the search for a community.

GP: Do you identify with any of your contemporaries in particular? Of course one thinks of Roethke and Lowell. Are there others?
SK: I feel close to a whole tribe of poets, young and old, but in the act of writing a poem, I have always felt alone.

GP: Do you have any favorite poems of your own? Which are they and why?
SK: A new poem is always the one I feel closest to, if only for a while.

GP: "The Wellfleet Whale" is different from most of your other poems. Was your writing process in that poem different from your usual procedure?
SK: "The Wellfleet Whale" had a long gestation period. I knew from the beginning, in September 1966, when the whale foundered in Wellfleet Harbor, that it was a significant experience, and I experimented through the years with various ways of conveying what I saw and experienced. All of them were failures. During that interval, I had an opportunity on Cape Cod to study other beached whales, went out on sightseeing watches, and read whatever seemed to me even remotely pertinent, until I began to feel I was part of the civilization of the whale. Fifteen years after the event, I was able to pull it all together and write the poem.

GP: You succeeded in converting all that information into a significant action. Can you comment on your guiding principle of organization?

SK: In the end, I turned to Greek drama—specifically Sophoclean tragedy—to help me solve the problem of the poem's architecture. Jane Harrison's *Prolegomena* clarified for me the main structural elements in the development of the action, from agon to recognition scene. It's a poem that wants to be read aloud, preferably in the open air. I guess I'm really thinking of an ancient amphitheater.

GP: You have translated Russian poets. How did you come to the Russian poets?

SK: I came rather naturally to them. After all, my parents were raised in Eastern Europe. My mother's forebears, who were fugitives from Spain, wandered through central Europe until they settled in Lithuania at the time of the Inquisition. Despite this heritage, I never heard Russian or any foreign language spoken in our household during my childhood. My connection with the Russian poets dates from the early sixties, when Patricia Blake, then a correspondent for *Time*, and the Oxford scholar Max Hayward, the outstanding Slavist of that period, persuaded a number of friends and acquaintances to undertake translations of Andrei Voznesensky's poems for an edition in English of his *Antiworlds*. This was the book that made Andrei famous in the Soviet Union and eventually everywhere else. There were six of us in that list of translators, and none of us, including Auden and Wilbur, knew a word of Russian, but we felt confident that we could rely on Max's literal versions and, if needed, his interpretation of the text. I felt the same way a few years later, when Max and I collaborated on the poems of Akhmatova, an exceptionally important book for me.

GP: Did the intimate contact with Akhmatova's poems affect your own work?

SK: I hope I learned something from Akhmatova about the management of an open style and the possibility of breaking down the barrier between the public and private poem. Perhaps I learned something more from the passion and humanity of her voice.

GP: You recently won the National Book Award for poetry with the publication of *Passing Through*, the poems of your later years, including your newest work. Thirty-six years before, in 1959, you received the Pulitzer Prize. Did that earlier recognition have a significant impact on you and your career as a poet?

SK: One doesn't write poetry for prizes, but I have to admit that the Pulitzer Prize actually changed the course of my life. It gave me self-confidence at a time when I needed it sorely. The manuscript for my *Selected Poems: 1928–1958* had been rejected by more publishers than I could bear to count before Atlantic accepted it. I had been through a bad period and I was tired of being called a "poet's poet." That sudden turn of the wheel did wonders for my morale.

GP: In regard to the poetry intrinsically, do you have any themes, concerns, subjects that matter a great deal to you and enter frequently into your work?
SK: Actually, I never think about themes when I am writing my poems. In the usual course of events, my poems spring from the occasions of the day, something perceived as beautiful or terrible or true. When that perception attaches itself to language and rhythm, I know I am on my way, but not with any foreknowledge of my destination. Whenever I yield to the temptation to explicate one of my poems, I am astonished at all the secrets I find buried in the text. Poets are characterized less by their subject matter than by their tone of voice, their ground of feeling. When I was still at school, I picked up a volume of Keats's letters and discovered the passage in which he spoke of "the holiness of the heart's affections." More than seventy years later, those words still light the way for me.

GP: As I look around your apartment, I see many striking works of art, including several by your wife, Elise Asher. You have written about some of your artist friends. Would you comment on that relationship?
SK: Like so many other poets, past and present, I have a feeling of kinship with painters and their art. During my youth in Worcester, my favorite haunts were the woods, the public library, and the local art museum, and it seemed almost inevitable that I should eventually marry into the world of painters. When that happened in the fifties in New York, I inherited Elise's friends and soon felt *very* much a part of the emerging generation of Abstract Expressionist painters just as they were preparing to step in the limelight. They were wonderful company—lively, articulate, ambitious, hard-working, hard-drinking, gregarious, outrageous, and ready at any hour to argue about anything. Eventually, of course, success and fame and hypertension took their toll. I'm thinking, in particular, of Rothko, de Kooning, Guston, and Kline—all of them gone now. But in the early years, they seemed to embody Blake's dictum that "energy is eternal delight," and

their elan struck me as irresistible and contagious. Painters, I think, have a special gift for friendship.

GP: Have you done any artwork yourself?

SK: I am never happier than when I am working with my hands. In Provincetown, where we spend a good portion of the year, my toolroom and garden compete for attention with my study. If there's any odd job that needs to be done around the house, I treat it as a challenge. There was a period when I produced a number of collages and assemblages and wire sculptures, but that was when I could make a bit of free time available. These days I seem to be busier than ever.

GP: Dante is a presence in your work. In "The Illumination," you address his apparition as "my Master and my guide." What is the source of your connection?

SK: My conversation, so to speak, with Dante began very early. Thanks to my immigrant parents, our house in Worcester was the only one in the neighborhood, as far as I knew, that could boast of an extensive library. It was there that I first encountered the plays of Shakespeare, each in a separate volume, bound in red cloth, with a critical preface and an appendix of historical sources. Other well-thumbed books that I recall were complete sets of Tolstoy, Dickens, and Thackeray; the poems of Browning, Tennyson, Wordsworth, Longfellow, and Whittier; a multivolume set of classic histories, including Plutarch, Gibbon, Grote, and Prescott; the *Century Dictionary*, unabridged; Spinoza and Maimonides; and the Holy Bible, leatherbound, both Old and New Testaments, with red-ink passages and marginal glosses. But the book that enthralled me most in that library was a folio edition of Dante in Cary's translation, with the Gustav Doré illustrations. Those visual images of Hell took possession of my imagination. I used to sit in that library with this enormous folio on my lap (I was twelve years old or so), terrified by that vision of the underworld. I had nightmares. So Dante was with me at a most impressionable stage. Later, at Harvard, I studied the *Divine Comedy* with C. H. Grandgent, the famous Dante scholar.

GP: The poet Gregory Orr, who has written about you, says the suicide of your father shortly before you were born is the central fact of your imaginative life, "that from which all else flows." Do you agree?

SK: Certainly the most traumatic event through my formative years.

GP: The poem "The Knot," which I find mysterious, does that have symbolic associations for you, and how did you come to write it?

SK: The poem's origin is quite simple, nothing mysterious about it. Over a period of years, in our place on the Cape, I couldn't help but notice a great swirling knot that kept bleeding through several layers of paint on the lintel of our bedroom door. And the more I studied it, the more I marveled at its persistence, as though it still had a buried life, a will to grow, to become branching pine again "out of the trauma of its lopping-off." As I lay in bed, only half-awake, it did not seem far-fetched to imagine flying into its boughs.

GP: All right, another deep, difficult poem, "King of the River." What kind of disintegration takes place within the narrator? "You would dare to be changed,/ as you are changing now,/ into the shape you dread/ beyond the merely human." Are you writing of madness there, or are you writing of some other kind of transforming experience?

SK: "King of the River" deals primarily with the aging process. The Pacific Northwest salmon gets done with it in only a few weeks. For humans, death is the most definitive of a long series of gradual transformations. That thought adds to the complication of feelings when I say in a later poem, "The Layers," "I am not done with my changes."

GP: Is "An Old Cracked Tune" in some way suggestive of Jewish alienation and suffering for you?

SK: The very first line, "My name is Solomon Levi" is borrowed from an ugly, anti-Semitic street song recollected from my college days. Coincidentally, Solomon was my father's first name. According to what I have learned, he was a Levite, and so am I by inheritance, descended from a tribe with a priestly function. Obviously, "An Old Cracked Tune" has some connection with my heritage. As for alienation and suffering, I believe that the people of the Diaspora carry the memory of exile in their blood. But don't forget that the singer of this poem does it with a dance.

GP: You were obviously raised to be conscious of Judaism as a religion.

SK: I was raised in a Jewish community in Worcester. In our household the emphasis was never on religious practice, but on the ethical tradition. And so it still remains for me.

GP: A tough question: Do you consider yourself a Jewish poet?

SK: My sense is that the noun "poet" does not require a qualifying adjective, either "Jewish" or "American" or "modern."

GP: Didn't the Nazi death camps of World War II have a large effect on you?
SK: Of course! Even Dante's vision of Hell hadn't prepared me for that monstrous reality.

GP: It doesn't seem to enter into your poetry directly.
SK: It's there, nevertheless, deep in the substratum of my poems. The one poem that seems to me great and terrible enough to evoke the smell of evil, the delirium, of the death camps is Celan's "Todesfugue." Only a survivor of the camps could have written it, one whose borrowed life ended in suicide. My most explicit approach to the genocidal horror of the Hitler years is my poem in honor of Dietrich Bonhoeffer, that true Christian, whose failed plot against the Fuhrer led to his death by hanging—yes, in an extermination camp. I call it, "Around Pastor Bonhoeffer."

GP: How would you characterize your faith? Is it an artistic faith, is it a religious faith?
SK: I am a nonbeliever, but with strong religious impulses and yearnings.

GP: Has the Bible influenced your poetry?
SK: The Bible—Jewish and Christian, as I've already indicated—was one of the first books that I studied, page after page.

GP: Here's a big question. How does one face death, and can poetry help?
SK: One lives and dies simultaneously. It happens bit by bit, every day. I have tried to report that dialogue. In my childhood I dreaded going to sleep, because I was terrified at the thought of losing consciousness. I am less fearful of death in my nineties than I was in my teens, for the natural cycle has its own reasons, even its own dark beauty. I consider myself lucky to have been given this life.

GP: America doesn't seem to listen to its poets. If America listened to its poets, what could it learn?
SK: Our American culture has no poetry written into its origin. We inherited our poetry—mostly hymns and heroic couplets—from England, and we've tended, since the onset of the Industrial Age, to regard the medium itself as superfluous or frivolous, if not dangerous. Whitman clearly per-

ceived that our myth, our great national myth, has to do with power, success, money; and he attempted to supersede it with a myth of Democracy
and of himself as Democratic Man. And the truth is that he died unhappy,
believing that he had failed, that his country had rejected him. We still need
to understand that a nation that alienates itself from the creative imagination has already begun to wither.

GP: You seem to agree with your mentor, William Blake, that the genius of
the poetic imagination is the most important gift. What do you hope to still
accomplish?

SK: Oh, how do I know? I want to record whatever I feel most deeply. And I
have plenty of unfinished business.

GP: What is the most amazing thing about life?

SK: Life itself is the most amazing thing in the universe!

GP: What is the most amazing thing about your life?

SK: Maybe it's that here I am, at this age, still loving this life as I did from the
very beginning, and wanting more.

GP: And finally, while many of your poems have an elegiac tone, you have
survived and lived a long, rich life. Have you found light within the darkness?

SK: Love and poetry are lights enough.

Openhearted: Stanley Kunitz and Mark Wunderlich in Conversation

Mark Wunderlich / 1997

American Poet 7 (Fall 1997). Used by permission of the Academy of American Poets, www. poets.org. All rights reserved.

Wunderlich: I'd like to begin with our location and ask you how you became a resident of Provincetown. What was it that drew you here?

Kunitz: From my early years, when I experienced a certain loneliness at the thought of becoming a poet in this culture, I have been driven to search for a community in which I could feel at home. There are other factors involved in addition to the need for companionship. In general, I've found that I am more at peace with myself when I'm in daily contact with the natural world, either in the country or by the sea, than in an urban situation. In the thirties, during the Great Depression, I acquired a run-down farm of more than a hundred acres, near Storrs, Connecticut, where the State University is now located. The sprawling old house had no heat or electricity or running water, but I managed to make it livable for the brief course of my first marriage. One of my sources of consolation was in the ritual of ploughing the fields with a yoke of white oxen. Afterward, I lived in Bucks County, Pennsylvania, until I was drafted for service in World War II.

Provincetown I came to more or less by accident through my marriage to the painter Elise Asher, who had rented a studio on the beach, smack in the middle of town. That's where we spent our first summer together, in 1957. Five years later we took possession of this property in the West End, where I terraced our hillside plot of sand facing the bay and began to invent a garden that continues to this day to occupy me as a work of imagination still in progress. "Stanley's Folly" is Elise's name for it. Provincetown, I might add, is a place where one is permitted to indulge in one's follies.

Wunderlich: What led you to found the Fine Arts Work Center?

Kunitz: It wasn't a solo operation by any means. I was one of a group of what you might call "concerned citizens" and friends of the arts who met irregularly in the mid-sixties to consider how to restore the town's historic prestige as a vanguard arts community. It was obvious that the older generation of artists was dying out and that the venturesome young were leaving, one by one, for what they perceived to be greener and more golden shores. As a departing painter of the New York School explained to me, "There's no place like Provincetown, but at a certain point, if you intend to make it, the Hamptons are where you have to be." I find it almost incredible now that out of those chaotic and argumentative sessions, inspired by a slump in the local economy, the concept of the Fine Arts Work Center should have evolved. We are still the only long-term residency program of its kind. Our commitment is to the discovery and nurture of exceptionally gifted artists and writers at that emerging stage when they are ready to work and live, in the company of their peers, outside the academic environment. Louise Glück, Susan Mitchell, Denis Johnson, and Yusef Komunyakaa, to name only a few, are representative of the writers who came here when they were unknown. We look for original talent and a diversity of backgrounds. It's a real gamble, for we have only the signs of early promise to guide us in our choice of applicants; but as the record of almost thirty years shows, we've been extraordinarily astute, or maybe only lucky.

Wunderlich: Over the years you've been responsible for blessing so many younger poets and for initiating them into the world of contemporary poetry. I'm curious to hear what that relationship to younger poets means to you, and also, I'd like to know who blessed you? Did someone initiate you as a young poet?

Kunitz: I felt very isolated as a young person, the son of immigrants, growing up in Worcester, Massachusetts, early in the century. In that period there was no possibility of conversation or even contact with older poets. In fact, I didn't know another soul with whom I could share my interests. Eventually, after my Harvard years, I gravitated to New York, the magnet city of the arts, where I found an editorial job and began to send out my poems. Among the first periodicals to publish me were *Poetry*, *The Dial*, *The Nation*, *The New Republic*, and *Commonweal*, but I was too busy and too shy to make friends easily, so I still felt like an outsider.

My life changed when, soon after its opening, Yaddo invited me to be a guest, much to my surprise. In that small summer group—there were only eight or nine of us—I was the child among elders. That was my entry, really, into the world of arts and letters. My first collection, *Intellectual Things*, was accepted by Doubleday, Doran shortly after. When it appeared in 1930, I was twenty-five. I made a vow then, many times renewed, never to forget how much the gift of friendship and encouragement had meant to me in my youth. As for my companionship with younger poets, I feel that I'm the one who's blessed in that relationship. Even if I wanted to sport with other poets of my age, where on earth would I find them? Besides "nonagenarian" is such an ugly word! I like to think that all the true poets—young and old, even the dead ones—are contemporaries.

Wunderlich: You said the greatest challenge that you faced was being in isolation. What do you think is the greatest challenge facing young writers today?

Kunitz: As a result of the proliferation of creative writing programs, summer conferences, and workshops, not to speak of the unprecedented availability of poets of established reputation as teachers of their craft, young writers need no longer feel neglected or isolated. I doubt whether any civilization has ever produced so many qualified poets as ours. That's something to boast about. Nevertheless, the general leveling of quality, what I have referred to as the democratization of genius, suggests to me that despite our advantages we are not living in a Golden Age of poetry, but at best a Silver Age. Perhaps it's time to question whether the conversion of poetry into an academic discipline is an altogether benign process.

Wunderlich: I think people often associate you with the organizations you helped found and shape—the Work Center, the MFA program at Columbia University, Poets House. How did your experience at Harvard shape your concept of the organizations you helped found?

Kunitz: At Harvard in my time, with its two percent quota for Jews and its general air of condescension to ethnic minorities and scholarship students, one had a definite sense of social stratification. Both the Work Center and Poets House are emblematic of the society I yearned for: idealistic, open-hearted, and free.

Wunderlich: That brings us to an interesting point. I'm curious to hear what you think about the poet's relationship to the political. Recently Adrienne Rich refused the National Medal of Arts, citing her disappointment with the government that has, she feels, turned its back on the disenfranchised of the country, and also pointing to the hypocrisy of a country that wants to bestow a medal on a poet with one hand, while doing away with funding for artists with the other. What do you make of the poet's relationship to the political?

Kunitz: I must confess it's somewhat awkward for me to respond to the questions you raise. In 1993, the first year of President Clinton's administration, I accepted the National Medal of Arts from his hands at the White House. If I had felt any qualms about doing so, they would have been allayed by the presence of William Styron and Arthur Miller, the two other literary recipients, both of them unimpeachable representatives of the liberal conscience. The president's recent intention to honor Adrienne Rich confirms for me that he remains a friend of the arts and a defender of free speech. Although I am fully aware of Bill Clinton's flaws, I fail to see how he can be held responsible for the trashing of the NEA by Jesse Helms, Speaker Newt Gingrich, and the Republican Congress. Blame them! This government of ours, we need to remind ourselves, is not a monolithic institution. All power does not flow from the top. Since I've thought a good deal about this subject, I'd like to add some further reflections:

• To live as a poet in this culture is the aesthetic equivalent of a major political statement.

• Beware of manifestos: they are the death of poetry.

• A poet is a citizen, like any other. One of the obligations of citizenship is participation in the political process.

When you accept an award for your poems, you do not imply that you endorse every action or belief of the donor: you accept it not for yourself alone, for ego gratification, but in the name of poetry and of the civilization inspired by the arts.

Wunderlich: In the debate concerning the survival of the National Endowment for the Arts, the charge of indecency turns out to be a major topic. How do you explain the persistence of so much controversy about the arts in our society?

Kunitz: The lingering influence of our Puritan tradition has led to an almost pathological native suspicion of the arts. To this day, in the political arena, the most successful conservative strategy is to wave the flag; attack immigrants, radicals, and intellectuals; and denounce indecent and subversive art in order to preserve the virtue of the average American family. A substantial portion of the American population seems not to know or care that the perpetuation of a free art in a free society depends on the prerogative to offend certain sensibilities.

Wunderlich: What is the role of poetry in our culture? We have so many media we can choose from—film, video, performance, etc. What does poetry have to offer the human spirit this late in the millennium? Why poetry?

Kunitz: Poetry is the medium of choice for giving our most hidden self a voice—the voice behind the mask that all of us wear. Poetry says, "You are not alone in the world: all your fears, anxieties, hopes, despairs are the common property of the race." In a way, poetry is the most private of all the arts, and yet it is public, too, a form of social bonding. It gains its power from the chaos at its source, the untold secrets of the self. The power is in the mystery of the word.

Wunderlich: What is the relationship of the self to your poetry? You spoke earlier about the mask. Is writing your attempt to penetrate the mask, and are you more successful at that now than you may have perceived yourself earlier? Is it easier now?

Kunitz: Yeats said that if you wear a mask long enough, it will become your face. That's the danger, of course. The hope is to do away with the need for the mask, to create a persona that grows with you, that is not fixed in one period in time. The evolving biological self is also an evolving spiritual self. I can see that the persona of my early poems is far different from the persona of my later poems, because I am different. And yet there is a continuity, a strain of selfhood, that runs from the beginning of the life to the end. As I put it in the opening lines of "The Layers": "I have walked through many lives,/ Some of them my own,/ and I am not who I was, though some principle of being/ abides, from which I struggle/ not to stray."

Wunderlich: Many of the poets you loved—your early influences—Herbert, Donne, Blake, Hopkins—I think of as essentially religious poets. What is your relationship to religion?

Kunitz: I do not subscribe to any organized religion, yet I think of myself as a religious person, and that's independent of any kind of faith or practice, or belief in God. While I was still in college I fastened on the phrase "the holiness of the heart's affections" in one of Keats's letters, and it has stayed with me ever since. To me, that's religion. "I am certain of nothing," he wrote, "but the holiness of the Heart's affections and the truth of Imagination." Though I

am in no danger of conversion, the poets you mention as early influences—
Herbert, Donne, Blake, Hopkins—still speak to me and light the way.

Wunderlich: You once described a poet's collected poems as his "book of
changes." What changes does your work now contain?

Kunitz: It's hard to speak about one's self while still in process. Certainly
through the years I've tried to simplify the surface of my poems. I've tried to
write more intimately than I did, in a more conversational tone. I have fewer conflicts, perhaps; yet the ones that remain are central to my existence.
Since I came to realize, in my middle years, that I was occupying two worlds
at once, that of my living and that of my dying, my poems have tended to
hover between them. More recently I expressed a desire to write poems
that are natural, luminous, deep, spare, "so transparent that one can look
through and see the world." That's pretty much what I still feel. I recognize
that there is a great area of unknowing within me. I try to reach into that
chaos of the inner life, to touch those words and images that will help me
face the ultimate reality. Such existential concerns tend to make me rather
impatient with the particulars of the day. At the same time I am aware that
it is out of the dailiness of life that one is driven into the deepest recesses of
the self. There is a transportation, to and fro, between these two worlds. The
moment that flow stops, one stops being a poet.

The Productions of Time:
Kunitz on Blake

Jason Shinder / 2000

Agni 52 (2000), 12–34. Reprinted with permission of the Literary Estate of Jason Shinder.

London

I wander thro' each charter'd street,
Near where the charter'd Thames does flow.
And mark in every face I meet
Marks of weakness, marks of woe.

In every cry of every Man,
In every Infants cry of fear,
In every voice: in every ban,
The mind-forg'd manacles I hear

How the Chimney-sweepers cry
Every blackning Church appalls,
And the hapless Soldiers sigh,
Runs in blood down Palace walls

But most thro' midnight streets I hear
How the youthful Harlots curse
Blasts the new-born Infants tear,
And blights with plagues the Marriage hearse.

SK: When I first read this poem from William Blake's *Songs of Experience* as an adolescent, I didn't fully understand the word "charter'd." I found little help in the dictionary. I didn't really grasp the meaning of the work until I moved from my native Worcester, Massachusetts, where I was born and raised, and came to New York. In Manhattan I saw particular buses parked in the street that were not available to the public, that had a "chartered" sign on the windshield. They had been hired. Blake was saying that the streets of London, even the Thames, were bought and paid for by the newly rising merchant class. They no longer belonged to the common people.

JS: You've often referred to Blake, in fact, as "The Poet of London." Why?
SK: You cannot separate Blake from London. He was born there in 1757, and he died there in 1827, seventy years later. In the course of his lifetime he had observed the evolution of London: its development from a fairly provincial capital to a bustling metropolis with enormous mills and factories looming over the landscape. At that time, London emerged as the capital of the world, particularly significant in that Britain was becoming a great empire in the forefront of the whole Industrial Revolution.

JS: So Blake observed the changes occurring in his city, and their effects on his fellow citizens.
SK: Precisely. Blake saw in each face the loss, as he perceived it, of his fellow citizen's individual imagination. People were in "manacles" as a result of the restrictions placed on them by Church, State, and the oppressive conditions of the newly rising factories. In his poem "London," you observe him walking the streets of London, observing all that is going on, while assuming the prophetic voice to give warning to individuals who were being drawn into the web of the new industrial life.

JS: "London," as part of *Songs of Experience*, was written in 1794, when Blake was thirty-seven. He had already written a good deal, including his first book, *Poetical Sketches*, most of the poems in *Songs of Innocence*, "The Book of Thel," "The French Revolution," and the beginning of *The Marriage of Heaven and Hell*. He seemed quite ambitious as an artist early in his life.
SK: That's very true. At the age of ten he had already left formal school to pursue his interest in drawing at one of the best art schools in London, the Henry Pars Drawing School. He was already having visionary experiences and was determined to be a painter. Fortunately his father, a shopkeeper, recognized Blake's determination and genius. He allowed him to focus on

learning his art. By the age of fifteen, Blake was already apprenticed to a master engraver, James Basire.

JS: I remember reading how Basire sent Blake into churches and church-yards and the tombs of Westminster Abbey to draw careful copies of the effigies of kings, queens, warriors, bishops, and so forth.

SK: Yes, and you know even then Blake proved to be too original to please his teacher.

JS: I'm wondering if Blake ever found it comfortable with his teachers and educational institutions—given his early and strong commitment to the in-dividual spirit and imagination.

SK: He was never that comfortable with any authority. After drawing school, for example, he attended the Royal Academy, and it was an unhappy, brief time. He felt like a stranger, despising the painters who were the favorites of the faculty of the Royal Academy. When he was told by his teacher to give up copying from Michelangelo, and to substitute Rubens instead, he blew up. The teacher said Rubens was a much more finished artist than Michel-angelo. And Blake responded, "How could he be finished when he never began?" He picked up his brush and palette and left the Academy, never to return.

JS: Would you say his devotion to his own work and vision created a sense of isolation from his contemporaries—Keats, Shelley, and Byron, for example?

SK: Yes. That's very true. He was definitely not a part of the literary com-munity. He was not really acquainted with the poets of his time. He was not recognized as a poet. In fact, he was considered something of a crank, an inspired madman.

JS: So who were his friends? What community, if any, did he feel close to?

SK: He was better acquainted with the visual artists, if any group. Remem-ber, he began as an engraver. And he did have some friends in political cir-cles, the working revolutionaries of the period. Instead of concerning him-self with the literary life, he spent a good deal of his time in social protest.

JS: What was he advocating for?

SK: You have to remember he was born into a very violent period. There were three revolutions that influenced him: the American, French, and In-dustrial Revolutions. He was engaged in all of them. He cared about the poor, wanted reform legislation, that sort of thing. He used to walk around the streets he talks about in the poem "London" wearing a red cap of the French Revolution.

JS: Wasn't his reason for finally leaving London—for a brief period—to fight in the French Revolution?
SK: It was the only time he left his native soil. The French Revolution—all the revolutions—were symbolic of Blake's lifetime fight against oppression of any kind. He believed religiously in the freedom of the individual for self-expression. He believed it was absolutely necessary to preserve the innocence of the child.

JS: Which he does magnificently in *Songs of Innocence and of Experience.*
SK: Indeed. They are central to the understanding of Blake. They are the poems, of course, most familiar to the world, especially to the young and the child in all of us. Their speech is universal. They are so simple, so lucid, almost transparent in their style, from the very first poem, "Introduction":

Introduction

Piping down the valleys Wild
Piping songs of pleasant glee
On a cloud I saw a child.
And he laughing said to me.

Pipe a song about a Lamb;
So I piped with merry chear,
Piper, pipe that song again—
So I piped: he wept to hear.

Drop thy pipe thy happy pipe
Sing my songs of happy chear,
So I sung the same again,
While he wept with joy to hear

Piper, sit thee down and write
In a book that all may read—
So he vanish'd from my sight,
And I pluck'd a hollow reed.

And I made a rural pen,
And I stain'd the water clear,
And I wrote my happy songs
Every child may joy to hear.

JS: Whom is he addressing in this poem?

SK: He's addressing not only children, but the child in man and woman, the child among us. The last line, "Every child may joy to hear," is a very prophetic statement. It sets the tone for the poems to come.

JS: Why does the child in the poem instruct the speaker to "write a song about a lamb"?

SK: Blake is thinking of the Lamb of God as a child, as a playmate. Of course, the lamb also implies the Christ figure. And it's also symbolic of childhood itself, the child in us that speaks of the innocence of the heart. The lamb is an essential image for Blake. As in one of Blake's best-loved poems in *Songs of Innocence*, "The Lamb."

The Lamb

Little Lamb who made thee
Dost thou know who made thee
Gave thee life & bid thee feed.
By the stream & o'er the mead;
Gave thee clothing of delight,
Softest clothing wooly bright;
Gave thee such a tender voice,
Making all the vales rejoice!
Little Lamb, who made thee
Dost thou know who made thee

Little Lamb I'll tell thee,
Little Lamb I'll tell thee:
He is called by thy name,
For he calls himself a Lamb:
He is meek & he is mild,
He became a little child:
I a child & thou a lamb,
We are called by his name.

Little Lamb God bless thee.
Little Lamb God bless thee.

SK: One of the beautiful things about this poem is the way the speaker lovingly identifies with the lamb, with the Christ figure.

JS: As you mentioned, the lamb is an image throughout. It surfaces again in the poem "The Little Black Boy," where the voice of God invites the souls of men and women to rejoice "like lambs" around his "golden tent."

SK: Once again the lamb is the angel of innocence and childhood. The lamb is an even more striking image in "The Little Black Boy" because the backdrop of the poem is so dark. You have to remember that this was a very early poem to be written about slavery. At that time the British were slave masters and traders. But slavery appalled Blake. He sees the black boy not only as representative of the victims of the slave trade, but of the victims of slave labor in the mills of England as well. These mills were largely worked by children and women, fifteen hours a day. So the black boy in the poem exploited by slavery is associated with the blackened face of the exploited chimney sweeper or the blackened hands of the children in the mills, or his own hands as an engraver. He imaginatively associates the little black boy with everyone who is oppressed.

The Little Black Boy

My mother bore me in the southern wild,
And I am black, but O! my soul is white;
White as an angel is the English child:
But I am black as if bereav'd of light.

My mother taught me underneath a tree
And sitting down before the heat of day,
She took me on her lap and kissed me,
And pointing to the east began to say:

Look on the rising sun: there God does live,
And gives his light, and gives his heat away;
And flowers and trees and beasts and men receive
Comfort in morning joy in the noon day.

And we are put on earth a little space,
That we may learn to bear the beams of love,
And these black bodies and this sun-burnt face
Is but a cloud, and like a shady grove.

For when our souls have learn'd the heat to bear,
The cloud will vanish we shall hear his voice,
Saying: Come out from the grove my love & care,
And round my golden tent like lambs rejoice.

Thus did my mother say, and kissed me;
and thus I say to little English boy:
When I from black and he from white cloud free,
And round the tent of God like lambs we joy:

I'll shade him from the heat, till he can bear
To lean in joy upon our fathers knee;
And then I'll stand and stroke his silver hair,
And be like him, and he will then love me.

JS: Blake's empathy must in some way have resulted from his identification with his own sense of being neglected and oppressed—of his struggle against the artistic and industrial fashion of his time that kept him unrecognized as an artist and in poverty.

SK: It's one of the reasons why his poems ring so true. His imagination was steeped in compassionate feelings for all those who were oppressed, victimized, or exploited, because he himself felt that way. You have to remember he made whatever living he could with his own hands as an engraver. But his engravings of his own poems did not sell; nobody wanted them. He had to farm out his services as a journeyman engraver doing hack work for others. And like other members of the working class, he was a victim of the newly rising industrial age. Engraving was becoming a dying art. He hoped to survive on his own, independently, but the struggle became more and more difficult, often desperate. His wife, Catherine Boucher, would sometimes place an empty plate on the table to remind him of their circumstances, but he never lost faith in himself, in his mission as a poet. Indeed, the humiliation, rage, and frustration underlying these circumstances fueled, in part, the fierceness of his imagination.

JS: Didn't Blake—in the midst of his lack of success as an engraver—invent a new process of etching poems?

SK: Yes. While Blake was readying the manuscript for his *Songs of Innocence*, the spirit of his younger brother—who had recently died allegedly—returned to impart to him the secret of how to make illuminated books by a process that involved etching in relief the poem and its accompanying illustration by applying acid on copper, then corroding with acid the blank areas of the plate, and finally coloring each impression by hand. It was a difficult and time-consuming process. The plates of his own work were produced only when they were ordered, and, as I mentioned, there weren't many orders. It is believed he had only thirty orders for *Songs of Innocence*, of which there are only twenty-six in existence today. But each was individually produced, and so no two copies could be identical. It also meant that the books are of unsurpassed beauty and today, ironically, priceless. He was, in fact, one of the great engravers in the whole history of the art.

JS: You've mentioned both Blake's younger brother and his wife, Catherine Boucher. Were these the most important people in his life, in helping him keep his faith in himself and in his mission as a poet?

SK: Blake's younger brother, Robert, died in 1787, when Blake was thirty. He was Blake's closest friend, whom he had taken in as an apprentice. When Robert fell gravely ill, Blake attended him night and day, to the point of exhaustion. At the moment of Robert's death, Blake saw the released spirit of his brother "ascend heavenwards, clapping its hands of joy." Afterwards, Robert became one of Blake's "Messengers from Heaven" from whom he received poems, visions, and secrets like how to produce illuminated books. His younger brother was forever an influence and a source of support.

JS: And his wife?

SK: His wife provided Blake not only with support throughout his life, but with absolute devotion. Blake was twenty-five when he married her. She was the illiterate daughter of a market gardener. In place of a signature their marriage certificate bears her mark. But with exemplary patience Blake taught her to read and write, as well as how to paint and draw in a style indistinguishable from his own. Throughout the years she became his collaborator, lending a hand in the execution of prints. Though their marriage produced no children, it was a rare companionship, as of two lovebirds. She died three years after Blake, at the age of seventy, the same age Blake was when he died. It was a rather long life at that time.

JS: His wife doesn't specifically surface in *Songs of Innocence*, but his affection for her seems evident in poems like "The Divine Image" that proclaim the beauty of the naked body and sensual expression.

SK: Yes. Blake was against oppression of any kind, including repression of our sexual desires. "The Divine Image" is a tribute to all human possibilities.

The Divine Image

To Mercy Pity Peace and Love,
All pray in their distress:
And to these virtues of delight
Return their thankfulness.

For Mercy Pity Peace and Love,
Is God, our father dear:
And Mercy Pity Peace and Love,
Is Man his child and care.

For Mercy has a human heart,
Pity, a human face:
And Love, the human form divine,
And Peace, the human dress.

Then every man of every clime,
That prays in his distress,
Prays to the human form divine
Love Mercy Pity Peace.

And all must love the human form,
In heathen, turk, or jew.
Where Mercy, Love & Pity dwell
There God is dwelling too.

JS: It's lovely, but a little darker than the earlier poems in *Songs of Innocence*.

SK: The poems in *Songs of Innocence* get a little darker as they move into *Songs of Experience*, which begin to concentrate on the evils of the world, the hardening of the soul, the afflictions of life. Blake felt that we were born in a state of innocence—in the image of the lamb—but that the experience of the world tended to corrupt and defile us, and to blight the natural innocence of the soul.

JS: Are you saying he was opposed to experience?

SK: No. He was not opposed to learning the ways of the world. He felt, in fact, that innocence could be fortified by knowing how to live with others in the environment. He wanted one's education in the ways of the world to strengthen the child within one, not to kill the child.

JS: Why do individual poems in *Songs of Innocence* have a counter poem in *Songs of Experience*?

SK: One poem does counterpoint another to highlight the contraries of innocence and experience, good and evil, to represent all the contradictions of one's life. For example, the first poem of *Songs of Experience*, "Introduction," counterpoints the first poem of the same title in *Songs of Innocence*. The voice is more prophetic and stern. It's very different from the naive and relaxed voice in the "Introduction" to *Songs of Innocence*.

Introduction

Hear the voice of the Bard!
Who Present, Past, & Future sees;
Whose ears have heard,
The Holy Word,
That walk'd among the ancient trees;

Calling the lapsed Soul
And weeping in the evening dew:
That might controll
The starry pole,
And fallen light renew!

O Earth O Earth return!
Arise from out the dewy grass;
Night is worn,
And the morn
Rises from the slumberous mass.

Turn away no more:
Why wilt thou turn away
The starry floor,
The watry shore,
Is giv'n thee till the break of day

JS: Now that the speaker of the poem is wiser, he claims that he is going to give us God's word so that we may correct our ways. It's a greater challenge for Blake than in the *Songs of Innocence*, and his voice seems stronger because of it.

SK: He assumes a more powerful voice in order to reinforce his conviction that man—in the midst of the ills of the world—is still capable of representing the divine spirit.

JS: He seems to become more forthright about opposing institutions that oppress, that would restrict his freedom. In "The Garden of Love," for example, he speaks of priests "binding with briars my joys and desires."

SK: That's one of my favorite poems of Blake's. It's certainly an exceptionally strong attack on the institutions of church and state. Blake believed in the free play of the body and the senses. He felt such expression was as much an expression of God as religious thought was, and he makes his point in "The Garden of Love."

The Garden of Love

I went to the Garden of Love.
And saw what I had never seen:
A Chapel was built in the midst,
Where I used to play on the green.

And the gates of this Chapel were shut,
And Thou shalt not writ over the door;
So I turn'd to the Garden of Love
That so many sweet flowers bore;

And I saw it was filled with graves,
And tomb-stones where flowers should be;
And Priests in black gowns, were walking their rounds,
And binding with briars, my joys & desires.

SK: Here Blake argues against the forces of religion and law that would bind the human spirit with "briars." He affirms once again the beauty of self-expression, the joy of the instinctual life, and the belief that the five senses are the chief inlets of the soul.

JS: The image of the chapel in the midst of the garden of love reminds me of the image of the worm in the midst of a rose in "The Sick Rose."
SK: It's the same theme in a more metaphorical vein. It's only eight lines, but they are among the most exquisite in English poetry.

The Sick Rose

O Rose thou art sick.
The invisible worm,
That flies in the night
In the howling storm:

Has found out thy bed
Of crimson joy:
And his dark secret love
Does thy life destroy.

JS: The rose is the rose of love.
SK: And the worm is the worm of guilt.

JS: What do you love most about the poem?
SK: There are many things, including the way this very poignant song lingers on the breath like a sigh, with its own intrinsic music.

JS: I'm always taken aback by the urgency in the first line.
SK: It's also there in his most famous poem, "The Tyger."

The Tyger

Tyger tyger, burning bright,
In the forests of the night:
What immortal hand or eye,
Could frame thy fearful symmetry?

In what distant deeps or skies
Burnt the fire of thine eyes!
On what wings dare he aspire?
What the hand, dare seize the fire?

And what shoulder, & what art,
Could twist the sinews of thy heart?
And when thy heart began to beat,
What dread hand? & what dread feet?

What the hammer? what the chain?
In what furnace was thy brain?
What the anvil? what dread grasp
Dare its deadly terrors clasp?

When the stars threw down their spears
And water'd heaven with their tears:
Did he smile his work to see?
Did he who made the Lamb make thee?

Tyger, Tyger burning bright,
In the forests of the night:
What immortal hand or eye
Dare frame thy fearful symmetry?

JS: There have been many interpretations of "The Tyger"—certainly as many interpretations of the poem as there are versions of it. It's certainly a very haunting, mysterious poem about the mystery of creation. What is the poem's primary glory?

SK: There are many versions of the poem. It was one that Blake worked on. He knew it was a central poem. And, yes, there are many interpretations, but somehow I think they all fail. The poem comes out of deep sources that cannot always be articulated. But without any doubt it is a poem—as you say—dealing with the whole mystery of creation, the awesome force, the principle of energy that gave us the cosmos in the beginning that still breathes within the human imagination. And that is one of the main glories of the poem.

JS: How would you briefly define the image of the tyger, for high school students?

SK: The tyger is an image of infinite power and dread not to be described as either good or evil.

JS: In the many versions of the poem, sometimes the tyger appears as an angel.

SK: Not exactly an angel. If you are referring to the illustrations that Blake drew for the poem—the ones that appear on the copperplates he engraved and then hand-colored afterwards—the tyger does take on different appearances because each copy of the poem is somewhat different from the others. There are a few copies in which the tyger looks like a tame pussycat. This might indicate a certain ambiguity in Blake's mind as to how he wanted the tyger to be seen. But in almost all the illustrations, the tyger is, as you would expect, a fierce creature, a raging beast of sorts.

JS: It's curious to note that Blake had several versions of the poem although he often claimed to have received his poems directly from God, or the voice of his dead brother.

SK: You don't expect a poet to be absolutely consistent. It is true, however, that Blake firmly believed he received his poems from sources other than himself. He wrote: "I am under the direction of messengers from heaven, daily and nightly." And in a letter he declared, "I have written this poem from immediate dictation, twelve sometimes thirty lines at a time without premeditation and even against my will." He also said—and this is his classic statement on his understanding of the sources of his poetry—"I dare not pretend to be any other than the secretary, the authors are in eternity."

JS: Blake maintained that he was writing as a vehicle of the divine spirit?

SK: At the same time that he accepted these gifts from heaven, he felt he couldn't help but improve upon them. "The Tyger" is a good example of this.

JS: Have you seen the original drafts of the poem?

SK: Yes. It should be noted that Blake left his manuscripts in a terrible mess, a state of chaos. In fact, it was really impossible to read Blake, that is the whole compass of his work, until the twentieth century, when serious work was done in examining the manuscripts and selecting the final versions, or what seemed the final versions, and trying to arrange them in some sort of meaningful order. It was a heroic task.

JS: A poem whose imagery seems intimately connected with that of "The Tyger" is "A Divine Image."

SK: You can see the connection immediately. The title itself is an ironic response to "The Tyger." It's one of the darkest poems Blake ever wrote.

A Divine Image

Cruelty has a Human Heart,
And Jealousy a Human Face;
Terror, the Human Form Divine,
And Secrecy the Human Dress.

The Human Dress is forged Iron,
The Human Form a fiery Forge,
The Human Face a Furnace seal'd,
The Human Heart its hungry Gorge.

JS: In this poem, and throughout *Songs of Innocence and of Experience,* Blake seems to speak to us through symbols.

SK: It is true that Blake lived by symbols and lived in a world of myth. At the same time, however, he believed that the discovery of symbols rests on clarity of perception, on looking at the world with the closest possible scrutiny. There is a wonderful passage in his prophetic work *Jerusalem* in which he says, "Labour well the minute particulars; attend to the Little Ones . . . He would do good to another must do it in Minute Particulars. General Good is the plea of the scoundrel, hypocrite and flatterer, for Art and Science cannot exist but in minutely organized Particulars." I think that is an observation that every poet, every artist, and every scientist needs to pay attention to.

JS: That passage is one of the many illuminating parts from his long, prophetic works, some of which I find difficult to understand. What do you see as the importance of these long, ambitious works?

SK: His prophetic books are extraordinarily difficult poems, representing his late work. Even scholars who have gone over every word and syllable have had a hard time interpreting them. It has to be understood that when Blake wrote these he was not—and never would be—a recognized poet. In addition, you have to remember Blake was a revolutionary spirit, a rebel. In fact, he was arrested once for speaking against the King. So as an unrecognized, poor poet and rebel, he began to feel—and rightly so—at odds with the government, with King George. This feeling motivated his need to write symbolically, to cover his tracks. Remember, there were extradition laws that were very harsh, and there was no doubt that Blake was frightened at the thought of being jailed.

JS: So the difficulty we encounter in Blake's prophetic works was in part his need to be secretive—to thwart those who might punish him for his views?
SK: He felt it necessary to invent a new mythology in order to be able to express his true feelings. It is part of the real difficulty of these poems. They have an elaborate architecture which is hard to grasp. And yet, Blake's prophetic works contain some of his greatest utterances.

JS: Blake created a world of his own in these long works.
SK: It reminds me of a significant statement Blake made in *Jerusalem*: "I must create a system or be enslaved by another man's." I think it explains a good deal about Blake's motivations and spirit behind his work—that fierce, independent spirit that he translated into the very fabric of his poetry.

JS: While working on his prophetic books, Blake continued to write lyrics. What are some of your favorite lyric poems by Blake not printed in *Songs of Innocence and of Experience*?
SK: There are many—some have actually been extracted from longer poems but have been printed as separate pieces. A lyric that anyone who has ever felt out-of-step or out-of-tune with the world can appreciate is "Why Was I Born with a Different Face?" It's actually one of those jottings that first appeared in his notebooks, obviously written in a rush and not intended for publication.

Why Was I Born with a Different Face?

O why was I born with a different face?
Why was I not born like the rest of my race?
When I look, each one starts! when I speak, I offend;
Then I'm silent and passive and lose every Friend.

Then my verse I dishonor, My pictures despise,
My person degrade and my temper chastise;
And the pen is my terror, the pencil my shame;
All my Talents I bury, and dead is my Fame.

I am either too low or too highly priz'd;
When Elate I am Envy'd When Meek I'm despis'd.

JS: What about the poem is most appealing to you?

SK: You can see Blake is feeling pretty sorry for himself, while at the same time he's a bit self-mocking. The poem reveals a tender and vulnerable side of him.

JS: Another lyric you've often mentioned as a favorite of yours is "And Did Those Feet."

SK: That lyric is actually from Blake's epic work *Milton*. It's a wonderful poem. It consolidates all the major themes of Blake. It represents what he stands for as a poet:

And Did Those Feet in Ancient Time

And did those feet in ancient time
Walk upon Englands mountain green:
And was the holy Lamb of God,
On Englands pleasant pastures seen!

And did the Countenance Divine,
Shine forth upon our clouded hills?
And was Jerusalem builded here,
Among those dark Satanic Mills?

Bring me my Bow of burning gold:
Bring me my Arrows of desire:
Bring me my Spear: O clouds unfold!
Bring me my Chariot of fire!

I will not cease from Mental Fight,
Nor shall my Sword sleep in my hand:
Till we have built Jerusalem,
In Englands green & pleasant Land.

JS: I've always found Blake's prophetic voice most engaging in his "Auguries of Innocence."

SK: In those verses Blake is trying to sum up his comprehension of the nature of the universe—so his voice would necessarily be prophetic in nature. In fact, "Auguries of Innocence" was one of the early poems of his that I read in my youth, and it has had a great influence on my own perspective of the world. Here are some of my favorite couplets:

> To see a World in a Grain of Sand
> And a Heaven in a Wild Flower
>
> Hold Infinity in the palm of your hand
> And Eternity in an hour
>
> A Robin Redbreast in a Cage
> Puts all Heaven in a Rage
>
> A dog starvd at his Masters Gate
> Predicts the ruin of the State
>
> The Strongest Poison ever known
> Came from Ceasars Laurel Crown
>
> If the Sun & Moon should doubt
> Theyd immediately Go out

I see all creation—and this stems in part from these couplets from Blake—as a single continuous web, all of whose single filaments are interconnected. If you touch the web at any point, certainly the whole web shudders. Everything that lives stands in connection with everything else on this planet. That is something Blake taught me.

JS: Would you say that that theme—of the marriage of opposites—is best developed in his epic satire *The Marriage of Heaven and Hell*?
SK: All of Blake's work deals with this theme—but in different ways. In *The Marriage of Heaven and Hell*—a foundation stone of Blake's canon, a masterpiece—the concept of the marriage of contraries is fulfilled as a philosophical argument. In the beginning of the poem, in the section entitled "The Argument," Blake makes his point very clear: "Without contraries there can be no progression. Attraction and Repulsion, Reason and Energy, Love and Hate, are necessary to Human existence."

JS: The poem seems unusually full of the senses.

SK: In order to see the whole world as he tried to see it in the poem, Blake felt it necessary to go back to the world of senses. He always begins with sensory experience. There is a sentence of Blake's which makes this point: "If the doors of perception were cleansed, everything would appear to man as it is, infinite." That's a sentence that has lasted throughout history, certainly among the poets. What he is saying is open your eyes, open all your senses, become as a child again and you will see the world as it is—its infinite and eternal perspectives.

JS: Does the sentence you quoted come from *The Marriage of Heaven and Hell*?

SK: Yes, from a section in the poem called "Proverbs of Hell." You have to remember that when he speaks of the proverbs of hell he means heaven, and when he speaks of heaven he means hell. It's an attempt to reconcile the concept of heaven and hell, of good and evil. So these are actually heavenly proverbs. Here are some that are essential to the understanding of the poem:

> The road of excess leads to the palace of wisdom.

> He who desires but acts not, breeds pestilence.

> A fool sees not the same tree that a wise man sees.

> He whose face gives no light, shall never become a star.

> Eternity is in love with the productions of time.

> No bird soars too high, if he soars with his own wings.

> If the fool would persist in his folly he would become wise.

> What is now proved was once, only imagin'd.

> The cistern contains: the fountain overflows.

> Every thing possible to be believ'd is an image of truth.

> The tygers of wrath are wiser than the horses of instruction.

Expect poison from standing water.

You never know what is enough unless you know what is more than enough.

Damn, braces: Bless relaxes.

Exuberance is Beauty.

Improvement makes strait roads, but the crooked roads without Improvement are roads of Genius.

JS: The proverbs remind me of your writings in the section "Seedcorn and
Windfall" in your book *Next-to-Last Things: New Poems.* Here are some of
my favorites:

Anyone who forsakes the child he was is already too old for poetry.

Be prepared for everything—even spontaneity.

We have all been expelled from the Garden, but the ones who suffer the most
in exile are those who are still permitted to dream of perfection.

SK: Blake is a great model for anyone who wants to write aphoristically, and
he has no rival in that sphere.

JS: When did you first discover Blake?
SK: I first read Blake as a teenager, beginning with *Songs of Innocence and
of Experience.* I became addicted to him and read everything of his I could
get my hands on.

JS: Wasn't the title of your first book taken from a poem of Blake's?
SK: Yes. When I was twenty-three years old and preparing my first book of
poems, which was published in 1930 (when I was twenty-five), I gave it the
title *Intellectual Things.* It's a phrase I took from Blake, which reads: "the
tear is an intellectual thing." Nobody understood what I meant by it. They
thought I was setting up the intellect, the mind, as superior to the body.
Of course, that is exactly the opposite of what I intended and what Blake
intended.

JS: Are there any poems from *Intellectual Things* which you feel have been particularly influenced by Blake?

SK: Yes, the poem "Single Vision." Blake gave me the title. But in a rather willful way I changed its meaning. He used it to attack the rational basis of science, particularly that of Newton with his theory of optics. Blake said, "([M]ay God keep us from single vision and Newton's sleep." I used "single vision" in a different way. My reference is to that single-minded determination to look honestly at the world and to be what one wants to be.

Single Vision

Before I am completely shriven
I shall reject my inch of heaven.

Cancel my eyes, and standing, sink
Into my deepest self; there drink

Memory down. The banner of
My blood, unfurled, will not be love,

Only the pity and the pride
Of it, pinned to my open side.

When I have utterly refined
The composition of my mind,

Shaped language of my marrow till
Its forms are instant to my will

Suffered the leaf of my heart to fall
Under the wind, and, stripping all

The tender blanket from my bone,
Rise like a skeleton in the sun

I shall have risen to disown
The good mortality I won.

Directly risen with the stain
Of life upon my crested brain,

Which I shall shake against my ghost
To frighten him, when I am lost.

Gladly, as any poison, yield
My halved conscience, brightly peeled;

Infect him, since we live but once,
With the unused evil in my bones.

I'll shed the tear of souls, the true
Sweat, Blake's intellectual dew,

Before I am resigned to slip
A dusty finger on my lip.

SK: It's a typical young man's poem. It has a lot of bravura in it.

JS: It's a powerful poem. Is there a poem from your later books which you
feel has a particular affinity with Blake?
SK: "The Knot." If you have any experience as a house painter you know that
it is difficult to paint out a knot. I used to stare at these knots in wood. And
it wasn't too long after I had written the poem that I came across a letter of
Blake's in which he said he would stare at a knot in a piece of wood until it
frightened him.

The Knot

I've tried to seal it in,
that cross-grained knot
on the opposite wall,
scored in the lintel of my door,
but it keeps bleeding through
into the world we share.
Mornings when I wake,
curled in my web,

I hear it come with a rush of resin
out of the trauma
of its lopping-off.
Obstinate bud,
sticky with life,
mad for the rain again,
it racks itself with shoots
that crackle overhead,
dividing as they grow.
Let be! Let be!
I shake my wings
And fly into its boughs.

JS: Stanley, above all, what matters most to you about William Blake?
SK: I suppose that above all what I learn from Blake is that the imagination
is a portion of the divine principle, that energy is eternal delight, and that
everything that lives is holy. I don't think that human liberty and imagination have ever been better served than by William Blake, and that's why I
love him. Here's what he says in *Jerusalem*, a passage I keep posted over my
writing desk:

> Trembling I sit day and night, my friends are astonish'd at me, Yet they forgive
> my wanderings. I rest not from my great task! To open the Eternal Worlds, to
> open the immortal Eyes of Man inwards into the Worlds of Thought, into Eterni-
> ty Ever expanding in the Bosom of God, the Human Imagination. O Savior pour
> upon me thy Spirit of meekness and love! Annihilate the Selfhood in me; be thou
> all my life! Guide thou my hand, which trembles exceedingly upon the rock of
> ages, While I write . . .

Index